THE PSYCHOLOGY OF GAMBLING

INTERNATIONAL SERIES IN EXPERIMENTAL SOCIAL PSYCHOLOGY

Series Editor: MICHAEL ARGYLE, *University of Oxford*

Other titles in the series include

THE PSYCHOLOGY OF GAMBLING

by

MICHAEL B. WALKER
University of Sydney, Australia

PERGAMON PRESS

OXFORD · NEW YORK · SEOUL · TOKYO

UK	Pergamon Press Ltd, Headington Hill Hall, Oxford OX3 0BW, England
USA	Pergamon Press, Inc., 660 White Plains Road, Tarrytown, New York 10591-5153, U.S.A.
KOREA	Pergamon Press Korea, KPO Box 315, Seoul 110-603, Korea
JAPAN	Pergamon Press Japan, Tsunashima Building Annex, 3-20-12 Yushima, Bunkyo-ku, Tokyo 113, Japan

First edition 1992

British Library Cataloguing in Publication Data
A catalogue record for this book is available from the British Library.

Library of Congress Cataloging in Publication Data
Walker, Michael B.
The psychology of gambling / by Michael B. Walker.
— 1st ed.
p.   cm.— (International series in experimental social psychology)
Includes bibliographical references.
1. Compulsive gambling.   2. Gambling—
Psychological aspects.
3. Gambling—Social aspects.   I. Title.   II. Series.
RC569.5.G35W35   1992   616.85′227—dc20

0 08 037263 5

Front cover illustration by Penny Berry Paterson

*Printed in Great Britain by
B.P.C.C. Wheatons Ltd, Exeter*

Contents

Preface

At least two books with the title of this one have been published previously (Bergler 1957; Halliday and Fuller 1974). Both made important contributions to understanding why people gamble excessively. Both took a psychoanalytic perspective and did not consider any alternative approach. Since the publication of those two books, the psychology of gambling has developed considerably along new lines and it is perhaps true to say now that the dominant explanations for excessive gambling are no longer psychoanalytic. The time appears to be appropriate for an account of these new ideas side by side with the recent development of psychoanalytic ideas.

Despite attempting to describe and critique psychological concepts associated with the explanation of gambling, there was a second, more compelling, motive behind writing this kind of book. One of the most recent ideas about gambling also appears to be one of the most promising. This is the idea that gambling is maintained in part by a set of false beliefs held by gamblers. It contrasts with the idea that gambling is maintained primarily by excitement or the idea that gambling is part of some deeper unconscious mechanism. This cognitive perspective is actually a set of disparate observations drawn from many sources but one that has not been advanced collectively before now. At this time, there are several people who hold similar ideas to those expressed in this book and are developing parallel theoretical accounts. Foremost among these are Robert Ladouceur in Canada and Mark Griffiths in England whose research is at the core of the sociocognitive theory presented in Chapter 5. Sociocognitive refers in part to the domain of psychology, social cognition, which deals with the key concepts used, but also in part to the fact that gambling takes place in a social context. Belonging to a gambling group may be another important factor maintaining gambling involvement. Much of the impetus for this idea comes from the observational work of John Rosecrance whose influence on this book is acknowledged with gratitude.

In many parts of the book criticism is levelled at the central role given to excitement or arousal as the core concept behind persistent gambling.

It just so happens that the foremost proponents of this view, Iain Brown in Scotland, Mark Dickerson in Australia and Durand Jacobs in the United States, I also count as my friends. Undoubtedly, they will think of ways to rebutt the arguments advanced here.

I would like to thank my students and friends who have kindly read or been required to read various chapters and who have given me valuable criticisms. In particular, I would like to thank Michael Argyle for his encouragement and critique. However, despite all of this assistance, there will be errors all of my own doing. I hope they are errors of detail and do not detract from the argument.

1

Questions and Directions

Gambling behaviour is an enigma. It is an area of human behaviour that is full of paradoxes. Most of all, it is a challenge to our best theories of human nature. Nearly all gambling is so structured that the gambler should expect to lose, all things being equal. So why does as much as 80% of the population in industrialised Western societies gamble? Again, some gamblers give up every thing of value in their lives in order to gamble: the family, the properties, the assets, their friends, their self-esteem. Why should anyone give up so much in such a futile cause? This really is the most important issue of all. Ordinary gambling is an interesting part of every human society, but it matters little if we fail to understand why it is so attractive to so many. But some small fraction of all those who gamble will destroy most of the things they value in order to continue gambling. It is of the utmost consequence to each such individual that we understand how it happened, what processes were operating, and how best their lives can be restored. It matters not just to that minority of gamblers who are endangered by gambling but to every member and institution within a society which takes responsibility for the welfare of its members.

Increasingly, gambling is being legalised throughout the world. When a community decides to legalise some form of gambling, they decide in favour of the benefits over the costs. The benefits usually consist of increased revenue to government and increased control over criminal activity associated with illegal gambling. Chief among the costs which will be tolerated is the increase in lives that will be ruined by excessive gambling. Interestingly, no accurate information exists concerning the numbers of ruined gamblers; there is no consensus about the psychological causes of the ruin; and, there is no cure to the problem. Those who decide to legalise gambling do so with little knowledge of the consequences to individuals for whom they are responsible. In some countries, such as Britain, there is an explicit attempt to restrict access to gambling and to restrict access to credit in order to reduce the incidence of excessive gambling, but in most countries there are few preventative measures in place. Presumably, the underlying argument that is accepted, in legalising gambling, is utilitarian: the greatest happiness for the greatest number. However, more knowledge is needed about the misery of the minority before this utilitarian inequality can be asserted with confidence.

Questions Needing Answers

Prevalence of Problem Gambling

How many problem gamblers are there and what is the nature of their problems? Is it true that some gamblers are ruined by gambling or is "ruin" too strong a word to describe their losses?

Relatively few attempts have been made to assess the social impact of legalising gambling and estimates of the increase in the incidence of problem gambling, when new forms of gambling are introduced to a community, are rare. Nevertheless, in a recent study of the social impact of establishing a casino in a major city, an attempt was made to estimate the increase in excessive gambling that would result (Caldwell, Young, Dickerson and McMillen 1988). Caldwell et al. estimated that a casino in the centre of Canberra, Australia, would produce 86 excessive casino gamblers. An excessive gambler was defined as one who met the following criteria: gambles once a week or more often; has lost more than he or she can afford six or more times; has lost more than planned on four of the last five sessions; usually or always chases losses; for whom gambling causes debts; who wants to cut back or stop gambling; and who has tried to stop gambling without success. It is clear that the criteria used fall short of "ruin". Furthermore, the estimate of the incidence of excessive casino gambling is relatively small. The implication is that financial ruin caused by casino gambling will be rare and Caldwell et al. (1988, p. 55) conclude that the impact on welfare agencies will be minimal: "not in sufficient numbers to make the increased demand readily assessable".

Have Caldwell et al. accurately assessed the incidence of excessive gambling? Is it true that the introduction of a casino has no readily assessable impact on compulsive gambling of the kind that increases the membership of Gamblers Anonymous? And how do we resolve differences of opinion about the prevalence of problem gambling, estimates of which range from 0.25% of the adult population (Dickerson and Hinchy 1988) to 2.8% of the adult population (Volberg and Steadman 1988)?

The Nature of Problem Gambling

There is no doubt that gambling causes problems. At the lower level, frequent gambling in casinos, betting shops and gambling clubs takes the gambler away from home, family and friends. For example, 12% of the adult population in Australia gamble in these ways at least once a week (MacMillan 1985). The hours spent gambling are hours away from the significant others in a person's life. There are gambling widows in the same way that there are golfing widows. At the other extreme, a gambler may lose not only all of the family savings, but all of the money that can be borrowed from all available sources and may steal, embezzle, and commit fraud until caught and imprisoned (Custer and Milt 1985). Why do gamblers persist with their gambling until they have lost everything? Is there a compulsion to gamble which is irresistible for some people? Can you become addicted to gambling? Is there a type of person who is prone to pathological gambling?

Explanation of Everyday Gambling

Most gambling is conducted through legalised, controlled games in which a percentage of the money invested is taken as profits or taxes. The consequence of this fact is that most gambles available to the public are not fair gambles in the sense that the money wagered is equal to the expected pay-off. Casino games, totalisators, bookmakers, clubs, and lotteries all take a percentage of the money invested and all are therefore unfair gambles, at least in principle. Why do people wager money in return for an expected loss? What is it about gambling which attracts people to a financial interchange which is not rational in objective economic terms?

The Diversity of Gambling Activities

The games in which people gamble vary a great deal. They vary in the extent to which the player can exercise skill to influence the outcome of the game: players will gamble on the outcome of a game of chess; bridge can be played for money; and, gambling is central to poker. Each of these games allow players to exhibit high levels of skill in the play. By contrast, numbers games such as various forms of lotteries, bingo and keno provide little opportunity for skill in the play of the game. Gambling games also vary in the rate at which an outcome is produced: from rapid repetitions in machine games such as draw poker and slot machines through to a period of weeks in major lottery draws. The size of the money won in relation to the bet varies from less than 1:1 for odds on favourites in horse and dog races through to more than 1,000,000:1 in some lottery games. And finally, the access to different gambling games ranges from open to everyone of any age, as is the case with fruit machines in Britain, through to the high roller rooms in exclusive casinos, where very small numbers of the population are permitted to play.

With such diversity in the types of gambling that can occur, is it reasonable to search for a common explanation of why people gamble? Dickerson, in particular, has urged caution in seeking broad explanations for problem gambling. What kind of theory should we look for and what should we expect to find? An all-embracing account which applies to all levels of gambling of all different types? A dominant model with contingencies ("applies where the following conditions are met ...") and exclusions ("applies to the following people or the following games ...")? A different model for each major type of gambling? We shall see that despite the high variation in different types of gambling the main kinds of explanation are global rather than specific.

The Personality of the Gambler

Is there a set of personality traits that are associated with, or predispose a person to, gambling? Are gamblers neurotic or stable? Achievement oriented or lazy? Do gamblers have an internal or external locus of control? Are they moral or amoral? Are they weak-willed? Are they intelligent of stupid? Is there any description which is generally true of gamblers or the people involved in any particular form of gambling?

Demographic Factors Associated with Gambling Involvement

Surveys of gambling involvement have revealed reliable differences between groups. These differences lead immediately to questions of why they should arise. Men are much more likely to gamble than women and make up a large majority of the membership of Gamblers Anonymous. Why are men especially attracted to gambling and is this difference likely to continue as women search for and obtain more egalitarian structures generally in society? The working class is more heavily involved in gambling than the more affluent middle class. Does gambling play a role in maintaining class differences? Religious affiliation is also associated with differential gambling involvement: in the United States it is claimed that the Jewish community is under-represented in Alcoholics Anonymous but over-represented in Gamblers Anonymous and, in Australia, evidence suggests that Catholics are more heavily involved in gambling than Protestants (Grichting 1986). National differences in gambling involvement have been found: Australians use more of their personal expendable income on gambling than do people of other nationalities (Haig 1985) and Australia has moved towards legalisation of gambling earlier and further than other countries (Eadington 1987). Why is Australia a nation of gamblers? Are there ethnic or racial differences in gambling involvement? Is there any evidence supporting the stereotype of Chinese as especially attracted to gambling?

The Role of Gambling in Society

Marx stated that religion was the opiate of the people. More recently the same claim has been made for gambling (Fuller 1974). Does gambling function as a means of distracting the working class from anger over their exploitation? Is gambling yet another mechanism for denial of death and avoidance of the dilemmas of existence? Or does gambling have its origins in games of skill and echo the simulation and re-enactment of the real life dramas of pre-historical hunting groups.

Major Psychological Controversies Concerning Gambling

Controversies abound in the area of gambling. Since most of the research into gambling behaviour is relatively recent in origin and since much of it is open to methodological criticisms (Dickerson 1984), it might be argued that the source of controversy is simply an absence of high quality observations and carefully designed experiments. While this state of affairs may contribute to the controversies that exist, it should be pointed out that similar controversies exist concerning alcohol consumption where a quantity of high quality research has been published over a longer period of time. Interestingly, one of the major controversies about problem gambling has a direct parallel in a major controversy concerning alcoholism: whether or not the problem is physiologically based.

The Explanation of Gambling Behaviour: Psychology, Sociology or Economics?

In attempting to understand why people gamble we can take one of two quite different perspectives: we may search for the explanation in the processes within the person or we may search for the explanation in situational contexts exerting control over the person. On the one hand we may try to describe the cognitions, feelings, motives, or physiological reactions within the person which determine whether gambling takes place. Or, on the other hand we might examine the social and economic factors which cause a person to gamble. Psychologically, we might say that a person will not gamble unless there is some pleasure or satisfaction that comes from the activity. Sociologically, we might say that a person will not gamble if no opportunities to gamble are present or if no opportunities to learn to gamble are present. And, economically, we might say that a person gambles when the anticipated utility of gambling exceeds that of not gambling. The controversy in this case is more apparent than real, since all of the perspectives can coexist. It is likely that some joint approach to understanding gambling will be more effective as an explanation than any one perspective alone. However, research and analysis within these disciplines often proceeds as if other perspectives were irrelevant or had nothing to offer.

Why Do People Gamble: For Money, Excitement or Some Deeper Reason?

Gambling is quite clearly about winning and losing money and one might expect that there would be little argument about the claim that individuals gamble in order to win money: the profit motive. However, gambling is set up so that each gambler should expect to lose and many gamblers do not give winning money as the reason why they gamble (Caldwell 1974). One of the common reasons given for gambling is amusement or excitement. A large number of writers on the subject claim that the thrill that comes with gambling is the main reason why people gamble (for example, Spanier 1987; Moody 1985; Brown 1985; Dickerson and Adcock 1987). Moody goes further to suggest that money could be dispensed with altogether.

How do we find the way back? Who will open a Disneyland type of casino, charging an entrance fee and letting people enjoy the fantasy of riding on chance without money value in the stakes?

(Moody 1985, p.328)

Opposed to the argument that arousal (excitement, thrill, fun, amusement) is the main motive for gambling, cognitively based theories argue that the money is central and that gambling is maintained by irrational thinking and misperception of outcomes and their causes which leads the gambler to expect to win (Langer 1975; Gilovich 1983; Walker 1985; Gaboury and Ladouceur 1988; Griffiths 1990).

Both the arousal and irrational thinking explanations suggest that the causes of gambling are easily observed and not hidden in the personality structure of the individual. However, psychoanalytic explanations propose that these accounts are superficial and miss the real energising mechanism. According to psychoanalytic theorists, gambling is associated with early psychological development though there is little agreement about the processes involved. Oral fixation (Maze 1987), Oedipal conflict (Bergler 1957), masturbation (Freud 1928), and the Secundus complex (Trompf 1987) have all been suggested as mechanisms for understanding gambling involvement. Thus gambling refers back to childhood events and a proper explanation must start there. By inference gambling is associated with personality differences.

A Medical Model or a Sociological Model of Gambling Involvement?

Considering the present state of our development, almost any concept of compulsive gambling one might choose to advance is likely to be controversial.

(Blume 1987, p.237)

Unfortunately, there is no consensus about what is meant by "medical model" and no agreement about what it means to say that a certain theory or treatment of gambling uses a medical model (Blume 1987). However, at the core of what is meant is the notion that there is something physically wrong with the individual that is causing the deviant behaviour or medical symptoms. When applied to gambling, this means that the individual is constitutionally predisposed to gambling and to a loss of control over gambling that is frequently called "compulsive". The constitutional predisposition is sometimes referred to as a disease but may include a disorder of neurochemicals, chronic displacement of arousal, personality disorder, or character defect. The central idea is that there is something wrong with the person that causes the excessive gambling and sets them apart from others who may also gamble but remain in control of their gambling. The compulsive, pathological, or addicted gambler is a type of gambler set apart from other gamblers by some physical condition other than that they have squandered some large amount of money.

The alternatives to the medical model are quite diverse and can only loosely be described as sociological. At the core of these theories is the notion that, under the appropriate conditions, anyone could have a problem with gambling. A problem with gambling results from the particular social development of the individual interacting with specific learning experiences involving gambling. According to one sociological perspective, there is no compulsive gambling type of person but only heavy gambling involvement. The particular problems which beset the heavy loser and lead to the label of compulsive or pathological gambler follow from the loss of money. The plight of the problem gambler is financial in origin. Other sociological models are not so radical but place the origins of problem gambling in the family background of the individual. Thus, one of the main distinctions between the medical and sociological perspectives is that the medical model describes a type of gambler who is distinct from other types of gamblers by being compulsive, pathological or addicted, whereas the sociological model describes gambling involvement as continuous from relatively low frequency financially non-dangerous through to high frequency heavy gambling that is financially dangerous (Dickerson 1984; Moran 1990).

Sociological theories include social learning theory which suggests that observational learning and vicarious reinforcement from the gambling of others are important aspects of how an individual becomes involved initially. Subsequently, gambling may become more frequent because of the excitement involved or in order to escape from painful stimuli in other parts of the gambler's life (Brown 1987). In some forms of gambling, such as horse racing, regular heavy gambling may be maintained by the positive rewards which come from belonging to a social network of like-minded individuals (Rosecrance 1986). Economic analyses of gambling stress the fact that the subjective value of large wins or large losses tends to be over-valued by many individuals (Eadington 1987). Finally, cognitively based accounts point to the false beliefs about gambling that many players hold: gamblers commit themselves heavily to the gambling enterprise because they believe, mistakenly, that they will win in the long run (Walker 1985).

Goals of Therapy for Problem Gambling: Abstinence or Control

The main means by which compulsive gamblers are aided to overcome their problems with gambling is through membership of Gamblers Anonymous. Gamblers Anonymous was established in 1957 and uses an approach similar to that in Alcoholics Anonymous. In 1984 the membership was 8,000 individuals in 380 chapters throughout the world. Members of Gamblers Anonymous believe that, "Compulsive gambling is an illness, progressive in its nature, which cannot be cured but can be arrested" (Gamblers Anonymous 1977). According to the beliefs of Gamblers Anonymous about the nature of gambling, a compulsive gambler must try to remain abstinent. No compulsive gambler can risk relapse by allowing himself even a single bet. Members are counselled to take each day one at a time and to attempt to complete that day without a bet. Perhaps because they have followed the lead set by Gamblers Anonymous, most treatment agencies and gambling clinics set abstinence from gambling as their goal (Blaszczynski 1988).

After the period of time in which an individual has been heavily involved in gambling, the goal of total abstinence might be expected to be a difficult one to achieve. Dickerson and Weeks (1979) suggest that the high drop-out rates that are often reported for gambling therapies may be related to setting as the goal, "stopping all gambling". Faced with never gambling again, the heavy gambler may look elsewhere for a solution to his or her problems. Although the notion that controlled low-level gambling might be an appropriate goal for therapy is alien to most treatment approaches based on the medical model, there is a growing number of therapists who are arguing that controlled gambling is both achievable and desirable for the problem gambler (Greenberg and Rankin 1982; Rankin 1982; Baucum 1985; Blaszczynski 1988).

The Fundamental Question

The fundamental question about gambling, for the student of human nature, concerns why one person bets within his or her means whereas another person loses far more money than can be afforded. It is a difficult problem to understand why people gamble at all, but far more difficult to understand why a person will borrow, steal, defraud, lie, break a range of promises, prove irresponsible, and commit a range of crimes all in order to gamble. Drug addicts have a similar range of behaviours and, perhaps for this reason, some observers have referred to gambling as the purest form of addiction. In order to demonstrate how difficult is the task of understanding the causes of problem gambling, we will examine the gambling histories of two individuals.

Bruce

Bruce suffered moderate levels of family loss during his childhood. His father was killed when he was one year old and at the age of three his mother left the boy with his grandparents. At about the same time his uncle lost his job, deserted his family, confessed to being a compulsive gambler, and was not heard from again. His paternal grandmother committed suicide when he was nine, his paternal grandfather died soon afterwards and his maternal grandfather died of cancer when the boy was eleven. Gambling began at the age of nine when his grandfather acted as bookmaker and took bets from the boy on the local races. By the time of his grandfather's death, the boy was keeping statistical information on horses and was developing a ratings approach to the assessment of true odds. Until the age of fifteen, his mother and stepfather were acting on his tips and placing bets as he suggested. Poker for small stakes began at thirteen years of age and continued on an occasional basis throughout adolescence. After particularly heavy losses on the horses at age sixteen, gambling on horses ceased. Bruce entered university and graduated with a degree in mathematics. During university studies, Bruce's involvement in poker became heavier with wins and losses equivalent to his weekly income. After moving into the work force, the involvement in poker declined and was replaced by an interest in blackjack. Blackjack play has remained an occasional leisure activity and the amounts won and lost have not reached dangerous levels.

Fred

Fred's family losses began before he was born. The family lived in Poland and most were killed in the Second World War. Fred's mother and father migrated to Australia at the end of the war. At the age of 14 years, Fred's mother and father separated. Gambling began at the age of five when he began playing Polish rummy with his mother and her friends. Although the stakes were low, the money meant a lot to him at the time. At thirteen, he placed his first bet ($4) on a horse. The horse lost. From school he went to university and completed degrees in Law and Commerce. During his university days he played poker with moderate stakes such that he might win or lose up to $300 in a day. He also played poker machines occasionally but his favourite form of gambling remained betting on horse and dog races. The early fascination with card games and horse racing did not remain harmless. By eighteen years of age Fred was going to the racecourse regularly once or twice a week and this continued over the next decade. At the same time, he was making more and more bets at the off-course betting shops. During this period money was being won and lost in growing amounts. His betting was still more or less under control and limited to a few race meetings each week. Many hours each week were spent preparing for gambling and actually making the bets. At one time, in his early twenties, he won $9,800 on the quadrella (pick four winners in four races). At twenty-eight years of age he married. This did not prevent the increasing amount of betting. As he lost more and more, he borrowed and stole the money with which he gambled. By thirty-five years of age he states that, he "had lost his ability to reason, communicate, love and be loved". At the same time his health deteriorated. Fred joined Gamblers Anonymous and has given up gambling completely.

The interesting thing about the stories of Bruce and Fred is the similarity of the early years leading up to regular and moderate gambling. Both began gambling early. Both suffered mild to moderate trauma during their childhood years. Both came from working class backgrounds but were sufficiently intelligent to complete university degrees. Both gambled moderately on cards. Both began betting on horses early and both lost money. Bruce's gambling remained moderate and still continues at low levels. Fred became more and more heavily

TABLE 1.1
A comparison of two gamblers on a range of characteristics

	Bruce	Fred
Age began gambling	9	5
Family gambles?	es	Yes
Compulsive gambler in family?	Yes	Yes
Childhood trauma?	Yes	Yes
Scholastic achievement	Tertiary	Tertiary
Socioeconomic class	Working	Working
Religion	Anglican	Jewish
Age of heaviest gambling	30	35
Size of heaviest loss in a day	$200	$2,000
Size of largest total debt	$1,000	$220,000

Despite the similarity in backgrounds, Fred is a compulsive gambler but Bruce is not.

involved until the gambling had to stop. With the help of Gamblers Anonymous, he has remained a nongambler.

Why did their gambling careers take different directions? Despite research suggesting that life traumas are an important factor (Taber, McCormick and Ramirez 1987), that is not the case here. The demographic descriptions are similar except for religion. Perhaps Fred's Jewish background is a factor. Is the difference to be found in the early childhood relations with the mother? Are there personality differences that are important: sensation-seeking and extroversion, for example? Or is it the details of the early involvement with horses that is important: rewards for involvement may have been present for Fred that were not present for Bruce? Given that the explanation of gambling involves a whole range of such factors, which are the important ones and which ones are of lesser importance?

Some Methodological Considerations

Studies of gambling behaviour are open to most of the criticisms that can be made of the experimental and observational methods used generally in the area of human behaviour. However, there are two methodological issues that are especially relevant to attempts to understand gambling behaviour: ecological validity and biased sampling.

Ecological Validity

Gambling occurs in gambling environments such as casinos, betting shops, clubs and the like. It may even take place at home as in the case where a horse-racing punter has a telephone account. It always takes place for real sums of money both as staked and as won. And a full understanding of gambling is likely to come from the study of the whole

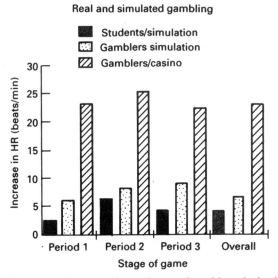

FIG. 1.1 Increases in heart rate for students and gamblers playing blackjack.

range of gamblers and not simply the novices. Thus, there is a great danger that studies conducted with students in simulated gambling environments for bogus money, small prizes, or course credit, will yield nothing of relevance to the real gambling of genuine gamblers in their natural environments (Anderson and Brown 1984; Dickerson 1986). Anderson, Brown and Dickerson point out that few studies using simulated gambling environments have attempted to verify that the pleasure, excitement and expectations felt in the genuine gambling environment are replicated in the simulation. For this reason, the Anderson and Brown study takes on special significance.

Anderson and Brown measured the heart rates of students playing blackjack in a simulated casino environment and genuine gamblers playing blackjack in both a real casino and the simulated casino in which the students played. Heart rate was measured three times for each deal: before receiving the first card, before receiving the second card, and before the result of the deal (dealer complete). The scores analysed by Anderson and Brown were the increases in heart rate relative to baseline heart rate measured during relaxation before commencement of the game. The results are shown in Figure 1.1.

Observation of Figure 1.1 reveals that the heart rate increase of student novices to blackjack in a simulated casino is small compared to the heart rate response of genuine blackjack gamblers in the casino. Furthermore, the blackjack gamblers did not find the simulated casino especially arousing despite the variety of props including an experienced casino dealer. These data are consistent with the interpretation that genuine gambling environments are significantly more exciting than the simulations used in laboratory experiments.

Anderson and Brown point to a number of ways in which gambling in the laboratory situation may differ from gambling in its natural environment. First of all the aspirations of gamblers in their natural environment may be quite different: a trip to the Bahamas if they win (by comparison, students' aspirations may be a percentage point credit towards their course grade or perhaps $10 or $20 if they win the game). Secondly, real gambling implies the risk of personal monetary loss whereas laboratory gambling usually does not. Finally, laboratory studies usually ignore personality differences and the way in which those differences interact with the actual gambling behaviour.

Biased Sampling

Much of the research on the fundamental question of why problem gamblers risk such great losses is conducted retrospectively with people receiving therapy for their problem. Many studies are based on questionnaires completed by members of Gamblers Anonymous or Gam Anon. Others use gamblers in treatment to analyse the differences between social and problem gamblers. The use of gamblers in treatment or gamblers who may not have gambled for many years, for studies of causation or even description of the phenomena of heavy gambling, brings with it the risk of two kinds of errors: errors of memory and errors of interpretation.

Errors of memory are always possible with retrospective data. However, for gamblers there is a complication which should not be overlooked. Gamblers are characterised as lying about the nature and extent of their gambling. Retrospective data may be contaminated by deceptions that have become "real" to the gambler. Errors of interpretation constitute an even more grave danger. Since nearly all treatments take place within a medical model of pathological gambling (programmes offered by Hand in Western Germany, Dickerson in Australia, and Sartin in the United States may be exceptions), we can expect that the gambler's experience will be reinterpreted in the rhetoric of pathological gambling. This point has been emphasised by Oldman (1978), in particular. Oldman argues that the notions of "compulsion to gamble" and "compulsive gambler" are not ones which are used by gamblers or croupiers to explain gambling behaviour. According to Oldman it is more appropriate to speak of habitual gambling and the financial losses that might be entailed (a similar conceptualisation underlies the work of Daley 1987 and Rosecrance 1987). The impact of a transition, from the language of the world of gambling and from the gamblers' own concepts of themselves within that world, to the language of the medical and psychiatric world and a reinterpreted concept of oneself as ill, may have major consequences for the results of surveys and questionnaires. For example, the blackjack player may believe that he has an edge over the dealer (Thorp 1962). During the period of long sessions and escalated gambling, the player may believe that winning is inevitable in the long run. However, as the losses mount, the gambler may become desperate, distressed and depressed. He or she may become preoccupied with the problem of recouping losses, may change tactics, may even change to another form of gambling. In treatment, the same gambler may concep-tualise his gambling as compulsive (it was not), out of control (it was not), as an escape from depression (the depression was a consequence not a cause), and himself as impulsive (nearly all of his behaviour was planned), thoughtless about his family (another consequence), and as addicted to gambling (despite the absence of a substance). If such a gambler fills out a questionnaire on almost any aspect of his gambling, the information given will have been distorted. Again the problem of reinterpretation of experiences may be emphasised with members of Gamblers Anonymous since the stance of that organisation is more dogmatic (Taber 1987) and members tend to focus on the lurid scenes from their most desperate hours rather than on the more typical behaviour from much longer periods in their gambling careers. The extremity of these stories may even prevent some prospective members from continuing to attend meetings (Brown 1987).

Thus, in the arguments that follow, more weight will be given to field studies of genuine gamblers than to laboratory studies of students and non-gamblers or retrospective studies of gamblers in treatment.

2

The Psychology of Everyday Gambling

Numerous authors have pointed out that gambling is not a homogeneous activity (Anderson and Brown 1984; Dickerson 1990). Different gambling games vary according to where and when they can be played, how frequently money can be staked, how much can be won with a single bet, and so on. However, perhaps the single strongest incentive to keep the accounts of different kinds of gambling separate comes from evidence that problem gambling appears to be much more closely associated with some games than with others (Hunter 1990). According to Hunter, the most addictive gambling games are those that have an element of skill. It is likely that the most dangerous games will be those in which there is sufficient skill to allow minor modification of the outcome but insufficient for the result to be determined in the gambler's favour.

Skill and Chance in Gambling Games

Gambling games can be located on a luck-skill dimension (Caillois 1960; Walker 1985). At the one extreme, lotto and lotteries are games of pure chance, although it has been argued that, even here, a minor element of skill may enter in the choice of the numbers (Allcock and Dickerson 1986). Allcock points out that extreme numbers (those that are very low or very high) are less popular in lotto. Thus, while a set of extreme numbers has the same chance of winning as any other selection, a winning combination of extreme numbers is likely to provide a higher return than other combinations since it is less likely that the prize will be shared. At the other end of the chance-skill dimension, chess and go are games of skill. Chance may enter in determining which player makes the first move but, thereafter, the game is determined by strategic play entirely controlled by each player. Games such as chess are preferred by convergent thinkers who are attracted by the problem-solving aspects of such games (Walker 1974).

For different reasons, neither games of pure skill nor games of pure chance are likely to be attractive to the heavy gambler. Games of skill provide a significant edge for the more skilful player, but the serious gambler needs more than an edge. Such a gambler requires an opponent who can be exploited and the chess Grand Master is unlikely to find any takers among the rank and file chess players. Perhaps the only scope for betting in chess involves side bets about who will win seemingly even contests, or, how many moves a superior player will take to demolish an inferior player. Ladbrokes, for example, offered odds on the outcome of the Fischer-Spassky World Championship match. Games of chance offer no significant edge to the serious gambler and thus are unattractive. While it is true that games such as lotteries and lotto attract large amounts of money, the amount invested by each player is typically small. One lottery ticket, costing one dollar, buys the chance of winning a large sum of money although the odds are heavily against success and the utility of the ticket is only about 64 cents. The purchase of one thousand lottery tickets does not bring the first prize appreciably closer but makes salient the decreased value of lottery tickets in economic terms (Quiggin 1987).

It is clear, from these observations, that the serious gambler will be attracted to games which involve an appropriate mix of chance and skill (Walker 1985; Vogelaar 1986; Hunter 1990). Such concepts are also popular in the construction of games for children. The Waddington research and development section, for example, believe that equal amounts of skill, chance and "venom" make up the formula for the successful children's game. Waddington markets Monopoly.

Horse racing is a popular basis for serious gambling, perhaps, because of the complex interplay of factors which combine to produce the final order of horses finishing in a race. A given horse has form, either over the short term or the long, which must be relevant to its chances in any given race. The quality of the jockey, the length of the race, breeding, age and sex are all likely to be contributing factors. Beyond these more static aspects, there are temporary and fluctuating factors such as the quality of the track and the current health of the horse. All of these factors, and many more, are available to, or may be estimated by, the punter. From this mix of information the punter must judge whether a given horse is being offered at favourable odds. Furthermore, when betting in the betting shop, the punter is pitting his or her skill and knowledge not against a mechanical adversary such as a roulette wheel but against the other punters who have access to similar information. If the mass of other punters make little use of all the information available, then a sizable edge may be available to the serious gambler (Allcock and Dickerson 1986). The edge available in gambling on horse races can be sufficient to fully support the professional punter (Mort-Green 1986; Scott 1987; Rosecrance 1988).

Gambling on Horse Races

Who is the most important person in the racing industry? The breeder? The owner? The trainer? The administrator? The bookie? The jockey or stablehand? No, it is none of these. The most important person is the mug punter.

(Williams 1990, p.145)

Many thousands of people in countries throughout the world are regular punters at horse races but little is known about who they are or how they choose to bet. A regular punter is one who attends race meetings frequently (at least once a week) and bets with serious intent. Perhaps all regular punters dream of becoming professional gamblers, but the reality of punting at the races is that about 95% lose money from their betting activities. It is probably this low rate of financial success that accounts in part for the attention that has been focused on problem gamblers. However, to regard all regular punters as problem gamblers is clearly an error. Of the thousands who have been gambling at race-courses for years, only a very small percentage reach a point where they come in contact with treatment agencies for compulsive gambling. The vast majority survive the losing streaks that beset all serious punters. Who are the regular punters that make up this vast majority? Are there different types of punter? Do they vary in betting strategies? Although any regular punter could answer these questions with certainty, this kind of information is not generally available. For this reason, a recent study of regular punters, conducted by John Rosecrance in the United States, is of particular interest (Rosecrance 1986).

A Typology of Punters

Rosecrance had a special advantage in his study of regular gamblers at the racecourse. He had gambled on horses for over thirty years and, in his own terms, he has "been there" and "put it on the line". His method of studying punters was participant observation. The main source of his information was eighty-seven focused interviews, with self-identified regulars, collected over sixteen months from the Hollywood Park and Santa Anita racetracks in the United States.

According to Rosecrance, the regular punters fall into five general types. He excluded all those who attended meetings fairly regularly but did not consider themselves punters, all those who attend meetings occasionally, and all those who were connected with the industry such as trainers, jockeys, owners, grooms and track employees. The five types of regular punters and their characteristics are shown in Table 2.1.

TABLE 2.1

A typology of self-identified horse racing punters

Type and percent of punters	Goals	Attendance	Betting style	Reaction to losing streaks	Employment
Pro 5%	keep on earning a living	everyday	overlay	takes it in stride	given up
Serious player 10%	earn a living	everyday	not consistent	upset	given up or occasional
Bustout 5%	action	whenever possible	long shots	resigned	casual
Regular 45%	recreation and friendship	regularly	exotic bets favourites	resigned	flexible retired
Part-time 35%	recreation become a pro	days off work most weekends	favourites	in stride upset	straight

(from Rosecrance 1986, p.86)

The Regulars

Most of the gamblers in the vicinity of the betting ring or totalisator are regulars. Many of them are older men who have retired from regular employment. They have been going to the races for most of their lives. If they have retired their incomes are severely reduced but they maintain their involvement by wagering smaller amounts and by backing favourites. They cannot hope for a big win, but their betting strategies allow them to continue their involvement while remaining within their pensions. What motivates these older retired men? A typical answer might be,

It's not really the money. I know I'll never make a big killing, but all my friends come here. If I didn't come to the track I'd be bored stiff.
(68-year-old, daily racegoer, Rosecrance 1986, p.91)

The regulars are happily retired. They enjoy the races and think that they are better off than many of their non-gambling friends whom they see as not leading fulfilling lives. Prior to retirement, they looked forward to the time when they would be able to go to the races every day without concern over wasting their time or their lives.

There is another kind of regular who is just as visible and no less well adjusted. The flexibly employed person has the kind of job that enables him or her to attend a race meeting on weekdays. Typically, they are self-employed but many drive taxis, work night shifts, or have occupations such as being a gardener that allow time in lieu. These regulars differ from the retired group in their approach to betting. They are not interested in safety first principles of betting on favourites but prefer more exotic bets such as quinellas, trifectas, and, at raceways in the United States, the Pick Six which requires the punter to pick six consecutive winners. The race meetings are an important source of interest for them and they would much rather talk about horses and courses than about their jobs or other aspects of their lives.

Regulars make up the largest single group of gamblers at the races; up to 50% of the gamblers are regulars. However, despite their heavy involvement with gambling, these gamblers should not be regarded as "sick". They are a happy, well-adjusted group of people. They do have losing streaks but they are resigned to that. The retired group know that losing streaks come to an end whereas the flexibly employed are willing to tolerate long losing runs in the hope of bringing off a big win. The regulars do not see themselves as compulsive gamblers, unable to control their betting and needing help. Nor do they lose sufficiently large sums of money to seriously deplete their resources.

The Part-time Players

The part-time gamblers typically attend weekend race meetings and are just as numerous as the regulars at those races. Regular employment prevents these gamblers from going to the races as often as they would like. Most of the weekend punters have white collar jobs and are reasonably satisfied with their employment. Nevertheless, full-time employment is often perceived as preventing the gambler from analysing the form as closely as might be wished or required. Many of the part-timers look forward to retirement and the possibility of becoming a regular gambler. Among the weekend punters there is a minority group who are less happy with their jobs and see their punting as more than recreation. These punters aspire to becoming sufficiently successful in their gambling that they can give up their jobs and become professional punters. Thoughts about horses and betting intrude into their regular employment. These gamblers find it hard to adjust to losing streaks and few of them are able to make the transition to professional status. The stability in their lives that regular employment brings is hard to give up. Whereas the typical weekend punter is able to accommodate losing streaks, those with ambitions to become pros tend to become depressed. When ahead, they hoard their winnings and plan for the day when they can resign from their jobs. Losing streaks destroy their ambitions.

The Pro

You have to win steady for at least two or three years. Anyone can get on a temporary winning streak. But if you can win fairly consistently for over two years and make enough to support yourself—you deserve to be called a pro.

(veteran racegoer, Rosecrance 1986, p.87)

Many punters aspire to professionalism but few succeed. Rosecrance estimates that the number of professional gamblers is as high as one in twenty. Professional gamblers frequently see themselves as investors and use the latest technology to enhance the profitability of their betting. The assessment of the chances of each horse is usually conducted at home with the use of computers and some gamblers may prefer not to attend the track. Other professional gamblers believe that it is important to see the horse before the race in order to judge whether the horse is in good health and spirits.

Those people who buy computer form or racing weekly or any other enterprise that collates factors, calculates odds and performance are very sadly misled because the computers and the form industry cannot tell you if the horse is fit.... Only by being on the course, evaluating the horse's condition then using your own judgment can produce results.

(J. Mort Green "The Butterfly", 1986, p.7)

It is clear that that there is no agreement about the relative merits of different kinds of information about horses among professional gamblers. However, they all share in common one characteristic: they do not bet unless they have established an "overlay" in the market. An overlay refers to the situation where the probability of winning as assessed by the gambler is greater than the probability of winning calculated from the odds quoted by the bookmaker or the totalisator. Professional gamblers seek to restrict their betting to overlays. Precisely how overlays are accurately assessed will be considered shortly. The main point of difference between the professional gambler and most other gamblers at the racecourse is that the professional has the knowledge and skill to calculate overlays accurately, and the self-control to avoid betting on races which do not provide a significant edge.

The Serious Punter

The serious punter is in a transitional role: he or she has given up regular employment and made the commitment to professional punting but has not been successful at the task for sufficiently long to be counted as a professional. Giving up regular employment is recognised as a brave and dangerous step by gamblers. The serious punters take this step but most cannot survive the losing streaks and are forced to seek regular employment again. Typically, serious punters lose the control over their gambling that is necessary for success when they encounter a run of losses. Their gambling becomes more and more erratic as they abandon one strategy after another, and more and more dangerous as they escalate their bets in an attempt to recoup their losses. Chasing losses is one of the aspects of gambling that is frequently used to describe compulsive gamblers (Lesieur 1984). The inability of serious gamblers to persevere with their chosen strategy in the face of losses is perhaps the main difference between them and the professional. Whereas the professional punter takes losing streaks in his stride, the serious punter is likely to become upset and lose control.

The Bustout

Rosecrance reports that this last category of punter is most likely to be found outside the racetrack gates waiting to be let in free. The bustout cannot spare the money for the racing form, the programme or the entrance fee. The little money that they have is conserved for betting. These punters usually do not have a regular job but exist by taking casual jobs of a low status kind. They are continuously in a state of poverty. Their betting simply depends on how much money they have in the pocket. The interesting thing about these punters is that they appear to have as much knowledge of form and true odds as do the regular or serious punters. However, their failure appears to lie in their betting strategies. They cannot wait, like the professional, for the right race on which to bet, and they have not got the patience to bet on favourites or near favourites like the older regulars. Despite knowing where the best odds lie, they are drawn to the horses with longer odds. When the bustout does bring off a big win, the money is not conserved but is soon lost.

It is not clear whether the bustout is the same person who will be found seeking help at Gamblers Anonymous meetings or at other agencies treating pathological gamblers. According to Rosecrance, about one in twenty on-course gamblers fall into this category: a much larger number of people than will be found in treatment for problem gambling. Whether or not the bustout is the same category as the compulsive gambler, one thing appears clear: these punters do not want to cut back or stop gambling. It is not that they are out of control in the sense that they feel compelled to gamble. It is more accurate to say that their strategy of betting is defective. The question that needs answering concerns what causes the defective strategy of the losing punter. Is it primarily inadequate knowledge of the facts (previous form, conditions in previous races, previous opposition and the like)? Do the punters begin with equivalent knowledge but vary in their ability to use that knowledge to derive the best bet? Or do personality factors intervene so that a need for action, for example, might be sufficient to tempt the punter from the best bet? Some answers are available in studies of the betting knowledge and skills of regular punters to which we now turn.

Handicapping Skill in Assessing Horses

Punter's lament: my horse ran so slowly they had to pay the jockey time and a half.
(Allcock and Dickerson 1986, p.13)

Horse racing is a well-developed industry in most countries in the Western world and an important part of that industry consists of the supports provided to punting. Newspapers provide guides to form; radio and television offer pre-race commentaries and post-race analyses; magazines devoted to the track evaluate systems and print columns by the expert tipsters; and punters seek out early form guides so that they have more time to make their selections. A vast amount of information is available to the avid punter to enable him or her to make informed decisions in each race. How much of the available information is used varies greatly from one punter to another. Many punters are satisfied to look through the field and make an inspired guess; others use systems which use more of the information; finally, the serious punters amalgamate many different factors combined in complicated ways in evaluating the field. Broadly speaking, there are two different ways in which punters attempt to win money at the races. The first way involves trying to select the winner, whereas the second involves trying to select the horse that offers the best odds in terms of its true chances. There are many different approaches and systems in each category and it is beyond the scope of this section to indicate the various kinds (for further information see Allock and Dickerson 1986; Drapkin and Forsyth 1985). However, as a simple example of systems which aim to select winners we might consider the "rule of three".

Whenever a three-year-old finishes in the first three in a weight for age (wfa) race, or within three lengths of the winner in these races, it should be followed for three starts, providing these races are against three-year-olds. If any of the next three starts are against older horses, no bets are made in that race and the horse is dropped after three runs unless it again runs well in a weight for age race and thus re-qualifies for a further three starts.
(Allcock and Dickerson 1986, p.33)

Similarly, a simple example of exploitation of favourable odds is the advice to back the favourite in the final race of a meeting. Analysis of betting markets suggests that short-priced horses are consistently under-bet while those with longer odds are over-supported (Bird and McCrae 1985). Thus, in general, shorter priced horses are better value than longer priced horses. To this general trend is added a trend over the meeting. As the meeting proceeds, the proportion of punters who are losing increases. The last race of the meeting is the last chance for punters to catch up. Thus many punters may be tempted to chase their losses by backing longer priced horses. This trend will lengthen the odds of the favourite perhaps to the point where it becomes a positively valued bet.

Most of the punters will lose on each race because the totalisator system scoops a certain percentage of the invested money (usually about 16%) before prices are set and winning dividends paid. Bookmakers set their prices so that a certain percentage of the money invested can be expected as a take after meeting the winning bets. Effectively, the attempt is made to offer each horse in a field at a shorter price than it merits. The possibility of beating the system and winning money at the races exists because neither the bookmaker nor the totalisator are able to calculate the true merit of a horse. The bookmaker combines an estimate of the merit of each horse with the need to cover the bets that are taken. Furthermore, some bets (such as those made by owners) may carry more weight than other bets of the same size. By contrast, the totalisator simply reflects the money wagered by the public which may or may not accurately reflect the true merits of the horses. Success in punting involves finding those horses for which the true chances of winning are significantly better than the chance represented by the odds offered. For example, if the odds offered on the totalisator are 7–2 but the true merit of the horse is even money, then the bet is definitely worthwhile. On the other hand, if the totalisator gives even money odds and the true merit is 7–2, then the bet should be avoided. The central question for the punter concerns how the true odds of a horse might be assessed. Assessing these odds is done by developing ratings based on the available information and is called *handicapping*.

Handicapping involves combining different types of information about a horse. Some of the factors involved are: ability, age, barrier draw, breeding, class, conditions, consistency, difficulty of recent races, distance, finishing times, fitness, recent form, gear changes, jockey, owners, sex, stable strike rate, track work, trainers and weight. Furthermore, different factors will have different importance on different tracks and in different countries. In the United States, the speed of the horse plays a central role in handicapping (Beyer 1975): overall speed, speed over the first quarter mile, and speed over the last quarter mile. In Britain and Australia, races are run on grass rather than dirt and speed becomes less important than weight and track conditions. Clearly, there is scope for many different approaches to ratings and not all punters will be equally effective in handicapping. In order to appreciate the complex reasoning involved, examine the following conversation with a track regular (S) in the United States:

E. Which horse do you think will win the next race?
S. The 4-horse should win easy; he should go off 3 to 5 or shorter or there's something wrong.
E. What exactly is it about the 4-horse that makes him your odds-on favorite?
S. He's the fastest plain and simple!
E. But it looks to me like other horses are even faster. For instance, both the 2-horse and the 6-horse have recorded faster times than the 4-horse, haven't they?

S. Yeah, but you can't go by that. The 2-horse didn't win that outing, he just sucked up.
E. Sucked up?
S. You gotta read between the lines if you want to be good at this. The 2-horse just sat on the rail and didn't fight a lick. He just kept on the rail and sucked-up lengths when horses in front of him came off the rail to fight with front runners (i.e. attempt to pass them on the outside).
E. Why does that make his speed any slower, I don't get it?
S. Now listen. If he came out and fought with other horses do you think for one minute he'd have run that fast? Let me explain something to you that will help you understand. See the race on June 6 (pointing to the relevant line of the racing program)?
E. Yes.
S. Well, if the 2-horse had to do all of this fighting (pointing to indications in the program of attempts to pass other horses), he'd run three seconds slower. It's that simple. There ain't no comparison between the 2-horse and the 4-horse. The 4 is tons better.
                                                                                    (Ceci and Liker 1986, p.266).

Intelligence and Handicapping Skill

It is clear that estimating the objective chances of each horse in a race can become a very complex calculation. Punters will show individual differences in their abilities to forecast a race accurately. However, those who can assess each horse's chances more accurately are better placed to exploit weaknesses in the prices offered by the bookmaker or the totalisator. How can we assess the handicapping skill of a punter? Unfortunately, we have no way of knowing the objective chances of horses. However, we do know the prices at race-time and we do know that the punter who is able to assess the real chances of each horse relatively accurately is likely to be able to assess the starting prices of each horse relatively accurately. Thus, a measure of handicapping ability can be calculated from how well the punter can predict the starting prices. We might give the punter the fields in ten races and ask him or her to forecast which horse will be the favourite and which three horses, in rank order, will have the shortest odds in each race. What qualities will the good handicapper possess? We can predict that they will have had years of experience, probably on a daily basis, looking over form, making selections, listening to or watching the races, and most importantly, learning from their mistakes. This suggests also that they will be highly intelligent individuals.

The relationship between handicapping skill and intelligence has been investigated (Ceci and Liker 1986). The subjects were thirty men who regularly attended harness races at the Brandywine Raceway in Delaware. These men were selected on the basis of extensive factural knowledge of harness racing and attendance at the races at least twice a week for the last eight years. In fact most of the men were at the track every day and would qualify as regulars in the typology suggested by Rosecrance. Given ten races to handicap, the performance of these thirty regulars was not homogeneous. One group of fourteen punters

TABLE 2.2
Correlations between IQ, expertise in selecting horses and experience at the game

	1	2	3	4	Mean	SD
1. IQ test score	1.00				100	15.3
2. Correct top horse	0.04	1.00			62%	32%
3. Correct top 3 horses	0.03	0.93	1.00		33%	30%
4. Expertise	0.05	0.97	0.95	1.00	1.5	0.5
5. Years of experience	−0.35	−0.19	−0.15	−0.18	16.1	4.0

From Ceci and Liker 1986, p.90.

was clearly superior to the remaining group of sixteen in predicting the favourite and the rank order according to odds of the three most favoured horses. The superior group was labelled *experts* and the remnant group *nonexperts*, although these terms are somewhat misleading in a view of the extensive experience of all members in the group. Each of the experts correctly picked the favourite in at least nine out of the ten races and correctly picked the top three horses in rank order in at least five out of the ten races. By contrast, the best of the nonexperts correctly identified the favourite in only five out of the ten races and selected the top three in only two out of the ten races. This clear partition into experts and nonexperts allows us to answer the question about the role of intelligence in skilled handicapping and also to assess in what way the experts are carrying out the task of handicapping differently to the nonexperts.

All thirty punters were given five of the ten WAIS subtests to provide a reliable measure of the intelligence quotient (IQ) of each person. Given that accurate handicapping involves complex processing of a large amount of information, we might expect the experts to be superior to the nonexperts in intelligence. Therefore, the results are surprising. There is no difference in the mean, range or variance of the IQ scores of the two groups. Table 2.2 shows the correlations between IQ, handicapping skill, and intelligence.

In order to examine the ways in which experts and nonexperts reach their conclusions differently, Ceci and Liker hypothesised that the experts would not only use more of the information but that they would combine the information in complex ways in order to predict how the race would unfold. Since it seemed unlikely that the complex interactions of the variables could be deducted from statistical analysis alone, Ceci and Liker decided to attack the problem differently. They interviewed the experts extensively about their methods and then tried to mimic the reasoning processes involved in order to obtain a rating on a seven-point scale ranging from high chance of losing (1) to a high chance of winning (7). This score was assumed to measure a factor, which Ceci and Liker called the interactive model variable (IMV), that separates the reasoning of the experts from the nonexperts. The reasoning used in scoring the IMV relies heavily on measures of speed in relation to the difficulty of the previous races in terms of class of competition and difficulty of moves in the race. In order to validate the scoring of this variable, they recruited the services of a professional handicapper.

The task they chose for their punters involved assessing 50 two-horse comparisons and estimating the odds for each comparison. The 50 two-horse comparisons were derived by pitting fifty different unnamed horses against a standard horse. The fifty one horses were described extensively using the *Early Form* guide format. Regression analysis of the odds for each comparison made by each punter showed that the IMV had a much larger impact on the odds for experts than for nonexperts. Since the IMV was derived from interviews with the experts, this is not surprising and simply validates the scoring of the IMV devised by the authors. However, the greater ability of the experts to handicap the ten real races suggests that the IMV variable captures some aspects of the different reasoning processes used by the experts.

The finding that intelligence and handicapping skill are unrelated is particularly interesting. How can we account for the fact that, despite years of experience, highly intelligent individuals have failed to acquire the same skill that less intelligent persons have in assessing the potential of horses?

A construction worker with an IQ of 85 who had been a regular at the track for 16 years, picked the top horse in terms of post-time odds in 10 out of 10 races and picked the top three horses in correct order 5 out of 10 races. In contrast, one nonexpert, a lawyer with an IQ of 118 who had been going to the track regularly for 15 years, correctly picked the top horse in only 3 out of 10 races and the top three horses in only 1 out of 10 races.
(Ceci and Liker 1986, p.262)

One way to explain the results is by asserting that there are different kinds of intelligence and that the WAIS (one of the most reliable, valid and widespread tests of general intelligence) does not measure or predict the cognitive skills involved in expert handicapping. Ceci and Liker favour this explanation and, indeed, the view that there are independent forms of intelligence has a long history (Guilford 1967) and has been revived in recent years (Gardner 1983). However, there are other possible explanations. We have already noted that there are two quite different approaches to backing horses at the races. Ceci and Liker are evaluating their punters with respect to a ratings framework. This would be inappropriate for punters who choose their bets based on picking winners. It is possible that the nonexperts do less well in a rating task simply because their methods are inapplicable to that task. Put simply, for the nonexperts, it may not be a matter of concern which horse is the favourite, but only which horse is most likely to win according to their system.

Another explanation can be advanced in terms of motivation. We know that 95% to 99% of punters lose money over the long term (Allock and Dickerson 1986). Each punter assesses the form in their own way according to their own system. It is also the case that gamblers may form biased evaluations of their outcomes (Gilovich 1983). Punters regard winners as proof that their methods work but losers as being caused often by factors outside the control of any gambler. Drapkin and Forsyth (1985) estimate that 40% of the factors that produce winners lie outside the realm of any system. Given that the outcomes of most gamblers are similar over time (mean of 16% loss on turnover), and given that punters are evaluating their own system as more effective than it really is, the motivation to change one's basic methods may be substantially reduced. According to this reasoning, the nonexperts may believe that they are being as successful as any other gambler using their own *nonexpert* methods. Why should they learn to use the data in the IMV way if they are apparently successful without those methods?

The Biased Cognitions of Punters

Two people are on a bus going to the races. One says to the other, "I hope I break even today." "Why is that?" "I really need the money."

(Williams 1990, p.150)

Betting on horse or dog races is attractive partly because of the wide range of knowledge the individual gambler can bring to the task. Theories and systems are widely available concerning how the gambler can gain an edge despite the negative expectation for the pool of gamblers based on the working principles of the totalisator. In New South Wales, the Totalisator Agency Board (TAB) pays out 84% of the money invested by punters as prize money. Thus, other things being equal, each TAB punter should expect to lose money in the long run. However, it is unlikely that most TAB punters think about their betting in this way. It is more likely that punters keep in mind the fact that one horse must win and that winning is not purely a matter of chance but depends on the quality of each horse in relation to its opposition. This in turn depends on a wide range of factors including, the current form of the horses in the field, the relative skills of the jockeys, the demands of the event and the state of the track, weather and so on. Precisely how all these factors can be combined to select a horse is a matter about which punters disagree, but it is reasonable to assume that many punters believe that their knowledge of these factors gives them an edge over the other punters with whom they compete (Zola 1963). The problem is complicated by the fact that winning against the totalisator is not just a matter of selecting the horse most likely to win, otherwise the great majority of punters would bet on the favourite. The task is one of rating the horses in relation to the field and then selecting that horse which is likely to provide the best yield. Since prices continue to fluctuate up until the start of the race, the best bet may not be known until the last moment.

Locating a strategy of betting, or system, is a matter that concerns many punters deeply. Systems are published and evaluated regularly in racing magazines (Allcock and Dickerson 1986; Matthews 1986) and punters will pay large sums of money for new systems or expert ratings (Scott 1987). Some of these systems are remarkably successful. Furthermore, the existence of professional punters provides evidence that it is possible for individual punters to beat the system. If an individual punter believes that he or she is smarter than the average "mug" punter, then it follows that an edge exists which through diligence and skill might be exploited. All those gamblers who bet on a horse because they have heard it is a "good thing" (Mort-Green 1986), or because they know a connection, or because the horse has a special name and so on, create an edge which the astute gambler might exploit (Walker 1985).

A range of factors might convince the novice gambler that he or she is going to win in the long run. Early success is held to be an important event and has been cited even as being a precursor of problem gambling (Custer and Milt 1985). According to Rosecrance (1987), the big win is certainly a factor in the history of many regular gamblers, although he finds no evidence that it causes problem gambling. Regardless of whether or not the gambler is successful early in his or her betting career, losing bets are matters that confront every gambler. Cohen (1972) points out that, for the occasional punter, losses do not cause a problem. The occasional punter hopes to win but expects to lose. The money invested is money already spent and the result of the bet does not have consequences for his or her self-esteem. According to Cohen, this state of affairs is not true for the serious gambler. Each bet is part of a pattern of bets which are expected to yield a positive return overall. Money lost is money temporarily taken by the TAB until the balance of wins over losses restores the profit which is expected. Winning bets demonstrate that the system being used is successful, but losing bets do not convince the gambler that the system is a failure. Losing bets are due to errors in implementing the system or to external factors beyond the control of any punter. The serious gambler is able to maintain the belief that he or she has a winning system in the face of mounting losses by biased evaluation of the outcomes. This may go as far as believing that some races are "fixed" illegally.

This kind of analysis is called "cognitive" because the factors asserted to be maintaining the gambling behaviour are beliefs, held consciously by the gambler, which combine to give the gambling an overt goal-directed character. The cognitive theory can be extended to explain problem gambling by assuming that the heavy gambler continues to believe in imminent success despite heavy losses through the use of biased evaluations. Since ultimate success is an event central to the gambler's self-concept and self-esteem, he or she cannot quit while losing. To do so would invalidate the core of the self-concept and initiate intense negative effects (typically, depression). Since the system being used is a winning system, it follows that borrowing, in order to continue gambling, recoup losses, and eventually show substantial profit, is justified. This spiralling use of resources has been described in detail by Lesieur (1979).

The cognitive theory leads to several expectations if heavy punters are compared with occasional punters. Heavy punters, relative to occasional punters:

1. have winning money as their main reason for gambling. The occasional gambler bets for a variety of social reasons and hopes to win, but the heavy gambler bets more heavily because he or she expects to win and intends to exploit an edge;
2. are more likely to expect to win. They believe they are smarter than other punters;
3. believe that they are better gamblers. This follows from their beliefs that skill is involved and that they have the knowledge to apply that skill;
4. believe skill is involved in making successful bets;
5. place their bets as late as possible before the start. This follows from the fact that the best bet in terms of expected yield is determined by the prices at the start of the race;
6. are more likely to change their bet selection at the last moment. This follows since the serious gambler is responsive to market fluctuations;
7. chase their losses. Since the serious gambler believes that his or her method of selecting and betting on horses is successful, losses can be recouped. Given a successful method, the most efficient approach to recouping losses is by increasing bet size;
8. are more likely to believe that races are fixed. Since their system of bet selection should be successful, it follows that frequent losses must be caused by external factors unknown to the punters. The wide publicity given to the occasional illegal venture, such as the Fine Cotton ring-in, strengthens such suspicions.

(Walker 1988, p.69)

In order to test these predictions, Walker interviewed 157 TAB patrons (people who bet on the totalisator) and categorised them as occasional, regular or heavy gamblers depending on whether they visited the betting shop less than once a week, once a week, or more often. Heavy gamblers were more likely to expect to win on the next race, thought they were better gamblers than other punters, were more likely to change their bet selection at the last minute, and were more likely to chase their losses. These results provide support for a cognitive view of the motivation to gamble.

The behaviours observed by Walker have been implicated as a cause of gambling losses in research by Solonsch. Solonsch (1989, 1990) developed a test of processing skill (for example, ability to rate horses accurately), knowledge of racing (for example, ability to read a racing guide), and behaviour (for example, knowing the correct bet to make on a horse). The subjects in the study were experienced punters on turf races in Canberra, Australia. The punters rated their own skill and gave information about their success at gambling over a period of time. The most important factor in determining the success of a gambler was his or her betting behaviour. Good betting behaviour involves: not betting on every race; making the right bet for the information held (place, win, each way, quinella, and so on); being consistent in applying the betting system (for example, not deciding or changing the bet at the last minute) and good money management (bet size appropriate to bank roll, not chasing losses). Bad betting behaviour was associated with the largest losses. However, good betting behaviour by itself did not give an advantage over the house. In order to win money it was necessary to combine high knowledge and skilful information processing with good betting behaviours.

Summary

Horse racing attracts a large following of gamblers in a wide range of countries. Such gamblers can be categorised by their involvement and success. These gamblers often show an ability to match their betting to their decreased resources when they retire from regular employment.

Gamblers at horse races vary greatly in their betting strategies and it is this aspect that appears to differentiate the less successful from the others. Compulsive gamblers are not recognisable as a group, although some aspects of gambling problems are seen in the betting behaviour of some groups. Although racing gamblers attempt to treat gambling as a skilful activity, it has been estimated that at least 40% of the relevant information which determines the winner of a race is not accessible to any gamblers. Furthermore, despite years of practice, regular gamblers may be very poor at assessing the chances of different horses. Despite the inadequacy of their systems and the associated information processing, regular gamblers continue to believe that their choices are better than the average punter. In fact, the characteristic that appears to be associated with the heaviest monetary losses is not lack of knowledge but the care with which the bets are placed.

Blackjack

Blackjack is a casino game which is closely related to the card games twenty-one and pontoon which are played by children and occasionally as social gambling in the home. The main difference between the social forms of the game and the casino form is that in the casino it is always the casino that is the dealer.

The players play against the dealer. Each player is dealt two cards and may request more (referred to as *hitting*). Each card scores its face value except that J, Q, and K count as 10 and Ace counts as either 11 or 1 at the player's choice (if A counts as 11 in the total of cards then that total is referred to as *soft*; all other totals are *hard*). The aim of the game is simply to obtain a total, the sum of the card values, which is twenty-one or less and which is greater than the dealer's total. If a player takes an extra card and thereby exceeds twenty-one, he or she is said to have *bust* and that player loses to the dealer the bet that has been made on the hand. The dealer has the advantage that he or she takes extra cards after all of the other players have completed their hands. Thus, if any player busts, the dealer is paid before the dealer draws extra cards even if the dealer, subsequently, also busts. However, the dealer must play by the casino rules which typically require the dealer to hit 16 or lower and to stand on 17 or higher. Since the dealer's strategy is fixed, the possibility of the dealer responding to the betting patterns and strategies of the players is eliminated and the dealer's edge is thereby reduced.

Betting at blackjack is straightforward. Players place their bets before a card is dealt. Each player receives two cards and must then decide whether to hit or stand on the total. Dealer receives his or her cards last after all the players have stood on totals less than 22 or have *bust*. Dealer hits or stands according to the rules for dealer and then pays out the sum bet by players who have won (by having a total higher than dealer's) or receives the bets of players who have lost (by having a total less than dealer's). In the case of a tie, the player retains the bet. Blackjack (A–10) is paid at 3–2 (the player receives one and a half times the bet). Depending on the casino rules, players may elect to *double down* in certain circumstances such as being dealt two cards that sum to nine, ten or eleven. When a player elects to double down, the bed is doubled. Typical casino rules specify that the player then receives one extra card and stands on the total. During a hand, if the dealer is dealt an Ace as the first card, players may elect to make an *insurance* bet. The insurance bet is up to half of the initial bet and wins if the dealer subsequently obtains a blackjack. Insurance bets are paid at 2 to 1 and thus a player can protect the bet on a good hand against dealer's possible blackjack.

Strategies for Blackjack

The feature of blackjack that attracts players most is, perhaps, the fact that the player can influence the outcome of the game by taking or avoiding extra cards. When should a player take an extra card? One strategy is to never take a card if that card could bust the hand. Thus, the player sits on 12 or above. We might call such a strategy "never bust" and it can be seen that it is a very conservative approach. The idea behind the

TABLE 2.3
Basic strategy for blackjack

	Player	Dealer
Hard stand	12	4,5,6
	13	2,3
	17	otherwise
Soft stand	19	9,10,A
	18	otherwise
Double	11,10	except 10, A
	9	3 to 6
Split	A's	except A
	2s, 3s, 7s	2 to 7
	4s	5,6
	6s	2 to 6
	8s, 9s	2 to 9 (not 9s if 7)
	5s, 10s	never!

From Tuck 1987, p.171. Soft stand refers to a score where Ace is counted as 11.

strategy is that since the dealer must draw to 16 or less, he or she will frequently bust and the player will win in all such situations. Another strategy, which we will call "mimic the dealer", involves playing to the same fixed strategy which the dealer is forced to follow: sit on 17 or more but draw to 16 or less. The idea behind this strategy is that what is good for the dealer must also be good for the player.

Since the dealer's strategy is fixed and the dealer's first card is known at the time at which a player chooses whether to draw another card, it is possible to calculate the probability of winning or losing depending on whether another card is taken. Thus, it is possible to draw up a grand strategy in which the decision to take another card or stay with the cards as dealt is specified for each possible up-card held by the dealer. This optimum strategy for the player is called "basic" and was first published by Baldwin, Cantey, Maisel and McDermott (1956). Subsequently, minor revisions have been made to basic strategy to accommodate the variations in rules of the game as played in different countries through-out the world (Tuck 1987). However, since the rules for blackjack are similar from one casino to another, the basic strategy is much the same independently of the author. Table 2.3 shows Tuck's basic strategy for casino rules which allow doubles on 9, 10, 11 and splitting of all pairs. Splitting refers to the situation in which the player has been dealt two cards with the same face value. The pair may be split into two hands and an extra card received for each hand. The bet placed initially is the bet on each of the split hands. Split hands may be re-split.

Although basic strategy is optimum based on the assumption that each card in the deck has an equally likely chance of being drawn ($p = 1/13$ for all values except 10, where $p = 4/13$), the equal likelihood assumption itself is false. In practice the number of cards in the shoe is limited and as the game progresses cards are exposed and removed from the shoe. Shoes typically contain from one (certain casinos in Reno and Las Vegas) to eight packs (Australian casinos) of cards in shuffled order. Thus, it is possible in a single deck, for example, for the four 5s to be dealt in the first round so that the probability of any further 5s becomes zero. In extreme cases, basic strategy may be far from the optimum set of decisions. Considerable effort has been expended in developing optimum strategies for the actual circumstance in which the shoe is unevenly depleted. These improved strategies are based on keeping a running count of the state of the deck in the shoe and will be called "counting" strategies. When the deck is known to be unfavourable to the player, the player places the minimum bet; when favourable, a larger bet is placed.

The first card counting methods were developed by E. O. Thorp in a landmark book titled *Beat the Dealer* published in 1962. Typically, card counters do not take each card value into account but concentrate on the cards that have a significant impact: the tens. Thus simple card counting is usually based on the ratio of other cards to tens: the smaller this ratio, the richer is the deck in 10s and the greater is the advantage to the player. The deck begins with a ratio 36 : 16 (2.25). As cards are played the ratio changes. If the ratio falls below 2.0, the deck has become favourable for the player and the bet size should be increased from the minimum. Since the deck is favourable to the player about 15% of the time (Wagenaar 1988), it follows that the larger bet size should be at least seven times the minimum bet size. When the ratio falls to 1.75, the advantage to the player is now +2.0% and larger bets are recommended. It is also the case that as the deck diverges further from the expected 2.25 ratio, the actual optimum strategy of play changes. The most important of these changes is that with favourable deck ratios, the player should insure when the dealer shows an ace.

More elaborate counting methods are available based on awarding points to low, medium and high cards and by keeping a running count of the unseen cards (Thorp 1962; Revere 1980). Furthermore, computers for keeping complete counts are available, although their use is illegal. One version of these blackjack computers fits in the false sole of a shoe and is operated by the toes: when the deck is favourable, a signal is delivered to the sole of the foot! Table 2.4 shows the expected profit or loss of the strategies that have been described.

The Contest Between Casinos and Blackjack Players

Thorp was a mathematician. Instead of playing blackjack, he went away and wrote a book about it, *Beat the Dealer* (1962), which has become a classic of gambling literature. It stands in relation to gambling rather as Einstein's theory of relativity does to physics—it changed perception of reality.

(Spanier 1987, p.5)

TABLE 2.4
Percentage profit or loss for different blackjack strategies

Strategy	% profit
Never bust	−8.0
Mimic the dealer	−6.0
Basic	−0.8 (Tuck's version)
Simple counting*	+0.5
Full counting*	+2.0

* Estimates of profit for counting methods depend on several factors.

Table 2.4 shows that a practised counter can expect to make a profit at casino blackjack in the long run. The reaction of casinos has been predictable: considerable effort is made to remove the blackjack counters from the game. Many casinos now use six and eight pack shoes which are harder to count accurately. In some cases, counting has been equated with cheating and legislation introduced to provide penalties for counting. In Reno and Las Vegas, many casinos have kept the one and two pack games but use frequent reshuffling when they believe that there is a counter in the game. Apparently, some casinos have also provided courses to teach their dealers how to count. Thus, when the deck becomes profitable for the players the dealer will reshuffle and ensure that the players are only playing blackjack that is favourable to the casino. However, we shall find in due course that the casinos have over-reacted to the threat posed by the card counters.

The conflict over blackjack began with Thorp's encounters in which it was demonstrated that card counting could produce considerable profits for the gambler. Thorp developed the ten-count method and gave the system a trial run in the Spring of 1961. In thirty hours of play, he transformed a bankroll of $10,000 into $21,000! The casinos reacted variously: some by shuffling frequently, others by refusing to sell him the chips needed to play. In particular, in most casinos throughout the world, one-pack blackjack gave way to blackjack shoes containing four, six or eight packs. The disadvantage of these larger decks is that counting tens becomes more demanding and variations in the distribution of remaining cards are smaller: the excessively favourable deck compositions that are moderately frequent with one pack are quite rare with eight packs. For this reason point-count methods are more commonly used now than Thorp's original ten-count method. Nevertheless, some casinos in Las Vegas and Reno realised that the relatively minor losses to card counters might be more than compensated by the profits obtained from the majority of gamblers who do not count. The advantage of a one-pack or two-pack deck is that more games can be played in the hour. Furthermore, it is likely that many of the card counters lose count or patience or know their system insufficiently well to profit. Others, competent in the short run, crack up under the pressure of the long hours involved. Although many card counters begin the long haul to their fortune, few ever reach their goal.

> It has been estimated that one out of every 20,000 players is a counter and of these only about one out of twenty is a winner.
>
> (Spanier 1987, p.17)

And in any case, a card counter in the Thorp tradition is easily spotted since they make the minimum size bet on most hands but occasionally make much larger bets as they attempt to take advantage of a favourable deck. Such players can be asked to play some other game at the casino or asked to leave.

Blackjack is a game that attracts stories and legends. One reason for this is that, as opposed to most other forms of legalised gambling, it is possible to win at blackjack through strategy and reason rather than relying on chance. Although claims of the profits made by card counters may be overestimated, there is no doubt that some gamblers have consistently won at blackjack and that professional blackjack gambling is a reality.

> The first of the system players, a much different personality from the others in the group and in no way representative, was a colorful individual known as "Greasy John." Large and obese, he acquired his name from his habit of coming to the casino with a large bag of very greasy fried chicken. He played for as long as twenty hours at a stretch, never leaving the table. The casino supplied the drinks, and innumerable meals of varying sizes could always be drawn from the huge bag of chicken. It soon became apparent that "Greasy John" wanted to play alone. As crowded as the casinos are, once he became a familiar face he did not have much trouble keeping other players away. His profanity and drinking drove off all but the hardiest of women players and finally the casinos forbade all women to play at the same table with him.
>
> Since Greasy John's hands were generally dripping with chicken fat, the cards soon became too oily to handle comfortably. Even though decks were changed frequently, the grease was sufficient to drive away the men players.
>
> Greasy John played for long hours day after day, and in a few months he became wealthy enough to retire. He suffered a heart attack and died shortly afterwards.
>
> (Thorp 1962, pp.173–174)

More recently, much has been written of the successes of another blackjack professional (Spanier 1987). Ken Uston and a team of counters won hundreds of thousands of dollars in a relatively short period of time. However, Uston himself was refused the right to play blackjack in the Atlantic City casinos. Clearly, the successful blackjack counter must not only obtain a high proficiency in counting the cards but must also play in such a manner that the counting is camouflaged. Point-count methods aid in this since the bet size can be varied systematically with the count.

TABLE 2.5
The average house advantage over blackjack players

Country	Author and date	No. hands played	% plays not basic	Loss wrt basic	House advantage
U.S. (Atlantic City)	Griffin (1987)	4,399	15	1.13%	1.63%
U.S. (Nevada)	Griffin (1987)	6,625	17	1.59%	2.09%
U.S. (Nevada)	Bond (1974)	940	16	—	—
Holland (Amsterdam)	Wagenaar (1988)	11,000	16–44	—	2.9%
Canada	unpublished	70,000	—	—	3.8%

Aspects of Everyday Blackjack Play

Regular blackjack players play the game weekly throughout the year wherever casinos are available. Some play every night that the casino is open. It is reasonable to assume that these regular players are proficient at the game; that their strategies will be variations on basic strategy and that many among them will use counting methods to minimise the edge that the casino holds. The occasional player who spends an hour or two in the casino at the blackjack table should expect to lose and we should not be surprised if his or her play is far removed from the basic strategy. But for the regular player, thousands of dollars a year and hundreds of hours of actual playing time are at stake. For this reason, the results of observational studies of regular blackjack players are very interesting indeed.

We should expect that the regular blackjack players would play basic strategy reasonably accurately for two reasons. First of all, blackjack is their game; they will have read Thorp's *Beat the Dealer* or some other equivalent book which specifies the details of the basic strategy and they have played thousands of hands of blackjack which would enable them to perfect their play. Secondly, blackjack played frequently with an inferior strategy will be expensive. Why pay $5,000 dollars in a year for one's entertainment or hobby when $1,000 will achieve the same involvement with the game? For this reason we will ask what is the error rate among regular blackjack players where basic strategy specifies the correct response.

One way of measuring the error rate is by comparing the actual choices of blackjack players with the choices advised by basic strategy and calculating the edge to the house for each hand. This edge can then be averaged over all of the hands observed to provide a measure of the edge to the house compared with basic strategy. Since basic strategy yields a known edge to the house of between 0.0% and 0.8% depending on the casino rules, the overall edge to the house can be estimated. This overall figure varies from country to country and within the United States (see Table 2.5).

From Table 2.5 it can be seen that the typical blackjack player is not playing basic strategy or is playing the strategy very badly. What kinds of errors are the players making when they deviate from basic? One argument is that some of the deviations from basic are not errors at all but correct actions made by counters who are adjusting basic to the distribution of the remaining cards in the deck. According to Griffin, this argument can be disregarded. Both Spanier and Griffin agree that there are so few card counters in the casinos that this explanation can be discounted. Thus, it remains to be explained why blackjack regulars deviate so often from basic. Prior to explaining why the players perform so poorly on average, it is important to note the type of errors made and whether there is any pattern to those errors.

The best analysis of blackjack errors is that published by Wagenaar (1988). Wagenaar recorded the blackjack decisions of 112 players in a small casino in Amsterdam. In order to be included in the study, each player had to complete at least 20 hands at the one sitting. Thereafter, the player was followed until he or she left the table. The number of hands played by different players ranged from 20 to 627. In each hand the player can be viewed as being confronted with the dealer's up-card and a total based on two cards of his or her own. If the total is less than 12, then the player requests another card. If the total exceeds hard 17, then all players sit. Thus, the player has a total of 12, 13, 14, 15, 16 or 17 and plays against dealer's up-card which can vary from 2 to A. The player must decide whether to stand or to request another card.

Wagenaar constructed a matrix (Table 2.6) showing the percentage of decision errors made in every combination of player's total and dealer's up-card. It is immediately clear that the errors in the boxes are generally larger than those in the other cells. The boxed cells represent those cases where the basic strategy advises that the player should draw an extra card but the player, in fact, stood pat. The unboxed cells represent those cases where the basic strategy advises that the player should stand but, in fact, the player takes an extra card.

Thus, in general, regular blackjack players exhibit a bias towards not taking an extra card when they should (43.8% errors) rather than taking an extra card when they should not (15.8% errors). Furthermore, a related feature of the errors also stands out in Table 2.6. The error rates are correlated with the size of dealer's up-card. In those cases where the player should take an extra card, he or she is less likely to do so the lower is dealer's up-card; and, in those cases where the player should stand, he or she is less likely to do so the lower is dealer's up-card.

The data in Table 2.6 represent the error rates for player's hands which total 12 to 17. On totals of 9, 10 or 11, players are permitted to double their initial bet if they wish and receive one extra card. Basic strategy advises players holding 9 to double when dealer's up-card is 3, 4,

TABLE 2.6
% of decisions that violate basic for hard non-pair hands

Dealer's card up

Players total	2	3	4	5	6	7	8	9	T	A
12	14.5	33.7	47.7	44.1	29.9	9.4	9.0	9.3	7.7	3.7
13	49.5	32.3	17.4	8.2	8.2	28.2	22.5	17.6	17.8	8.3
14	24.5	10.4	4.0	1.3	4.8	35.7	38.1	39.1	47.4	27.8
15	6.3	3.6	2.5	4.1	3.5	77.6	78.4	63.9	71.5	48.8
16	3.0	0.0	0.0	0.0	0.0	89.7	86.2	82.8	89.6	71.6
17	0.0	0.0	0.0	0.0	0.0	0.0	1.2	0.0	0.5	1.2

From Wagenaar (1988, p.23). The boxed figures are those in which the player following Basic is required to hit. In the other cells Basic players will stand.

TABLE 2.7
% errors for doubling and insurance

Doubling	Number of situations where doubling was permitted = 1,307
Player incorrectly doubles	20.5% of occasions
Player incorrectly fails to double	36.9% of occasions
Insurance	Number of players observed = 112
Percentage of players who always insure	12.5%
Percentage of players who sometimes insure	47.5%
Percentage of players who (correctly) never insure	40.0%

5 or 6; holding 10, players should double except against dealer's 10 or A; and, holding 11, players should double except when dealer is showing A. Table 2.7 shows the relevant error rates.

Players are also permitted to insure against dealer obtaining a blackjack (A, 10) when dealer's up-card is A. The insurance is allowed to be up to half the value of the initial bet. If dealer obtains a blackjack, the player who made the insurance bet wins twice the size of the bet and thus covers the loss of the initial bet. Since insurance bets favour the house by 7.7%, basic strategy advised players never to accept the offer to insure. Thus, when players do insure they make an error. The error rate is shown in Table 2.7.

In all cases, the players are exhibiting conservatism. Standing when an extra card should be taken, not doubling when doubling is advised, and taking out insurance unnecessarily all constitute an attempt to stay in the game. Not taking the extra card avoids the possibility of busting; not doubling avoids risking more money; and insurance guards against dealer's blackjack.

The Thinking Behind Blackjack Decisions

Bond (1974) asked 14 players the following six questions:

Question	Correct answer	No. incorrect
1. When do you take the insurance?	Never	13
2. What do you do when you have 7–7 and the dealer has a 6 up?	Split the pair	12
3. Do you hit 12 when the dealer has 6 up	No	7
4. What is the minimum hard standing number you ought to have if the dealer has 8 up	17	0
5. Over at Casino X, they let you double down on hard 9; when do you do that?	When dealer has 2–6	
Do you always double on 10 and 11?	Yes except 10 against dealer's 10 or A	5
6. When do you split a pair of 9s?	Always except against dealer's 7, 10 or A up	11

From Bond 1974, pp.421–422.

From Bond's results it is clear that many players do not know when to split pairs and that many players have the wrong idea about the value of insurance. Furthermore, Bond's observations of play led him to the conclusion that many players incorrectly stand on A–6 (soft 17). Unfortunately, Bond's questions give further data on players' strategy errors but do not clarify why the errors are made. However, with respect to the question of insurance, players often said that insurance should be taken "when the cards are running right". This suggests that some players believe that they can predict the run of the cards and detect those occasions when dealer is going to turn over blackjack.

The strategies and beliefs of regular blackjack players have been further exposed in a questionnaire based study published by Wagenaar,

TABLE 2.8

Statements with which blackjack players agree

Statement	Mean rating
1. A bad player can spoil the game for everyone	1.61
2. You only know whether your decisions were correct after the round is over	1.96
3. If you are very unlucky on a particular day you should quit playing	2.25
4. When I lose with 20 points I feel worse than when I lose with 13 points	2.28
5. A bad player often asks for too many cards	2.33
6. When you play on two boxes you may protect one with the other	2.35

From Wagenaar 1988, p.36.

Keren and Pleit-Kuiper (1984). 77 regular blackjack players recruited from a casino in Amsterdam completed a questionnaire consisting of 45 questions about blackjack with which they could agree, disagree, or remain indifferent. A six-point scale was used to code degree of agreement ranging from 1 (strongly agree) to 6 (strongly disagree). Where the mean rating for an item fell between 1.0 and 2.5, blackjack players were judged to be in general agreement with a statement and where the mean rating fell between 4.5 and 6.0 the players were judged to be in general disagreement with the item. Table 2.8 shows the strategy oriented items with which the players generally agreed.

The statements listed are those that enlighten concerning the nature of the regular blackjack player's thinking about the game. Other less relevant agreements and disagreements have been omitted. The six items listed point to an entirely different perspective on blackjack from the thinking behind basic strategy. According to basic strategy, each of the statements in Table 2.8 has little to recommend it. A bad player does not spoil the game: if the player makes the wrong decision on some occasions and thereby rearranges the deck so that you lose where you should have won, then on other occasions the wrong decisions will rearrange the deck so that you will win where you should have lost. With basic strategy, the play of the others in the game is unrelated to the performance of that strategy. Similarly, a decision is not right if it wins or wrong if it loses (statement 2), but is right if it conforms to basic and wrong otherwise. Similarly, the result on any number of previous hands is independent of the result on the very next hand. Even 30 losses in a row, as unlikely as that event is, has no relevance for success or failure on the next hand or next thirty hands. Statement 5 is particularly revealing. Table 2.7 shows that the most frequent error made by blackjack regulars is to stand when they should hit. A basic strategy player who hits in such cases will be perceived as a bad player by the other players even though he or she is correct and they are wrong. The ratings given to these six statements suggests that it is not adherence to the principles of basic strategy but another approach that is used by many blackjack players: belief in luck and conservatism in play.

The Role of Luck

To add to this poor beginner's misery, the dealer was having a very strong run of luck. Every player at the table was losing heavily.

(Thorp 1962, p.17)

Wagenaar's regular blackjack players are displaying an obvious self-serving bias. When a good player wins, the result is deserved no matter if it came about through another's incorrect play of the cards. However, when another player plays badly by asking for too many cards the game may be spoiled for the other (better) players. It will be spoiled when a good player loses because a poor player has taken one card too many. Such players ignore the role of the bad player when the "wrong" cards they receive lead to a win.

These regular blackjack players also have the illusion that they can control luck, by playing on when their luck is in and by quitting when their luck is out. These players appear to conceptualise luck as a personal characteristic that comes and goes rather like emotional moods. No wonder that they believe that a bad player can spoil the game for the others: a bad player takes too many cards and may change the run of good luck for the others!

Statements 2 and 4 in Table 2.8 illustrate another perspective on the game which is far removed from the thinking behind basic strategy. The players are clearly unconcerned with the long-term correctness of decisions but see each hand as a contest with the dealer which may be won or lost depending on the decision made by the player. Thus, you may stand on 13 or hit 13 depending on your judgement concerning the likelihood of the next card being a 10. Most players will not hit 13 against dealer's 7 or 8 if there has been a run of small cards but will hit 13 if they are convinced that the next card is not a 10. Thus a player finds out the accuracy and correctness of his or her decisions after the hand is complete. A player may dislike holding 13 because of the possibility of busting on the next card. 13 is too far from 21 to be comfortable but large enough to bust with 9 or 10. By contrast, holding 20 brings with it a sense of elation: dealer is unlikely to beat this hand. Thus when 20 is defeated, the player feels cheated whereas when 13 is defeated the player may think that it is his or her own fault for not hitting.

Playing two boxes is favoured because one box protects the other (statement 6). If you have bad luck with one box you are likely to have good luck with the second box. Thus playing two boxes evens out the fluctuations in luck. Such reasoning is clearly in error. If the strategy you are using has an expected loss of 3%, then playing two boxes means that you will lose twice as fast in the long run.

Summary

Blackjack is a game that the player can win. By using basic strategy as the starting point and modifying that strategy as the composition of the remaining deck changes, card counters are able to extract an edge over the casino. Professional gamblers with blackjack as their game can be found wherever casinos exist, but it appears that card counting is relatively rare. Most regular blackjack players not only fail to count the cards as they are played but they also deviate significantly from basic strategy, the only zero-memory strategy which will minimise their losses. In particular, most players tend to stand when they should hit rather than hit when they should stand. Questionnaire data reveals that players make these sub-optimal decisions because they perceive themselves as being engaged in a hand-by-hand contest with the dealer. Through good judgement they can gain an edge over the dealer whereas through bad luck the fruits of their good judgement can be lost. Thus players believe that they should persist when their luck is in but quit when their luck is out. Since the characteristics of good play can be specified, the game is a good example of the extent to which players can bring about their own losses through the false beliefs they hold. These false beliefs are held tenaciously. Despite playing thousands of hands, the beliefs which bring about gambling losses are maintained in the face of failure.

The Game of Poker

Card games are of special interest. The rules of many card games allow for skilful play. The mixture of skill and chance ensures that a diverse set of players will be found gambling on the outcomes, each hopeful that he or she will have the skill and good fortune to be a winner. In this section we will concentrate on poker.

At a certain shared level of skill, poker, like chess, is a psychological combat. It depends finally on your insight into your opponent's state of mind . . . .
(Alvarez 1979, p.12)

The poker player is betting either that he or she has a better hand than the opponents or that the opponents will not be willing to continue betting. The game thus has three main components: evaluation of the winning chances of your hand; determination of a betting strategy appropriate to the situation; and estimation of the strength of the opposition. The complete poker player must have not only a sound knowledge of hand improvement probabilities but also the ability to estimate joint probabilities; not only good money management but also the ability to anticipate the strategic thinking of others; and, not only a knowledge of the hand improvement potential of the opponents but also the skill to monitor and interpret the unintentional clues they give to their hand strengths. It is not surprising then that advocates of the game claim that poker is a game of skill. World championships are held and won by characters with names such as "Amarillo Slim". Yet even Amarillo Slim could not win against a novice if the cards were wholly unfavourable. Since chance plays such as large part in each game, it is possible for the less skilful to win from time to time; and the occasional win may be sufficient to convince the less skilful that they are good players and that their fortune is about to be made.

The skills that we have listed for the complete poker player are demanding and we might be sceptical that any person, even the world champion, could attain such skills. Furthermore, the evidence available about human abilities suggests that we are poor at estimating joint probabilities, inaccurate in estimating the relative values of risky actions, error prone in our impressions of others, and insensitive to nonverbal communications. Poker provides an activity where the truth of such claims can be tested.

Strategy Decisions in Poker

There are two major categories of poker: draw and stud. In draw poker, the cards in a hand are seen only by the player who holds them. Each player discards unwanted cards and receives replacements in the draw. In stud poker some of the cards for each player are dealt face up whereas others are dealt face down (the hole cards). In any round of betting, each player has the option of betting or folding the hand. If a previous player has already bet, then the next player who wishes to bet must place an equal amount ("calling") or greater amount ("raising") than the previous player. Betting continues until all who remain in the pot have called the largest amount bet by any player. When all cards have been dealt and the final betting round is complete, the best hand wins the pot.

Typically, the amount bet corresponds to the quality or potential of the cards held. However, to bet in such a fashion cannot be the best strategy of play. If the size of bet always reflected the quality of hand, then the other players would fold early following a large bet and the pot would remain small. Thus, a player attempts to keep the other players uncertain about the quality of the cards held by sometimes betting on poor or worthless hands as if they were high quality ("bluffing") and by sometimes simply calling, rather than raising, with excellent cards ("sandbagging"). The optimum strategy of play will involve just the right amount of bluffing and sandbagging to ensure that other players remain in the pot when good cards are held and the betting is accelerated ("driving"). Clearly, the optimum strategy for any given player will depend on the strategies adopted by the others in the game. If the other players are playing loosely by staying in too many pots, then the amount of bluffing required is reduced. If the other players are playing tightly, then more bluffing is necessary to teach them to stay in the pot. Clearly, in actual play little can be said, of a general nature, about how much to bluff or how much to sandbag. However, if it is assumed that the other players are excellent players who will exploit any defect in one's own strategy, then we can ask what is the optimal strategy under these conditions.

If each of the players is an expert, then each player will adopt the same strategy: the best play when playing against other players who mirror one's own qualities. This is the situation in which game theory can be used to define the strategy which minimises the maximum expected loss. Such a strategy is called a minimax strategy and has the quality that no matter what strategy the opponents adopt, there is no weakness that can be exploited. While the principles of game theory are well understood, the practical matter of solving poker games for the minimax strategy is held up by the complexity of such games. Simple forms of the game have been solved (Von Neumann and Morgenstern 1944; Karlin 1959; Walker 1974) and in these solutions the distributions of bluffing and sandbagging are specified. The value to the complete poker player of game theory solutions is that they provide baseline information on features of the game, such as bluffing, which can be used to anchor estimates of the optimum strategy in any actual game. Unfortunately, we do not yet know the minimax strategies for important games such as five-card or seven-card stud.

In stud poker, each player receives a certain number of cards before the first betting round. For example, in five-card stud each player receives two cards: the first down (hole card) and the second up. In seven-card stud, the player receives three cards of which the first two are hole cards. Thus, the initial decision that each player must make concerns whether to bet or fold. Schemes for making this decision vary from player to player but perhaps the most well-known account is given in *The Education of a Poker Player* (Yardley 1980). Yardley's advice for five-card stud based on the first two cards is to bet if both cards are 10 or higher (for example, 10 A or J Q) and to bet on A X and K X where X indicates any card below the 10. Similarly, the seven-card stud, Yardley advises betting with any three of a kind, any two pairs, any pair with the A or K, and any three-card straight or flush. These rules are based on experience rather than calculation and do not go uncriticised. In the introduction to Yardley's book, Alvarez (1979, p.11) writes, "This is an iron-clad system when playing against weak players who do not understand the odds or the endless finesses possible. Against strong players

TABLE 2.9
The probabilities of drawing poker hands in five cards

Hand	No. of such hands	Probability
Royal flush	4	0.000002
Straight flush	36	0.000014
Four of a kind	624	0.0002
Full house	3,744	0.001
Flush	5,108	0.0019
Straight	10,200	0.003
Three of a kind	54,912	0.02
Two pairs	123,552	0.049
One pair	1,098,240	0.4
Bust	1,302,540	0.5

Based on Allock and Dickerson 1986, p.78.

who know 'the book' and have the necessary discipline it may be less immediately effective since they will recognise your tactics and simply fold when you bet." Thus, Yardley's advice may be too conservative for poker among the experts.

The probabilities of drawing different poker hands in five cards are easy to calculate and have been known for a long time. It is simply a matter of counting the different card combinations that yield a given hand and then dividing by the total number of combinations of five cards.

These probabilities apply to the chance of drawing different hands in general and enable us not to expect good hands too often, but they have little bearing on the actual decisions a player must make during the game. Typical decisions are of the kind, "If my opponent has a pair of sevens against my ace and king, what are my chances of winning?" Fortunately, in the years since Yardley's book was published, progress has been made in the calculation of the probabilities of partial hands becoming winning hands after receiving the extra cards (Crossman 1987; Hyndman 1987). The probability of drawing three cards to A K and beating a hand composed of three cards drawn to 7 7 is 0.3. The unfortunate side of the development of exact probabilities for continuing and winning under varying situations is that the amount of information which must be stored in memory is vast. Furthermore, the hole cards in stud poker ensure that player characteristics remain central to forming winning decisions: holding 7 8, one player bets where another does not. Thus, though the probabilities of one hand improving to beat another might be known, players will continue to be confronted with calculations of winning chances which must be made on the spot. A typical situation occurs as follows. In five-card stud, three players may remain in the pot with hands as follows:

Player A	©	A	J	7	8
Player B	©	A	4	4	3
You	K	Q	10	10	9

Either player A or player B might beat you depending on their hole cards represented by ⓒ. In order to assess your winning chances you must evaluate the probability of beating hand A, evaluate the probability of beating hand B, and calculate the joint probability of beating both hands. Are experienced players able to evaluate such situations accurately?

Decision and Inference in Poker

The question of whether human beings can integrate information of a probabilistic kind is very interesting. Studies of risk suggest that estimates of probabilities made by people may be systematically biased. The popularity of lotteries suggests that people may overestimate the probability of very unlikely events, whereas the propensity to take out insurance of various kinds suggests that people may underestimate very likely events (for example, that the house will not be destroyed by flood). In some cases, human decision making has been modelled successfully by incorporating bias functions of probability (Edwards 1954; Quiggin 1987). However, in general, human decision making has failed to match up to the rational decisions prescribed by utility theory (Lee 1971). One possibility for this failure is that the subjects in studies of decision making under risk have been placed in novel situations in which the sources of information are unfamiliar and the transformations of information unpractised.

To be specific, decision making has been studied in environments for which the statistically sophisticated researchers have appropriate models, whereas the statistically naive subjects have none. While it is undoubtedly true that people perform poorly under these circumstances, it does not follow that their performance will be poor in familiar environments for which they have developed appropriate models.

(Lopes 1976, p.218)

Poker is a game of decision making under risk where regular players may have acquired years of experience with the tasks involved. Thus it is of interest to investigate the decision making behaviour of experienced poker players to see whether they are able to combine probabilistic information consistently and accurately. Lopes (1976) conducted such a study using experienced poker players as the subjects and five-card stud as the context.

The subjects in the Lopes study were shown pairs of five-card hands held by two opponents. In every case, the subject held a pair of sevens and the task was to assess the probability of winning and to nominate a bet that should be made against those hands. One of the opponents was characterised as conservative whereas the other was characterised as an average player. For each of the opponents' hands the amount bet by the opponent on that hand was shown. This amount ranged between 1 cent and 25 cents. Thus the subject may be presented with two cards with information as follows:

CONSERVATIVE PLAYER

© Q_S 6_H 5_C 2_S where © is the hole card

and Q_S is the queen of spades

amount bet = 6¢

AVERAGE PLAYER

© A_H J_C 4_D 3_D

amount bet = 15¢

Since the subject holds a pair of sevens, the conservative player can win if the hole card is a Queen and the average player will win if the card is an Ace or Jack. Since the conservative player has wagered only 6 cents, it is likely that the pair of sevens will win. The probability of beating the average player is less than the probability of beating the conservative player. Ignoring the characterisation of the conservative player, there are three cards out of forty that will enable the hand to win. Similarly, for the average player, there are six cards out of forty that will enable the hand to win. The probability that the pair of sevens will beat the other two hands is given by:

$$\text{prob (7 7 wins)} = [1 - \text{prob (Q Q)}] * [1 - \text{prob (A A or J J)}]$$
$$= \quad 0.925 \quad * \quad 0.85$$
$$= \quad 0.786$$

However, this calculation does not take into account the likelihood, which can be inferred from the size of the amount bet, that an opponent has made a pair. In the example given, it seems likely that the conservative player has not made Q Q but the 15 cents bet by the average player suggests that in this case a pair might have been made. Subjectively, we might revise our estimates so that the subjective likelihood that the conservative player is beaten (SL_C) is about 0.99, but the subjective likelihood that the average player is beaten (SL_A) is about 0.5. Then the subjective likelihood of beating both hands with 7 7 is about 0.5. The same calculations can be carried out where the conservative player bets more and the average player bets less. If the conservative player bets 13 cents then we can be more confident that he or she has made Q Q and so the subjective likelihood of winning with 7 7 is decreased. Furthermore, if the conservative player bets 20 cents and the average player bets 23 cents on the following hands then the subjective likelihood of the 7 7 winning is substantially decreased.

CONSERVATIVE PLAYER

© Q_S 10_H A_C 2_S
Amount bet = 20¢

AVERAGE PLAYER

© K_H J_C 9_D 8_D
Amount bet = 23¢

As before, we can estimate the actual chances of winning as follows:

$$\text{prob (7 7 wins)} = [1 - \text{prob (Q Q, 10 10 or A A)}] * [1 - \text{prob (K K, J J, 9 9 or 8 8)}]$$
$$= \quad\quad 0.725 \quad\quad\quad * \quad\quad\quad 0.70$$
$$= \quad\quad 0.575$$

However, the betting now inclines us to believe that both of the opponents have made their pairs. In this case the subjective likelihood of winning would be markedly decreased.

Lopes used three different conservative hands in combination with twelve different average player hands. The strength of the hands could be determined by knowing how many of the up-cards were higher than 7 (denoted by H) and how many were lower than 7 (denoted by L). Lopes was able to deduce that the player's subjective likelihood of winning was based on the multiplicative rule: the subjective likelihood of beating both hands depended directly on the subjective likelihood of beating one hand multiplied by the subjective likelihood of beating the other hand. These results are important because they demonstrate that the experienced poker player is able to use probabilistic information in the game of stud poker in an accurate and effective way. However, it is important to remember that the task which Lopes gave to her subjects differed in important ways from stud poker as it is played in reality. First of all, the players did not know how the betting had unfolded prior to the current position. Secondly, the cards were dealt in such a fashion that high cards were not duplicated across hands. Finally, and most significantly, there was no real opponent and thus no opportunity to judge from nonverbal cues whether a player was likely or not to have made a winning hand. According to Yardley, this last source of information is particularly important.

Nonverbal Leakage in Poker

I could see Monty, his face clouded in anger over some argument by the players, yelling, "Deal! Goddammit, deal!" Then he pounded his right fist on the table. His *right* fist! That rang a bell. But what bell? Then quickly I knew. Monty was left-handed. When excited he pounded on the table with his *right* fist. Yes, I must be right. At times—it must have been because of tension—he bet with his *right* hand. Of course. When he was bluffing, he shifted his cards from the right hand to the left and bet with the right hand.

(Yardley 1980, pp.21–22)

Poker has contributed many words and concepts which enrich everyday language, but perhaps none so well known as the *poker face*. It is commonly assumed by players that control over one's body during play is just as important as the strategic decisions to bet and to fold. If the body betrays the good hand, then the opponents who can read the nonverbal messages will fold and the pot will be so much the smaller. Poker players refer to unintended behaviour that telegraphs information about hand quality or intention to bet as a *tell* (Hayano 1980). However, the belief that nonverbal leakage is an important factor in poker does not imply that it is so. Players spend much of the time looking at the cards, at the pot, and at their own stacks of chips but relatively small periods of time watching their opponents (Walker 1974). On the other hand, inexperienced players at five-card stud examine the hole card more frequently when it does not match the up-cards than when it does, whereas experienced players typically look once only whether or not the hole card helps their hands (Mahigel 1969; Walker 1974). Thus, it appears that there may be nonverbal leakage of a useful kind, but it is not clear that players look sufficiently often to make use of that information.

Among experts, we might expect that experience will have enabled each of the players to have eliminated or camouflaged any nonverbal leakage. If nonverbal leakage can be used by the skilled player against the naive player, then the naive player will also have the opportunity to learn from the experience and modify his or her self-presentation. On the other hand, if each player attends only to his or her own nonverbal behaviour, then nonverbal leakage may remain present but unexploited. Do the expert players emit cues which might be received by those with eyes to see? Mahigel had the credentials to examine this question as a participant observer. Apart from observing the play very carefully, he also surveyed fifteen expert players for their views on the role of

TABLE 2.10
Nonverbal leakage of hand quality in poker games

Nonverbal behaviour	Interpretation of cue
Move chair forward, lean forward, bring hands or cards nearer game centre	Good hand: confident of winning
Withdrawing from game centre	Weak hand
Alertness—no sign of fatigue; body is tense, head high, eyelids fully open	Good hand
Body oriented towards opponent	Good hand: wants to compete
Looking at the opponent's chips	Good hand: assessing how much to raise
Attending closely to the dealer rather than cards or other players	Weak hand
Neglect of own cards; rarely refers to own cards	Good hand: easily remembered, player is confident
Neglect of own chips	Weak hand

From Mahigel 1969, pp.41–53 and Hayano 1980, pp.114–116.

unintentional communication at the poker table. Fourteen of the fifteen affirmed that they could usually tell the strength of opponents' hands by *reading* the players. However, they also claimed that this skill did not transfer from the poker table to other social situations. What are the cues which give away the strength of a hand? Table 2.10 lists the cues and their interpretation.

Mahigel's results suggest that there is a wealth of information at the poker table concerning hand quality which is available through the nonverbal channels. His observations support Freud's famous dictum, "If his lips are silent, he chatters with his fingertips; betrayal oozes out of every pore." However, participant observation at this level is only one step removed from anecdote and observer and informants alike may be reporting nothing more than an illusory correlation. Illusory correlation refers to the fact that pairs of items which have some distinctive quality appear to occur more often than in fact they do. In one study, Chapman and Chapman (1967) gave subjects a set of drawings from the Draw-a-Person test with the subject's psychological symptoms also included on the sheet. The drawing characteristics were randomly paired with the psychological symptoms. Students looked through the sheets and were then asked what drawing characteristics were diagnostic of which psychological symptoms. The students *discovered* many of the same relationships that professionals use in their diagnoses such as the idea that enlarged eyes go with paranoia or that no hands on a drawing indicates psychological withdrawal. Similarly, Mahigel and Hayano may have *discovered* the truth of many of the claims about nonverbal leakage which are common in poker folk lore. Until further evidence becomes available, it may be wise for us to suspend judgement on the value of nonverbal leakage in poker.

Professional Poker Players: Profit or Piffle?

Expert poker players can survive on winnings at the game. There is no doubt that the game supports professional gamblers in the United States (Hayano 1977, 1982, 1984) and elsewhere (Walker 1987). Hayano studied poker players at the clubs in Gardena twelve miles south of Los Angeles. Several thousand players might attend these clubs in one evening. Most of these players are neither professionals, cheats, nor compulsive gamblers. About one third of the players are women. In an early study of the poker playing in these clubs, thirty-one women, chosen at random, were surveyed (McGlothlin 1954). The survey included the Bell Adjustment inventory which yields scores on home, social, job, health, and emotional adjustment. The scores of these poker-playing women can be compared with the norms for the general population. McGlothlin found that the poker players were significantly better adjusted than the general population on the social, emotional and home adjustment scales. This is a surprising result, since one might expect that better adjusted women would stay within traditional female roles and that only socially deviant women would frequent the poker clubs on a regular basis. On the other hand, poker is an absorbing interest which may give meaning to the rest of a person's life.

If playing poker can be classified as a hobby, it is quite possible that it may contribute to good adjustment by combating boredom. In our society, many middle-aged women find that time weighs heavily on their hands, and the resulting boredom is often a contributing factor to conflicts in various facets of their lives. To the extent that the game of poker offers a stimulating activity to occupy the participant's time and interest, it may well be an adjustive factor.

(McGlothlin 1954, p.147)

McGlothlin's data is supported by Hayano's observations. According to Hayano (1977, p.558), "Most pros do not fit the picture of the dandified Broadway gambler. They dress in conventional leisure clothing, drive modest automobiles, and live in rented apartments in the greater Los Angeles area." Hayano estimates that there are about 100 to 120 full-time poker players in the Gardena clubs at any one time. For these professional gamblers, playing poker is serious work. One of Hayano's informants expressed this clearly:

Most people think that poker is a game. It isn't man. It's work. You have to work at it like anything else and you get payoffs. You can't just sit down and play. I go and think about the players and the game for a while and draw up a game plan. I don't like to play long hours because I'm concentrating and figuring odds all the time. Hell, I work less hours a month than a doctor, and I can take vacations any time I want to. This is what I want to do. This is my career.

(Hayano 1977, p.560)

In order to profit regularly from poker, apart from skill at the game, two other ingredients are necessary. The first is that there must be losers. Professionals cannot afford to play among themselves: in any zero sum game there must be both winners and losers. Who are the losers and why do they continue to play? The professionals prefer to play against *loose action* players: those players whom Yardley identified as coming into the pot on inadequate values and who stay to *see* their opponents despite knowing they have lost. Loose action games are exciting, the pots larger, and the profits for the professional are that much greater. Why do the losers continue? One view is that they are compulsive gamblers, but this is possibly far from the truth for most poker players. Another possibility is that the losers are *buying* other rewards: simply to take part with the big-time players may be sufficient incentive in itself (Zurcher 1970). Furthermore, loose play is often rewarded by status within the game. Bluffing is the essence of poker and to win pots by bluff receives the highest acclaim. Thus, in a so-called *friendly* game of poker, the big losers may be regarded as the most exciting players or even the players who embody the finest aspects of the game.

The second ingredient which the successful poker player must have is self-control. From time to time all players lose control and begin to play wildly. This loss of control is sometimes called *steam* (Hayano 1982, p.187) and sometimes *tilt* (Browne 1988, p.4). The most common causes of going on tilt are bad losses and needling by one's opponents. These situations are inevitable in long sessions of poker. As a result, players lose their control over betting, change their strategies and sometimes chase opponents who have got through to them with their needling. Browne (1988), in a participant observational study of lowball poker, identified successful emotion work as a key attribute of consistent winners at the game. Emotion work refers to the ability to shape and redirect one's feelings rather than denying or escalating the conflict. Successful emotion work may consist, for example, in convincing oneself that the needler is not worth listening to. Whereas consistent winners go on tilt for two or three hands before regaining control, losers may be on tilt for hours, days, or weeks.

Poker is a game at which the good player can be consistently successful. Professional poker play is reality not myth. There is sufficient skill in the game to enable casinos and card clubs to organise tournaments, but a sufficient role for chance so that, over a short term, even the novice can aspire to win against the experienced player. Superficially, at least, striking similarities are apparent with bridge where tournaments are also held and chance can elevate the weaker players to success in the short term.

Summary

Success at the game of poker involves both skill on the part of the player and chance in the allocation of cards. The players believe that the skill lies in the assessment of the probability of improving hands when further cards are received, strategies of betting, and ability to read the quality of hands held by opponents. There is evidence that regular poker players do develop these skills, although there is some suggestion that the role played by skill in the determination of the outcome of a game or a session is over-rated. Although nonverbal leakage of information is given an important role, it is not clear that many regular players actually notice the cues. Again, some players consistently lose either because they bluff too much or too little. Finally, the fact that professional poker players may require as much as 30 hours play in order to win money indicates that the edge is slight. In casinos, where a percentage of the pot is paid to the house, the edge held by good players is reduced still further. In fact, observational studies suggest that a more important factor than technical skill may be the temperament of a player. Under stress, a player may lose control over the quality of play. At these times, too much is risked too often and heavy losses may occur.

Bridge: Gambling with Finesse

Bridge has a large following throughout the world. It is a well-organised game with State and National Boards controlling its overall development and local clubs catering for the thousands of enthusiasts. Bridge tournaments are organised at the National, State and Club levels throughout the Western world. Although bridge is a popular game, it is primarily played as a game of skill for points and status ranking rather than as a gambling game for money.

Poker and bridge are both card games but, in most other structural aspects, are quite different. Poker is, essentially, a gambling game. It is difficult to imagine the game being successfully transformed to a non-gambling format. Even children place matchsticks on the outcomes. The betting for the pot is an integral part of the game and much of the skill of the game lies in the manipulation of bet size in relation to the quality or potential of the hand held, the size of the pot, and the number and nature of the players remaining in the pot. Players may raise the current bet in order to drive out weaker hands that otherwise might stay in the pot, or may raise the current bet to drive the pot into an accelerating rate of increment, depending on the contextual factors. By contrast, bridge is typically played for points and not for money. The game would exist as a competitive form of entertainment if no money ever exchanged hands based on the results. The gambling aspect of bridge is incidental to the game.

Given that bridge is not, primarily, a gambling game, it is important to realise how money becomes involved. Bridge has three major forms: teams, duplicate, and rubber. In duplicate, the partnership pairs sit either North-South (NS) or East-West (EW) throughout the competition. Most of the NS pairs play most of the EW pairs at some time in a session. The hands played by a given pair are reserved for play by all, or most, of the other pairs sitting in the same direction. Thus, the performance of all EW pairs can be compared for the same cards but against different NS pairs. Similarly, the NS pairs can all be compared on the same hands. This structure emphasises the skill component of the game at the expense of the luck component. In teams, a team is composed of a NS pair and an EW pair. The NS of team 1 (NS1) plays the EW of team 2 (EW2) across a set of hands. The same hands are then played by NS2 against EW1. In this way, the role of chance is substantially reduced and the game becomes, like duplicate, primarily a game of skill. Rubber bridge contrasts with duplicate and teams by no allowance being made for the quality of hands drawn. Each hand is played once only and so a given pair may, through chance, receive a sequence of weak hands or a sequence of strong hands. Thus, even expert pairs will fail against novices if the cards they receive are sufficiently poor. However, over a period of time, the role of chance can be expected to decrease and the more skilful pair can be expected to amass more points. Gambling enters rubber bridge based on a set rate per points scored. Much of bridge for money is played at rates of between 10 cents and $1 per hundred points. A rubber, which typically lasts about half an hour, involves a minimum of five hundred points and may involve several thousand points.

While skill is difficult to assess across games, comparisons can be made in terms of the time taken to learn the rudiments of the game and the size of the literature attempting to pass on skills involved in playing the games. Poker is the name for a large class of games played according to a similar principle of hand rankings. Thus the game may be played with five- or seven-card hands and with a full deck including jokers or a shortened deck excluding various lower denominations of cards. However, despite variations in whether cards are exposed for some or all to see, the aim remains the same: to hold the highest ranking hand in the pot. Conceptually, the mechanics of the game are sufficiently simple for children to master and many children play for matchsticks or cents. By contrast, bridge is typically not played by children, and not played at all by children as a gambling game. Knowledge sufficient to play poker at a tolerable level of competence can be acquired very quickly, whereas a tolerable level of competence in bridge typically takes a course of lessons lasting many weeks. Again, both games have books available which seek to increase the skill of the reader (for example, in poker, Yardley 1957; and in bridge, Mollo and Gardener 1977). However, judging by the books available on library shelves, the number of books concerned with skill in bridge appears to be much larger than the number concerning skill at poker.

Given that expert bridge players have a significant edge through skill over their opponents and that rubber bridge is so popular, a question of considerable interest concerns the extent to which rubber bridge for money is able to support professional or semi-professional players. Is the edge too large to be attractive to the professional gambler?

Playing Bridge for Money

Professional gamblers, typically, do not advertise their success very widely. For taxation purposes, professional gamblers are required to declare their winnings. However, it is possibly the case that very few gamblers declare themselves to be professionals. In any case, those who play bridge for substantial sums of money keep a very low profile. Club managers typically claim that very little bridge is played for money, and the money involved would not amount to any more than a minor increment to funds obtained from other sources such as employment. Perhaps for similar reasons, serious poker players are equally difficult to locate.

The approach used by Walker (1987) in collecting his information proceeded for both poker and bridge through a contact person who nominated others that might fall in the professional or semi-professional categories. A professional gambler was defined as one who, year by year, obtains more than 50% of his or her income from a given gambling game. Thus, a professional bridge gambler is a person for whom most of his or her income comes from bridge for money. A semi-professional bridge gambler is one whose income from bridge, including a substantial component from rubber bridge for money, makes up 50% or more of his income. The best bridge players obtain money from prizes in major tournaments, by teaching bridge to beginners and intermediate players, by writing magazine and newspaper columns, by playing for a top bridge team in return for payment by a sponsor, and, usually but not always, by playing rubber bridge for money.

Six professional or semi-professional bridge players and five professional or semi-professional poker players were interviewed. All six of the bridge players and three out of the five poker players were categorised as professional or semi-professional gamblers. The bridge players

Table 2.11
A comparison of the characteristics of serious bridge and poker gamblers

Question	Bridge	Poker
Number in sample	6	5
Professional status	2	0
Years playing seriously for money	12–20	2–30
Hours spent playing per week	20–30	7–18
Income per year from gambling game	$15,000–$30,000	$10,000–$15,000
Number of hours to be confident of winning	4–24	3–50

typically enjoyed rubber bridge played at a rate of $5 or more per hundred points. All of the bridge players had a rank of Grand Master, or higher, in competitive bridge. All three of the serious poker gamblers played in the inaugural Australian championships. Table 2.11 summarizes the central results.

Table 2.11 shows a certain similarity of profiles of gamblers across bridge and poker. On the whole, the bridge players, compared to the poker players, had been playing for longer, played more hours per week, and made more money from the game. Interestingly, most rubber bridge is played during the day while most poker is played during the evening. Both groups chose player reading and card reading as the main factors associated with making money at their game. However, these terms mean different things to poker players than to bridge players.

Player reading in rubber bridge refers to the perception of the playing capacities of the others at the table end, and in particular, one's partner. The expert, playing with a weaker partner will, for example, bid directly to game on occasions when more subtle techniques would be appropriate. Underbidding and overbidding by partner may have to be compensated. Thus, player reading in bridge refers to the perception of the skills of the others at the table. In poker, player reading refers to the skill the expert has in reading small changes in the betting styles of the others at the table. Yardley (1957) gives the example of an otherwise competent poker player who changed hands for betting when under stress and Walker (1974) showed that looking at the hole card in five-card stud varies with quality of holding for inexperienced but not for experienced players.

Card reading in bridge refers to the ability to deduce from the bidding and from the play to the early tricks, where unseen cards are located. This skill is particularly evident in the play of experts and is frequently the basis for the award of brilliancy prizes at the international level. Card reading in poker refers to the ability to deduce from the betting, on the current and previous pots, what cards individual opponents are likely to hold.

One final point is worthy of note. Most of the bridge gamblers also gambled seriously in some other way: three in betting shops and three at poker. By comparison, one poker player gambled in the betting shops, one played blackjack seriously, and one played rubber bridge.

Games of Skill: General Conclusion

When we search for commonalities across gambling games we cannot help noticing first the diversity between different forms of gambling. The skills involved in picking the winner of a horse race are quite different from the skills involved in card games. And although gambling games involving playing cards are superficial, since the same materials are used, the actual skills involved in successful play are quite different from game to game. Nevertheless, despite the obvious differences between the games, there is one feature of the play which appears to be similar across games. Each of the games surveyed involves real skill if the gambling is to be successful. Players are aware of the need for skill and strive to attain skill. However, in each type of game, the players proceed to choose strategies which are often inferior while at the same time believing that the game involves more skill than it actually does. The potential role of skilful play is over-estimated and the actual skill used is less than believed. In each type of game, regular players can be found whose strategies for that game are seriously defective. However, the failure of their strategies does not lead to change and improvement. Rather the gambling outcomes appear to be assimilated to the existing belief structure and biased evaluation of outcomes used to support beliefs which are false.

3

Gambling on Games of Pure Chance

By definition, a game of pure chance allows the gambler no opportunity to apply skill or to influence the outcome. Thus most of the gambling games that we shall investigate in this chapter only approximate pure chance because in most instances players can influence the outcome of their bets. Lotteries are games of pure chance, but lotto and keno allow the gambler to choose the numbers and thus place the fate of the bet in the gambler's grasp. Perhaps surprisingly, even this low level of involvement makes possible better choices and worse choices for the numbers entered. Similarly, standard slot machines are games of pure chance since the player can exert no control over the fate of his or her bet, but many fruit machines allow holding reels and nudging reels and this is sufficient for an element of skill to become possible. Video poker machines allow even more skill because the gambler makes the choice not only of which cards to hold but also for which poker hand to play. Finally, roulette appears to offer many possibilities for skilful play through the wide range of systems available. In fact all systems are of equal value in roulette and all would be expected to lose in the long run. Nevertheless, not all systems are equal in the danger they pose to the bank roll of the gambler and the choice of system belongs to the player.

Number Games

Lotteries have a long history and are currently very popular in many countries. A ticket is purchased for a small, insignificant sum of money. That ticket represents the chance to win a large, highly worthwhile sum of money. The gamble is not fair because the chance of winning is so remote that the utility or expected value of the wager is much less than the unit of wealth expended in buying the ticket. Typically, about 60% of the revenue from the sale of tickets is returned in prizes. That means that the value of a ticket costing one unit of money is about 0.6 units. Why then do people buy lottery tickets? When asked, the typical response is, "to win a lot of money" (Sullivan 1972; Weinstein and Deitch 1974; and Walker 1985). This answer does not make much sense in terms of objective utility and so economic analysis is often based on the notion of subjective utility which is nonlinear with objective utility (Machina 1982; Quiggin 1982; and Chew 1983). The subjective probability of a very low probability event, such as winning the lottery, is overestimated by the people that take part: the ticket purchased in the lottery represents a better chance in the mind of the player than it is in fact. According to another view, probabilities receive very little attention in any case by most of the people who buy lottery tickets (Walker 1985; Brenner and Brenner 1987). According to this view, the attractiveness of lotteries is a property of the uneven distribution of wealth in capitalist societies. In such societies, large numbers of people from the working class have chronic financial problems: mortgages, repairs, and the general cost of living. The lottery is the only source of income of sufficient size to relieve the chronic poverty. The dollar invested in the lottery buys the only chance of the good life for vast numbers of people. The cost of buying that chance is minor. Yet another view holds that some people are attracted to risk. It is not the economic imperative or the misjudged probability but the fact that the act of taking risks itself is positively valued by some people. According to this view risk-taking is a personality trait and buying lottery tickets a matter of taste (Arrow 1970).

Our analysis of lotteries will be directed toward a clearer understanding of why people take part: the subjective probability, poverty, and risk-taking explanations lead to different expectations of which groups in society will be more likely to become involved. However, there are other interesting questions which we shall also explore. How should a lottery be constructed to be most attractive to the public? What happens to the lottery winners: Do they continue with their involvement in gambling or do they take the money and give up gambling? Is it possible for a lottery ticket buyer to be a compulsive gambler, and, if so, how big a problem do they represent?

Who Buys Lottery Tickets?

There is no doubt that lotteries are more popular with the working class and poorer sectors of society than with the middle class and more affluent sectors (Kaplan 1988). Perhaps the best method of obtaining a profile of the people who buy lottery tickets involves examining the characteristics of those who win the big prizes. This is the approach used by Kaplan in a series of studies. In the 1988 study, Kaplan reports the responses to a questionnaire mailed to the 150 people who had won one million dollars or more in the Ohio State Lottery since its inception in 1974. Since lotteries are random draws from among the entrants, it can

TABLE 3.1
A comparison between Ohio lottery winners and the U.S. population on age, education and occupation

Age (years)	Lottery winners percentage	U.S. population percentage
19–39	19	50
40–49	28	14
50–59	27	13
60–64	14	6
65 and over	12	16

Education (years)	Lottery winners percentage	U.S. population percentage
0–8	6	15
9–11	16	13
H.S. graduate	60	38
1–3 years college	6	16
4+ years college	11	19

Occupation	Lottery winners percentage	U.S. population percentage
White collar	32	54
Blue collar	55	37
Service	13	14
Farmers	0	4

Kaplan 1988, p.175.

be assumed that those who win the lotteries will be distributed in the same way as those who enter the lotteries. Table 3.1 shows the age, educational, and occupational profiles in comparison to the adult population in the United States. Observation of the table shows that lottery winners are much more likely to be older, less highly educated, and from blue collar rather than white collar occupations. Lotteries are a source of revenue for governments and it can be seen that the less affluent sectors of the community are contributing the major share of this revenue. Economists describe such revenue as regressive taxation since those with lower incomes pay more (Clotfelter 1979; Johnson 1985).

How can these clear differences in involvement with lotteries be explained? One possibility is that the less educated sectors of the community are less aware of the extent to which lotteries are poor gambles. However, the clear under-representation of the 19–39 year group argues against this explanation. Another explanation is that the lottery prize means less to a rich person than to a poor person. $50,000 for $1 at poor odds is not especially attractive to the millionaire when a similar sum can be obtained by rock-solid investments. However, the same sum of money is extremely attractive to the low income earner who is under severe economic stress. In economic terms this decreasing attractiveness of $50,000 with increasing wealth is described as decreasing marginal utility. The decreasing marginal utility of money for the wealthy makes them risk-averse: they are less interested in gambles but more interested in insurance. The poor, with less to preserve and with greater needs, will be risk-attracted: they will be motivated to gamble and will not take out insurance. However, one problem for this kind of explanation is that many people both take out insurance and also buy lottery tickets (Quiggin 1985)! Another problem is that if a lottery ticket appears to be an attractive purchase to someone, then we should expect that that person will keep buying lottery tickets until the change in his or her wealth is sufficient to make further purchases unattractive. But people do not behave in this way—they typically buy one or two tickets at a time. In Kaplan's study, 50% of the lottery winners spent less than $10 per week on lottery tickets.

The notion of risk aversion linked to wealth makes sense in general terms but does not explain the behaviour of individuals. First we must explain why just one or a small number of lottery tickets is attractive to those who invest in lotteries and then we must explain why it is the older, less educated, blue-collar worker who is attracted. We can assume that each person who buys a lottery ticket knows that the chance of winning is very small indeed. Small prizes may have been won by the player or the player may know of friends who have won small amounts. However, the small number of big prize winners ensures that each person knows that the ticket purchased buys only the merest possibility of winning the top prize. Objectively, ten tickets give ten times the chance of one ticket. However, subjectively, such discriminations are difficult to make. Ten tickets afford simply a very small chance of winning the big prize. Therefore, it will be more attractive to the individual to buy ten single tickets in ten different lotteries and thus have ten chances of winning the ten different big prizes than to buy ten tickets in the one lottery and have only one very small chance of winning one prize. Consistent with this outlook is the extra time involved. A ticket a week for ten weeks extends the fantasy of winning for ten times the length of time that ten tickets in one week affords.

Now we must explain why the three different groups we have mentioned are over-represented. Why is it that older rather than younger individuals buy lottery tickets? If we allow that risk-aversion with increasing wealth explains why, in general, the less well educated working class are over-represented, we must still explain why the older groups are involved as well. Since wealth increases with age up until the retirement years, an explanation in terms of poverty and risk-attraction will not succeed.

Perhaps the best explanation for the age effect has been given by Brenner and Brenner (1988). Brenner and Brenner argue that frustration of life goals is a significant factor that has been omitted from analyses of involvement in lotteries.

People's willingness to take risks, to deviate from customary behavior, is triggered when such behavior fails significantly to produce the expected results. Such failures cause those who bear the brunt of failures to fear a decline of their relative standing in society, and who subsequently pin their hopes on undertaking risks they shunned before: sometimes playing games of chance and, at other times, venturing into entrepreneurial or criminal acts.

(Brenner and Brenner 1988, p.3)

When we examine the impact of age in the light of this formulation, it can be seen that two individuals with the same income but who differ in age will not react to their wealth in the same way. The younger person will perceive that current income is a step towards increasing income in the future, whereas the older person will perceive that current income is not likely to increase significantly and may fall with retirement. The older man will realise that he is poorer than the younger man and less able to provide for himself in old age or to leave an inheritance for his children. But by gambling he can change his prospects.

The interesting aspect of Brenner and Brenner's financial frustration theory is that it makes further predictions which can be tested. Who will gamble more, the parent in a small family or the parent in a large family? Given the same income, the greater the number of children the poorer is the family and so parents with larger families would be expected to be more involved in buying lottery tickets. An analysis of lottery winners in Michigan for the years 1973–80 revealed that the average number of children was five.

Brenner and Brenner argue that the statistical analysis of lottery involvement may be misleading because heterogeneous data may have been pooled. Their analysis indicates that an important distinction must be made between those who buy tickets on a regular basis and those who buy tickets spontaneously. The regulars may include the older, less educated, working class, whereas the spontaneous buyers may be those younger individuals who have suffered some kind of setback: lost their job or failed to get a rise, for example.

The well adjusted middle class salaried employee may lose his job for a variety of causes that lie partially or wholly beyond his control . . . excessive gambling may appear as one of the by-products of this sequence.

(Devereux 1949, p.807)

The evidence again appears to support Brenner and Brenner's predictions. About 50% of ticket buyers invest in a ticket on a regular basis, whereas the remaining 50% buy their tickets spontaneously (Sylvestre

TABLE 3.2
Catholic and Protestant involvement in Loto-Canada

Religion	Winners percentage	Canadian population percentage
Catholic	67.8	47.3
Protestant	28.9	43.4

Based on Brenner and Brenner 1987, p.12.

1977). Furthermore, there is some evidence to support the claim that lotteries are more popular in times when unemployment is high. In Quebec in 1982, unemployment had reached a record high (15% unemployed). A poll conducted at that time showed that people were buying lottery tickets with money formerly spent on beer and wine (Brenner and Brenner 1987). Similarly, dissatisfaction with work and with income appears to be associated with buying lottery tickets (Tec 1964; Brunk 1981). Thus, it appears that buying lottery tickets may be a way in which people suffering financial stress try to cope with their situation.

It is not only the poor or frustrated groups in society that are over-represented in lottery involvement. Analysis by Kaplan of the big prize winners in the Loto-Canada competition for the years 1974–78 revealed that Catholics are more involved in lottery gambling than are Protestants (Table 3.2).

The high Catholic involvement is consistent with the results of research elsewhere (Grichting 1986). Why are Catholics more heavily involved than others in playing the lotteries? Perhaps the explanation is that the Catholic Church has always been more tolerant of gambling and other vices. Gambling is acceptable provided that it is done in moderation and does not diminish the ability to meet one's responsibilities in the home and elsewhere. Indeed, a Catholic bishop in 1923 is reported as saying that gambling was "approved by God, who ordered Moses to distribute the promised land to the twelve tribes by means of a lottery" (Inglis 1985). By comparison, the Protestant Church has strongly disapproved of gambling. Acquiring money through gambling stands in direct confrontation with the Protestant work ethic and evangelical Protestants have consistently opposed a trinity of vices: sexual immorality, drink and gambling (Inglis 1985).

It is clear that our understanding of why people buy lottery tickets cannot be simplified to stating that lottery tickets are a matter of taste. A personality dimension such as orientation to risk cannot function as a full explanation when involvement in lotteries is associated with situational factors such as financial stress. In any case, offering a personality type as an explanation is empty unless it can be shown first how the personality was acquired and secondly how it relates to a specific activity such as buying lottery tickets. The fact that so many people both buy lottery tickets and take out insurance argues against any simple attribution to personality types or dimensions.

It is also clear that economic analyses miss some important aspects of lottery involvement. The notion of subjective or anticipated utility (Quiggin 1987) makes clear that the poorer sectors of the community are likely to perceive lottery prizes as more valuable than the more wealthy sectors, but it does not explain why the majority of people spend relatively small amounts on the activity or why as many as 50% of players buy their tickets spontaneously and irregularly. The factors that mediate lottery involvement are psychological as well as economic: lotteries provide a chance of reversing unequal allocation of resources in society. The person who purchases a lottery ticket also purchases the solution to their immediate problems, at least in fantasy.

Lotto Games

In a lottery, the player must be content with the ticket number purchased. If the kiosk does not have the number you would like there is little you can do. In lotto games, the player chooses the numbers and so has more control. The control is apparent rather than real since the outcome of a lotto game is purely a matter of chance. Nevertheless, if a person believes that in some way he or she can select numbers which are more likely to win then involvement in the game becomes considerably more attractive.

Businesses have been developed in recent years which promote books and pamphlets as well as devices that purportedly tout systems and schemes for selecting lucky numbers or handicapping numbers, and charts and computerized programs are hawked for the serious student who believes he or she can lower the odds and beat the lottery by rational calculation.

(Kaplan 1988, p.180)

Is there any way in which lotto players can improve their chances? Typical lotto games require the player to select a small group of the numbers from a larger selection. For example, Australian lotto asks the player to select six numbers from the range 1 to 44. A single lotto ticket contains four such selections and costs $1–10. The chance of winning is less than one in a million. Furthermore, if you pick the winning six numbers then you must share the prize with any other fortunate entrants. Nothing can be done to improve your chances of picking the winning numbers, but care in choosing the numbers can reduce the probability that you will have to share the money with others. Most people select middle order numbers (10 . . . 40) or numbers towards the middle of the coupon. Thus the thoughtful player selects low or high numbers and chooses numbers at the edge of the coupon. By choosing numbers in this way, the chance of winning is not altered but, should your numbers win the prize, the number of other players with whom you must share the prize is decreased (Allcock and Dickerson 1986).

All methods of selecting numbers appear to have equal merit in terms of the probability of selecting the winning numbers. Since the player can exert no influence over the probability of winning, random number machines will be just as effective as other methods and less time consuming. In many lotto games, machines are provided for just this purpose and are usually quite popular. In Ohio, about 40% of entrants in lotto allow a machine to randomly select their entries. Clearly, this kind of gambling stands in antithesis to the scientific handicapping of horses, the cold calculation of odds at poker, or the skills of the expert bridge player. Why does a person enter a game in which the play is random, the result is random, and the only involvement is to hand over money with effectively no chance of winning?

Lotto is one of the most popular gambling games of all (Macmillan 1985). Part of that popularity comes from the same source as the popularity of lotteries: the game offers a low cost chance of winning an extraordinarily valuable prize. However, part of the popularity may also come from the way in which the game is marketed. In Australia, the winning lotto numbers are drawn live on television and lotto is also heavily advertised on television. Thus, winning at lotto is made salient to Australians in a way that is difficult for other forms of gambling to match. The televised draw highlights the simplicity of winning while at the same time hiding the huge audience of participants (losers) who are watching. Thus, an individual's assessment of the possibility of winning may be distorted from the realistic "no chance at all" (Robin Hood in the football stadium). At the same time, the advertising clarifies just how valuable the prize is and suggests all the benefits that may come to the winner. Playing the game costs very little money which brings the over estimated probability of winning the over valued prize within the reach of most people.

Demographically, a similar pattern of involvement in lotto is found as in lotteries. The working class sector of society is over represented and the middle class under represented in ticket sales and in the addresses of winners (Walker 1985). While it is likely that similar explanations for this difference given for lotteries also applies to lotto, the use of television adds another possibility. Since television viewing is greater in the working class sector, the impact of the television based marketing of this form of gambling may be heightened for this group.

Despite the similarities between lotteries and lotto, one major difference affects the involvement of large numbers of people. In lotto, the player can choose the numbers which will be entered. Many people believe they have special knowledge of the lucky properties of numbers. Perhaps it is a lucky birth date or perhaps it is a set of numbers derived by astrological methods. The use of such knowledge to gain insight into the winning lotto numbers might, appropriately, be called magical thinking. For people with such knowledge, the random number generator holds no attraction. However, such knowledge brings with it the possibility of *entrapment*.

Entrapment in Lotto Games

By picking the same numbers week after week, a lotto player may become entrapped. Entrapment refers to commitment to a goal that has not been reached. The resources expended thus far, without reward, motivate a person to continue expending resources until the goal is reached. The numbers that are entered on the coupon each week are known to be lucky. Sooner, rather than later, they will win. Each week the lotto draw brings the lucky day a step closer. Each draw increases the commitment of the player. The lucky day cannot be predicted but the player knows that each week it comes closer, like crossing off the days on a calendar. At every step, the opportunity is there for the player to stop playing lotto and cut his or her losses. But should the player stop, the lucky numbers may be the winning numbers the following week. The special knowledge and the perseverance will have been wasted. The prospect of stopping and thereby missing the big prize is too daunting for many players who persist with their numbers week after week. The player is entrapped and the entrapment becomes greater as the weeks pass. People can reach a point where holidays cannot be taken unless arrangements are made for the weekly coupon to be completed and entered.

The phenomenon of entrapment has been studied experimentally by Brockner and Robin (1985) whose work is discussed in detail in Chapter 5. The phenomenon appears to be widely applicable to different forms of gambling although it is specially relevant to lotto. Slot machine players may become entrapped by playing the same machine every session. A change in machine may cause the player to miss the jackpot to which they have committed their resources. Blackjack players may become entrapped by a certain seating position at the table and roulette players by "special" numbers. Even horse racing gamblers are susceptible to simple forms of entrapment. One punter, known to the author, would select the horse which was likely to win a race and continue to bet on that horse, meeting after meeting, until it did in fact win. Once having started its betting strategy he was entrapped despite the changing conditions and changing odds from one race to the next. One horse became a legend in Australia and its name has become slang for a person with little common sense. The horse, called "Drongo" was entered in many races but never won a single race. Such a horse could spell disaster for an entrapped punter!

Bingo

Bingo is undoubtedly one of the most popular gambling games in many countries (Kallick, Suits, Dielman and Hybels 1976; Downes, Davies, David and Stone 1976; MacMillan 1985) but little empirical data has been gathered about the motivations of those who play or the causes of continuing to play regularly and for long periods of time. The exception to this claim is a recent study based on participant observation by King (1990). King made the observations at fourteen bingo parlours which were mainly in Ohio in the United States. The participant observations yielded accounts of the play and outcomes which were further supplemented by interviews with twenty players.

King was able to observe frequent use of magical and superstitious strategies. Players commonly have hunches and feelings about their own or their friends winning. In the minds of many bingo players, these feelings are often confirmed by the occurrence of the foreseen outcome.

As PF sat down at our table he said, "I have a feeling someone at this table is going to win tonight." Sure enough, someone did. It happened to be Red. We congratulated him after he won. PF said, "See! I knew someone would win."

(King 1990, p.50)

The belief that feelings and hunches are frequently supported by the unfolding events is, perhaps, a good example of illusory correlation: we remember the hits but forget, or underestimate, the number of misses. According to King, bingo players are aware that their "special powers" do not always work. This awareness has an important function in allowing players to disclaim any undue influence when they are especially lucky. Players are keen to do this because bingo is seen as a charitable game which players engage in for healthy, social reasons and not as a selfish game in which players are trying to make money.

Bingo players believe in luck as an attribute which can be enhanced or diminished by a person's actions. Lucky numbers are common as exemplified in the following statement:

During a conversation about winning, a player said, "Fives are lucky for me. All week I've been finding hidden five dollar bills in the money customers give me. I gave them back. The customers were grateful. (pause) I win a lot at poker with three fives."

(King 1990, p.53)

Any colour, object or circumstance may be lucky for a given player. However, commonly a great deal of luck surrounds the use of the

sed to mark the bingo cards and the seat in which one chooses
perstitious practices of this kind have been observed in a wide
ᵣₐₙ𝓰ₑ ₒf gambling games (see, for example, Henslin 1967).

Summary

The numbers games include lotteries, lotto, bingo and roulette. They are
games of pure chance since the outcome is unpredictable and the
gambler has no opportunity to influence the result. There is no role for
skilful play. Nevertheless, numbers games are very popular despite the
relatively large cut taken by the house in most games (roulette being the
exception). The attractiveness of the games appears to lie in the large
prizes that are offered. These prizes are particularly attractive to
segments of the community in which there is either chronic or acute
financial stress. Despite the inability of gamblers to influence the
outcome of games through skilful play, the use of systems, the application of special knowledge, and belief in superstitious practices are
common in numbers games. The gamblers also frequently believe that
they are "lucky". Thus gamblers playing numbers games behave as if
these games of pure chance can be influenced and appear to believe that
they themselves have the special knowledge or characteristics which
increase their chances of winning.

The Attraction of Slot Machines

What is more they assume human traits like the greedy mouth, the pot belly and the
sphincter from which spills a diarrhoea of coins.

(Hersant 1988, p.10)

Not all gambling machines are slot machines. The slot machine is
characterised by the insertion of a coin, the action of a chance mechanism (for example, the spin of the reels), and a payout depending on the
outcome. Although video card games and certain fruit machines appear
to follow a similar principle, they differ from the slot machine in one
important attribute: the player has the opportunity to interact with the
machine in some way that influences the outcome. In fruit machines of
the "Hold 'em" type, the player has the option of holding some or all of
the symbols in place for a second spin. Similarly, in draw poker some or
all of the cards may be held for the draw. This interaction with the
machine is important because it adds a small element of skill to what
otherwise is a game of pure chance. Thus, in discussing the psychology of
gambling on machines, a distinction will be made, in this section,
between slot machines, fruit machines and other gambling machines
such as video draw poker. In later chapters, slot machines will be used as

the general term representing all coin in the slot games whether they involve an element of skill or not.

Slot machines, perhaps more than any other gambling game, attract the ire of the anti-gambling lobby. The legislation of the machines has been difficult to achieve in most countries where they now operate. In the sociology of games, the slot machine is given a very low rank. Huizinga (1950) omitted to discuss them at all and Caillois (1961) could see no reason why people would play such games. Caldwell, one of the early explorers of the motivation to play slot machines, described the play of the machines as the "epitome of non-skill gambling".

The player has to insert a coin and pull the handle. There is no way that he can influence the outcome. The poker machine (slot machine) not only determines the result, but pays out in the event of a win. The banker, the Cabinet Minister, the housewife, and the labourer are all equals before the poker machine, for skill and experience count for nothing.

(Caldwell 1974, p.16)

Despite the lowly regard with which sociologists hold the play of slot machines, the truth of the matter is that wherever they have been legalised, slot machines have become one of the most popular forms of gambling. What makes the slot machine so popular with so many people? Unlike the racing game, there are no professional slot machine players. There is no basis for viewing the slot machine as a sound financial investment. As a first step towards understanding the motivation of the slot machine player, we shall review the reasons they give for playing.

Reasons for Playing Slot Machines

Amusement

Caldwell (1974) surveyed a sample of 300 slot machine players concerning aspects of their use of the machines. The main reason given for playing the machines was neither winning money nor achieving jackpots, but rather amusement. Nevertheless, about 20% of the players claimed that they were winning money by playing while a quarter of the sample reported losing more than they had intended. More recently Dickerson and Walker (Dickerson, Fabre and Bayliss 1986; Walker 1988) have surveyed slot machine players with results that were remarkably similar to those obtained by Caldwell. As in Caldwell's results, the majority of players reported playing for entertainment or to be sociable rather than to win money. Similarly, about 20% of those playing reported winning in their last session while 40% reported spending more than they could afford on the machines at least once.

These results suggest that the motivation for gambling on slot machines is different from that for betting on horses. Slot machine players report playing for amusement and excitement rather than to win money. Leary and Dickerson (1985) provide data suggesting that arousal is higher in high frequency players than low frequency players. Thus, *amusement* or *entertainment* might be best understood as inclusive terms representing measures and reports of players that the activity of playing slot machines is amusing, exciting, arousing and rewarding as an activity in itself. Slot machines are played for entertainment whereas betting at the races is seen as a potential way of winning money. This difference is consistent with the perception of skill associated with the two different forms of gambling. The results of Dickerson et al. and Walker show that over 40% of betting shop punters believe that bet selection is primarily a matter of skill whereas only 12% of slot machine players believe that the way they play has any influence on the amount they win. These differences in approach to playing are consistent with the view expressed elsewhere that the mix of chance and skill in gambling on horses is particularly attractive to the serious gambler. However, if the slot machine player is not serious about winning, can we believe that he or she is serious about being entertained by the activity?

It has been suggested by Daley (1987) that slot machine players "are buying time". The function of the time might be leisure, social involvement, escapism or relaxation. Thus, the player spends time on the machine because this activity is intrinsically rewarding quite apart from the money involved. If it is assumed that the player starts with limited financial resources, then, other factors being equal, we can predict that they will choose their machines in such a way as to maximise their playing time. Daley points out that the newer type of multi-coin machines have the potential to reduce slot machine playing time by as much as 80%. According to Daley, regular players will prefer single-coin machines over the newer multi-coin or multi-line machines because they allow enjoyment of a longer playing period.

Daley compared the playing rates on two types of machines (single-coin and multi-line) in 600 clubs throughout New South Wales, Australia, during a one-month period. Whereas 269 million dollars was invested on 3,400 single-coin machines, 335 million dollars was invested on 2,400 multi-line machines. Clearly multi-line machines proved popular with large numbers of club patrons, although possibly these machines were not as popular as the manufacturers had expected. The fact that multi-line machines are so popular, despite an average reduction in playing time of 50% (Daley 1987, pp.239–240), suggests that Daley's argument concerning maximisation of playing time, as a major motivation for the majority of players, is incorrect. Daley provides data showing that there is a drift from higher denomination coin machines to lower denomination coin machines. This may well represent the actions of some players to extend their playing time in this way. However, the argument that slot machine players are primarily concerned with "buying time" appears to be invalidated by the continuing popularity of multi-coin and higher denomination single-coin machines.

Social Interaction

Walker (1988) asked punters in betting shops and slot machine players in clubs whether they came with a friend or not. Whereas 73% of punters reported that they went to the betting shop alone, only 41% of slot machine players went to the club alone. One possible interpretation of this difference is that clubs, in general, and slot machine playing, in particular, represent a social milieu in which the company of others is a significant part. 55% of the sample of slot machine players were aged 50 years or more. It seems reasonable to assume that people attend clubs in groups rather than as individuals for social reasons and that slot machine playing for many people may be simply an extension of the social group into an area other than eating and drinking. Older people who may have retired or whose families may have left home would have more time to spend in clubs and perhaps more need to spend time with friends (having lost the company of family or work mates). From this perspective slot machine playing for a large number of older people may be motivated neither by the hope of winning money nor by the excitement of playing the machine but rather because the activity legitimises the time spent in the company of peers. While attention appears to be focused on the machine and its outcomes, the conversations that continue with others throughout the course of playing may be of greater importance. Furthermore, by being engaged on a parallel activity with other players, each player can feel a sense of fraternity and group solidarity.

Although the social interaction perspective makes sense of the involvement of some older groups of people in the activity of playing slot machines, there are several reasons why this perspective should not be considered central to understanding slot machine playing in general. First of all, many people play the slot machines alone and reject attempts at conversation. Secondly, if conversation was the main motive for playing the machines, then the higher quality time available at coffee tables nearby would surely lead to a drift away from the machines. Finally, Caldwell (1974) has discussed the social rules which surround the activity of playing slot machines. Strict rules of access to machines are held in place by social consensus. If the machine was simply an excuse for social interaction, we would not expect these rules to be so rigorously imposed. Players would not need to protect their machines against interlopers if, in fact, any machine would fulfil the social function.

To Win Money or Jackpots

Gambling explicitly involves risking money in order to win money on an outcome that is wholly, or partly, determined by chance. By definition, gamblers are attempting to win money. However, legalised gambling is so constructed that the public who invest their money must lose. Thus, although some gamblers will win, the expectation of nearly all gamblers should be that they will lose. Why then do people gamble? Typically, gamblers give other reasons than winning money when asked. However, Baudot (1988) echoes the common-sense view when he states that the slot machine player is seeking his or her fortune. Despite the rational expectation of losing which is realistic for the structure of the game, it may well be the case that the majority of regular slot machine players are waiting expectantly for their fortune. Despite the smaller prizes, the motivation of the slot machine player may not be greatly different from that of the lottery player.

The expectation that one will make one's fortune by playing a slot machine is irrational when viewed objectively. When asked about the chance of winning on slot machines, most players know the conclusion reached by objective analysis. Why then do they continue to play? One possibility is that each slot machine player thinks that he or she will be the lucky one. According to this perspective, the explanation of why the slot machine player perseveres with the machines involves personal and erroneous cognitions. That heavy slot machine players believe that they have special means of influencing the machines is consistent with the practices observed among regular players. One common practice involves placing a few coins in several machines in order to select the one that is going to pay back more often and more money. Some players maintain certain "essential" levels of credit in the machine whereas others engage in superstitious behaviours such as holding certain denominations of coins in their hands while playing.

Cognitively based explanations of heavy gambling, in general, assume that the gambler holds a set of invalid beliefs which are maintained by a biased interpretation of the evidence (Walker 1985). Specifically, heavy gamblers believe that they can "beat the system" and make money. They believe that through logic or special insight they have an advantage over other gamblers. They believe that there is more opportunity to use skill or special knowledge in picking the outcome than there is in fact. They discount losses as being caused by factors beyond their control but count wins as evidence that their system or special knowledge is working.

Thus, despite losing large sums of money, the gambler can continue gambling with the firm expectation that shortly the gambling investments will begin to pay, the losses will be erased, and a small fortune will be acquired. Thus, a cognitive perspective is consistent with "winning money" as the reason for playing slot machines. Of course, slot machine players may not give "winning money" as the reason for playing because they are well aware of the objective futility of such a goal. Both Caldwell and Dickerson found that slot machine players reported playing for amusement and entertainment rather than as a way of making money. Furthermore, Walker (1988) found that 77% of heavy slot machine players report that there is no skill involved in playing slot machines. Slot machine gamblers report losing on the whole and expect to lose on the next machine they play. The reasoning involved in believing that you will be the lucky player under such circumstances has been referred to as *irrational thinking* (Gaboury and Ladouceur 1988).

Irrational Thinking and Slot Machine Playing

According to the cognitive theory, heavy gamblers have a set of beliefs which maintain their gambling despite losses. In games which have a skill component, the heavy gambler exaggerates his or her skill. However, slot machine playing is generally acknowledged as involving no skill and leading to an inevitable loss of money. According to the cognitive theory the heavy slot machine player privately accepts another belief: that his or her special knowledge of machines will provide a winning edge. In particular, slot machine players do not believe that all machines are equal from a payout perspective and they also believe that machines can be influenced to make a payout more probable. Until the work of Robert Ladouceur it was difficult to see how such a theory could be tested.

There is a wealth of anecdotal evidence suggesting that irrational thinking may be common among slot machine players (Caldwell 1974). Players can be observed trying a range of machines for short periods in order to avoid the "cold" or "hungry" machines and to find one that is "paying". Some players talk to their machines, and most players take precautions to prevent other people from playing *their* machine. The fact that players zealously guard *their* machine while they change money suggests that few of them believe one machine is as good as the next.

Ladouceur (Gaboury and Ladouceur 1988; Ladouceur and Gaboury 1988) introduced a method of studying the cognitions of gamblers while they play, which does not rely on the questionnaire approach. The player is required to say aloud what he or she is thinking while playing the machine. By studying the selection of bets made during the game of roulette and using the thinking aloud method, Ladouceur found that irrational thoughts predominate in the strategic thinking of the player.

TABLE 3.3

Rate of irrational thinking in playing video amusement machines, video poker and slot machines

| | | Type of machine played | | | |
		Video amusement	Video poker	Slot machines	Total
Preferred machine	Video amusement	0.012	0.066	0.139	0.072
	Video poker	0.012	0.118	0.170	0.100
	Slot machines	0.017	0.199	0.379	0.198
	Totals	0.014	0.127	0.229	

Each cell gives the proportion of irrational statements out of the total number of statements averaged across the players.

By irrational thinking, Ladouceur means beliefs such as the gambler's fallacy ("If my choice loses this time it is more likely to win next time"), personification of the machine ("This machine is making me mad on purpose"), and illusions of control ("I am getting good at this game. I think I've mastered it").

Gaboury and Ladouceur asked ten subjects, who were not regular gamblers, to play a Bally slot machine. The subjects were given 200 chips and did not play with their own money. 70% of the verbalisations were irrational. Gaboury and Ladouceur conclude that most cognitions associated with gambling on slot machines are irrational.

Ladouceur's results suggest that irrational thoughts may play a central role in maintaining gambling in games of chance. However, most of Ladouceur's published work has thus far used students as subjects in artificially created game environments. It is not clear that his results and conclusions can be generalised to slot machine playing *in situ*. Walker has extended Ladouceur's research by studying the link between irrational thinking and heavy use of slot machines at the site of the gambling (Walker 1989, 1990). The subjects were university students who reported playing slot machines, video poker machines, or video amusement machines at least twice a week throughout the year. Each group of players (nine preferring each type of game) played all three types of game with their own money for half an hour. It was hypothesised that gamblers whose preferred style of gambling is the slot machine will exhibit higher levels of irrational thinking than the other groups; that slot machines would induce more irrational thinking in all players than would the other games; and that an interaction effect would occur whereby when slot machine players are playing their preferred machine, the level of irrational thinking would be higher than anticipated. All three hypotheses were supported (see Table 3.3). Furthermore, when only rational and irrational thoughts about how to play the machine are

TABLE 3.4

Irrational strategic thinking as a proportion of all strategic thinking in playing video machines, video poker and slot machines

| | | Type of machine played | | | |
		Video amusement	Video poker	Slot machines	Totals
Preferred machine	Video amusement	0.083	0.380	0.606	0.356
	Video poker	0.133	0.576	0.657	0.456
	Slot machines	0.150	0.815	0.803	0.589
	Totals	0.122	0.590	0.689	

Each cell gives the proportion of irrational statements out of the total number of strategic statements.
From Walker 1990.

included (excluding purely descriptive statements), 80% of the verbalisations were irrational (Table 3.4), thus confirming Gaboury and Ladouceur's result.

Studies using Ladouceur's thinking aloud technique demonstrate that the verbalisations of slot machine players often reflect ideas about slot machine action and how the machines can be influenced that are false. However, this approach to the study of slot machines is purely correlational. It does not follow that irrational thinking causes persistence in playing the machines. It is equally possible that irrational thinking is an interpretation of the experience of playing and that other, possibly non-cognitive, factors cause the play itself. Furthermore, superstitious behaviours and the accompanying verbalisations would be expected according to learning theory based behavioural analyses.

A Behavioural Approach to Persistence and Impaired Control with Slot Machines

In textbooks of psychology, the slot machine is frequently used as an example of operant conditioning in human beings. These machines reinforce the pull of the lever or the press of the button according to a probability schedule. Similar schedules have been very effective in maintaining bar pressing behaviour in animals. The negative utility of the behaviour (the fact that, with continued play, money will be lost) is a schedule of punishments which conflicts with the positive reinforcement schedule. However, Skinner (1974) argued that the partial reinforcement schedule is so powerful that the behaviour will persist despite the negative utility. Of course, individual differences in response to the slot machine provide a problem with such an account. Why do some players persist with play on a regular basis whereas others play irregularly and for shorter periods of time? According to Dickerson and Adcock (1987), arousal is the important variable which must be added. Physiological arousal is subject to a wide range of individual variation and its responsive to stimulus variation. Conditioned arousal may act as a reinforcer.

Guided by such considerations, much of Dickerson's subsequent research (Dickerson 1990) has focused on locating, empirically, the determinants of persistence and impaired control in playing slot machines. Dickerson makes two distinctions of importance. First of all, the factors that determine whether a session of play starts may well be different from the factors that determine whether or not it continues. Secondly, among the factors that control whether or not the play continues, internal factors should be separated from external factors. Internal factors are those within the player such as physiological arousal, cognitions, mood and emotion. External factors are those outside the player, primarily the machine events in the course of play but also the availability of funds, time of the day, and the like.

The major study reported by Dickerson involved sixty-four slot machine players who were categorised as high frequency, medium frequency, or low frequency players. High frequency players played the slot machines once a week or more often, whereas low frequency players played less than twice a year. The subjects in the study played with their own money and were free to stop whenever they wished. As would be expected, the high frequency players played faster and continued for longer (average, 40 minutes) than did the other groups. Low frequency players continued, on average, for 13 minutes. The physiological arousal of the players, measured by heart rate, was monitored continuously together with each play and its outcome. Wins were divided into small wins of up to 50 credits and big wins of more than 50 credits. Every five minutes and after every big win, subjects completed a short questionnaire in which they rated their subjective state of excitement and assessed their likelihood of winning.

The interesting results concern the effects of small and big wins on rates of play and differences in the stability of rates of play between the different groups of players. Small wins increased the rate of play for all groups, but this increase was maintained for longer by the high frequency players than the other two groups. By contrast, big wins decreased the rate of play for all groups. Unfortunately, the break up of play in this case cannot be attributed unambiguously to the big win itself since big wins were immediately followed by a disruption to play when the questionnaire was filled out. Dickerson discounts the questionnaire because the slower rates lasted for up to three minutes. However, some interaction between the large win and filling out the questionnaire cannot be ruled out. For example, the questionnaire forces the player to attend to his or her excitement in response to the big win and to turn his or her attention away from the machine itself.

Differences between the groups in the structure of play are also interesting. Low frequency and medium frequency players show little consistency in their rates of play from one minute to the next. However, high frequency players keep up a relatively constant rate of play in the absence of pay-outs. This rate of play increases with small wins over the course of one or two minutes but then drifts back to the baseline rate. Only big wins disrupt the rate of play. The failure to find major effects in the measures of physiological arousal, subjective excitement, and expectation of winning points to the relative importance of machine events in determining variations in the play of slot machines. Dickerson has drawn the following general conclusions concerning the influence of different factors on impaired control in the play of slot machines.

(1) Learning. Learning has a major impact on impaired control. People who play the slot machines frequently build up stereotypic rates of play which are responsive in different ways to small wins and big wins. Players are probably unaware of the fact that they play faster after small wins.

(2) Cognitions. Cognitions have little or no role in controlling the play of slot machines or maintaining play within a session. Expectations of winning are not related to the rate of play or the length of the session. Cognitions are viewed as explanations that players give after the event for why they have continued to play the machine. Irrational explanations therefore will be found mainly towards the end of a session.

(3) Arousal. Arousal is not casually related to impairment of control and has no clear relationship to the speed of play or changes in play rate. Even big wins caused only small increases in heart rate. This failure to find arousal based effects would be explained if players are simply "killing time".

(4) Prior mood. This variable has a major impact on the length of the session. If the player begins the session in a depressed mood, the session lasts longer.

(5) Personality. No clear effects for personality differences have been found, although there is some suggestion that both the horse racing punters and the slot machine players are relatively low on sensation-seeking.

Unfortunately, Dickerson's conclusion concerning the strong impact of learning and the weak impact of cognitions on impairment of control in slot machine playing may be premature. Dickerson has not demonstrated impairment of control in high frequency players but the reverse.

High frequency players are less disrupted by machine events than are low frequency players. High frequency players maintain their rate of play despite the length of a losing sequence, whereas the play of low frequency players is more unpredictable from one minute to the next. Even the disruptions to the high frequency player's rate of play following a big win may be caused by the unwanted intrusions of the observer. Thus, high frequency players show greater stability in their play than low frequency players.

Dickerson did not measure irrational thinking and so the effect of this variable on persistence or rate of play cannot be assessed. In fact, Dickerson's only measure of cognition was a rating obtained every five minutes concerning the expectation of winning. Not only is this an impoverished measure of the complexity of thoughts uncovered by Ladouceur and others, but in sessions of length 13 minutes (low frequency players) or 40 minutes (high frequency players), one score every five minutes is unlikely to provide sufficient data to draw a valid conclusion in even this limited domain.

Why do sessions last longer for high frequency players than low frequency players? It is very likely because they allocate more money to the enterprise. Why they should do this may have much to do with their goals in playing the machines and with the irrational cognitions associated with reaching those goals. If Dickerson's work has any implication concerning the role of machine events in determining the length of a session or impaired control over play, it is likely to involve the observation that high frequency players maintain their rate of play despite the absence of wins. It is this learned ability to disregard the losses that is important. Where the low frequency player is unlikely to persist through a bad sequence, the high frequency player is able to do so. But the important learning in this case is not within the session but across sessions: the high frequency player learns that even the longest of bad runs must end. This is precisely the kind of experience that may become associated with irrational thinking.

Summary

Slot machines have been described as the epitome of non-skill gambling. Yet slot machines are popular throughout the world and are a major source of revenue in casinos. The central question for the psychology of gambling concerns why some people play the games regularly, sometimes every day of the week. Excitement and arousal appear to be absent and the best studies of slot machine playing have failed to show a central role for physiological arousal. Playing the machines as a basis for social interaction may be a primary motive for some players, especially the elderly, but does not explain the strong rules that forbid using another player's machine. Research based on having gamblers verbalise their thoughts while playing the machine have shown that the majority of strategically oriented statements are false. Regular slot machine gamblers appear to believe a number of things about the way in which slot machines operate and can be influenced which are false. These beliefs have been called irrational thinking and may be the basis of the explanation of why slot machine players persist through long losing sequences.

Fruit Machine Players

The inordinate commercial success of slot machines is one of the most disconcerting enigmas posed by contemporary amusements.

(Fischer 1990)

Fruit machines are common throughout Britain in amusement arcades and in cafés and fish and chips shops. Typically, the fruit machines are placed in the same area as video amusement machines of the "space invaders" variety. It is common to see children playing both the video amusement machines and the fruit machines. According to Ide-Smith and Lea (1988) the average age at which children begin playing fruit machines is between eight and nine years and according to Fischer (1989) the majority of children in Britain have played fruit machines by the time they have settled into secondary education. Perhaps this tolerance of gambling by children is linked to the fact that the machines are played for 10p or less per turn for a maximum return of £2 in money. This level of gambling may be perceived by many people as not dangerous.

The siting of fruit machines in amusement arcades, side-by-side with video amusement machines, ensures that these machines are played primarily by the young. In this way they differ from the slot machines of the United States which are found exclusively in casinos and played mainly by adults, although it has been noted by Jacobs (1989) that a considerable amount of illegal teenage gambling on slot machines takes place in casinos. Furthermore, while women make up a majority of the slot machine players in clubs in Australia (Dickerson, Walker, Legg-England and Hinchy 1990), boys make up the majority of fruit machine players in England (Fischer 1989). Again, this is consistent with the siting of fruit machines together with video games in arcades.

Perhaps the most extensive investigation of adolescents' playing fruit machines is provided by Fischer from Plymouth in England. Fischer (1990) provides a sociological explanation for heavy adolescent involvement with fruit machines. Fischer's data comes in part from eighteen months in which she worked part-time in the change box of an amusement arcade. According to Fischer, fruit machines have a similar social function for children as non-gambling games such as marbles and computer games. It is not the monetary gains that are important but the acquisition of self-esteem and recognition among peers for the prowess shown. If it is agreed among the players that there is some skill possible in the play of fruit machines, then it follows that the acquisition of such skill can become a basis for status within the social group. One of the adolescents observed by Fischer was much admired by his peers because he had memorised the reel sequences for one machine. Thus, if the reels showed ♣♣Ó, this particular player would know how many nudges were necessary to achieve ♣♣♣ and thus obtain a payout. Thus, fruit machines are no different from other forms of children's play in the social function they serve: they become an arena of contests through which social hierarchies are worked out.

Against this sociological explanation of the attraction of fruit machines is the observation of Brown (1990) that large numbers of children play the machines alone and not with their peers. Adolescents who play the machines regularly show by their explanations for playing that the fruit machines are exerting a similar attraction to that of slot machines for adults.

If you win you sort of think the machine is paying out, so you put more in, you think you've got a chance until you put your last one in.

When you get over a fiver you think, "Oh hell, I'll get it back," so you just keep putting it in. Because you want your money back, you keep going down and down.

(From Graham 1988, p.20)

Fischer allows that heavier use of the machine may be associated with a different motivation: that of beating the machine. It is likely that, at this point, the play of the machine may become a problem for the adolescents involved. Also, something of a problem for Fischer's analysis is a result obtained by Griffiths (1990) with a questionnaire administered to sixty-nine adolescent fruit machine players as they left an arcade. Griffiths asked the adolescents their reasons for playing the fruit machines. The main reason these adolescents played was for fun (84%). To win money was another popular reason (48%). Only 2% indicated that they played to impress their friends and only 18% played because of the challenge. Thus, the explanation given by Fischer for the attraction that fruit machines have for adolescents is not supported by what the adolescents say. However, it may well be the case that adolescents do not fully understand their own motives and that they give answers of a socially desirable kind.

Video Poker: the Second Generation of Slot Machines

In the standard slot machine, there is no opportunity for the gambler to influence the machine. The handle is pulled or the button pressed, the reels spin, and the result obtained. By contrast, in video poker machines, the gambler can influence the outcome. Five cards are displayed and the player can elect to hold whichever cards he or she wishes. The cards which are not held are replaced in the draw and the outcome determined by the quality of the hand held. Typically, video poker machines pay out only for two pairs or better. Again, typically, the player is offered double or nothing after a win depending on the colour (black or red) of a randomly chosen card. The best strategy for playing video poker has been published in various places. This strategy specifies which cards should be held in every possible situation. It is interesting to note that the double or nothing part of the game is the only fair bet. The edge to the house is typically in the range 4% to 10% depending on the laws in the part of the world concerned. It is also interesting that the element of skill involved, although small, has been important in terms of legal decisions. In setting up casinos in Queensland, Australia, the State Government prohibited the inclusion of slot machines in casinos but allowed video poker machines because in the latter case some skill was involved.

Dumont and Ladouceur (1990) investigated the motivation of regular and occasional video poker gamblers by questionnaires administered during and after play. As would be expected, regular gamblers, who played the machines at least once a week, were more motivated to play than the occasional gamblers. Their reasons given for gambling included, to try one's luck, for the fun of it, for the thrill, and to win money. This last reason, winning money, appears to be irrational given the structure of the game. The more often a gambler plays video poker the less likely he or she is to win. Nevertheless, some video poker players insist that it is possible to win if the game is played correctly. Dumont and Ladouceur investigated the rate of irrational verbalisations among their sample of video poker players, but found no difference between occasional and regular players. However, in their method, statements "were judged irrational if they make reference to something other than chance such as . . . personal control". Since video poker is an interactive game in which players do influence the outcome, it is possible that some of the explanations given for skilful play by the regular gamblers were incorrectly categorised as irrational.

Although Dumont and Ladouceur report that winning money is a motive for some video poker gamblers, it is likely that more video poker gamblers are playing to win money than report so. Since nearly all regular gamblers lose money over time playing the game, it would not be surprising if many avoided the real reason for playing (making money) and reported instead that they played for fun or thrills (a reason that is difficult to falsify). However, if we assume that the reasons given by regular video poker gamblers for playing the machines are representative motives, then it would be interesting to know which motive is most associated with the development of gambling problems. Data collected by Hunter (1990) is relevant to this issue.

Hunter has investigated problem gambling among 250 gamblers who sought help in a hospital in Las Vegas. Given the wide range of gambling games available in Las Vegas, it would not be surprising if a similar spread of games was at the centre of the problem gambling. Hunter's results are remarkable. Out of 110 female gamblers, 95% reported only gambling on video poker and out of 140 male gamblers, 74% reported that video poker was their problem. Although there are many reasons why statistics of this kind may not generalise from Las Vegas to the rest of the world, the fact that video poker causes problems for so many people suggests that there is some aspect of video poker than encourages gamblers to persevere with the game. By comparison, Hunter found that very few of the gamblers had any problem with the traditional slot machines. When Hunter investigated the motives for playing, he did not find that these problem gamblers were playing for fun or for the thrill. Rather, they believed that they were good players who knew how to win at the game. Furthermore, it seems likely that these heavy video poker gamblers are relatively skilful at the game since they gamble for astonishingly long sessions. One gambler reported playing for 72 hours. Even if such session lengths are greatly exaggerated, the fact that heavy gamblers can maintain rapid play for hours suggests that the edge to the house for the optimum strategy of play is very low.

Irrational Thinking Among Fruit Machine Players and Video Poker Players

Using the same approach that Gaboury and Ladouceur used with slot machine players, Griffiths (1990) from the University of Exeter, has examined irrational thinking among thirty regular and thirty non-regular fruit machine players. The regular players played once a week or more whereas the non-regular players played once a month or less. The average of the sample was twenty-three years and so is comparable to the subjects used by Gaboury and Ladouceur and by Walker. However, by contrast with Walker's study, the subjects were given money with which to play and lasted on average ten minutes. Half of the subjects were placed in the thinking aloud condition.

Interestingly, the regular players obtained more plays on the machines for their money than did the non-regulars, suggesting that there is an element of skill involved in playing fruit machines. When Griffiths examined the statements of the regular and non-regular players in the thinking aloud condition, he found that the regular players produced significantly more irrational verbalisations (14% of all statements were irrational) than did non-regular players (where only 3% of statements

TABLE 3.5
Irrational thinking among video poker and fruit machine players

	% irrational verbalisations while thinking aloud	
	Fruit machines (Griffiths 1990)	Video poker machines (Walker 1990)
Regular players	14.0	11.8
Non-regular players	2.5	6.6

From Walker 1990; Griffiths 1990.

were irrational). These results are consistent in the direction of the difference with those obtained by Gaboury and Ladouceur but contrast with the results of both Walker and Gaboury and Ladouceur in the rates of irrational thinking obtained. However, this inconsistency is resolved when we examine the methods used by the three studies in assessing the rate of irrational thinking. Gaboury and Ladouceur analysed only those statements which referred to how the machine was being played whereas Walker and Griffiths analysed all of the utterances whether they were about the play or not. Although the rate of 38% irrational thoughts found by Walker for slot machine players is higher than the 14% found by Griffiths for fruit machine players, this is not the correct comparison to make. Since fruit machines have a "hold" mechanism and involve an element of skill, they are therefore more similar in structure to the video poker machines than to the slot machines studied by Walker. Thus the best comparison is between, on the one hand, the regular video poker players and the video amusement players (non-regulars playing video poker) from Walker's study and, on the other hand, the regular fruit machine players and non-regular fruit machine players from Griffiths' study. The comparison is shown in Table 3.5. Clearly, despite the different machines and the different cultures, there is good agreement between the results of Griffiths and Walker.

Griffiths' data is particularly interesting because he was able to make further comparisons on sub-categories within the irrational thinking category. Compared to the non-regulars, the regulars engaged in more personification of the machine. Examples of personification include, "The machine is laughing at me now" and "The machine knows what I'm thinking now." Regular players exhibited more swearing at the machine and more talking to the machine. One subject in Walker's study held conversations with a little man in the machine who apparently controlled the fate of each play. Finally, regulars provided significantly more irrational explanations for their losses. In Walker's study, one subject, after a long losing sequence, claimed that the symbols spelled out SATAN: the devil was in the machine.

Griffiths also found that regular players made more references to skill than did non-regular players. This is consistent with the proposition that where a form of gambling allows an element of skill, heavy gamblers will be found to over-value the skill component. After the game was over, Griffiths asked the players questions concerning the role of skill in playing the machines. Regular players were significantly more likely than non-regulars to place skill as equal or more important than chance and to rate themselves as having more skill than the average player.

Summary

Video poker, although similar to the conventional slot machine in many ways, differs by allowing the gambler to interact with the machine. The gambler chooses which cards to hold and which cards to have replaced at the draw. This choice allows for variations in skill that cannot occur in a conventional slot machine. It is this element of skill which appears to make this form of gambling particularly attractive. Although the gambler cannot win in the long run, the element of skill may well be the basis for maintaining a belief that the gambler has an edge and money can be won. Beliefs of this kind are present in gamblers for whom video poker play has become a problem. The evidence available suggests that video poker may be a greater cause of problem gambling than any other game.

Roulette

The prima donna of casino games. Talented, attractive, temperamental and full of history. Literary accounts of the game and its consequences abound. Yet it is a tough game, with no percentage that is not against the player.

(Allcock and Dickerson 1986, p.68)

Although casinos have a history stretching back into the nineteenth century, it is in the second half of the twentieth century that they have developed worldwide. A wide range of games are played with distinct variations from one culture to another. In this section we will concentrate on roulette which is one of the best known games of all. Although roulette and blackjack are core games in any casino, they stand in sharp contrast. Both are games which have attracted a lot of research aimed at understanding the motivations of gamblers. Roulette is a game of chance for which there is, in principle, no system that can provide an edge. By contrast, the game of blackjack has developed as a battlefield in which the casino attempts to maintain its advantage against an array of impressive techniques which are used by players to gain an edge. Why do people play these games? We can be sure that the answers for roulette will be quite different from the answers for blackjack. Roulette and blackjack share in common the fact that the players tend to remain quietly concentrating. They differ from craps and two-up which produce a noisy group of players who are keen to make themselves heard. Based on this observation alone, it seems likely that different casino games attract different kinds of people according to temperament.

There are many questions to answer about the game of roulette and those who play it. A ball spins around the roulette wheel and lands on a given number and colour. Thirty-six numbers are red or black but the zero is green. When the ball lands on the zero, the house wins all bets placed on the other numbers and their combinations. The house advantage is one number in thirty-seven (2.7%) if we ignore the American wheel on which there are two zeros. In some casinos the house advantage is cut further by the addition of a prison rule: bets are held until the next throw which determines whether your bet is lost or returned (1.35% advantage). The interesting question is simple: with such a small advantage to the house, why do so many people lose their total savings at the game (Leigh 1977)?

Oldman (1974) has pointed to the many and varied ways in which roulette players attempt to choose the winning numbers. Systems often focus on betting strategies such as the Martingale. The Martingale is well known to children everywhere in its simple form. A losing bet can always be covered by a larger bet on the next play. Thus, we might decide that the wheel is favouring *rouge* at this time. We place $2 on red. If this loses we next place $4 on red. Each loss is followed by doubling the previous bet. This doubling-up strategy ensures that when red eventually wins, the bet made recoups all the previous losses and leaves a $2 surplus. Thus, the player is guaranteed to win, in principle.

Reverse systems follow the opposite approach. In the reverse Martingale, for example, the initial bet is, say, $8. If this loses, the next bet is $4; and, if this too loses, the next bet is $2. Wins increase the bet size to double the previous bet. If the $2 bet loses, the cycle begins again at $8. The idea here is to have a system in which small bets are made when the outcomes are generally unfavourable and in which big bets are made when the outcomes are favourable. When the player hits a run of wins, the betting becomes dramatic and a fortune can be made (Leigh 1977).

With such systems available, why has roulette become known as a dangerous gambling game. How is it possible for a person to lose his or her fortune at such a game when the advantage to the bank is so small? The answer lies in the structure of the game and the psychology of the individuals who play it.

The size of bets that players make increases over time (Ladouceur, Mayrand and Tourigny 1987). The reason for this may be found in the twin concepts of the law of effect and the phenomenon of chasing. The law of effect suggests that when the outcomes have been favourable so that the player is ahead, they are encouraged to continue. Furthermore, with larger bets the profit can be increased. This echoes the reverse systems philosophy. Chasing refers to the outlay of progressively larger bets when losing to recoup one's losses. This echoes the simple Martingale and other classical betting strategies. Thus, over time the bet size can be expected to increase. This in itself is not sufficient to cause a player to lose a fortune. The important factors concern the upper and lower limits for betting.

Casinos typically set an upper limit and a lower limit to the bet size. The upper limit poses a problem for the Martingale and similar methods. Since, past a certain point, doubling up is not permitted, there is little the gambler can do to recoup losses. At the other extreme, when all of the available funds have been expended, there is little the gambler can do to regain the losses. As the betting size increases and the length of the gambling session increases, it becomes increasingly likely that the gambler will reach this final state. Thus, one reason why roulette can produce large losses within an evening is the poor money management primarily associated with chasing losses. Good money management is ensured by the use of reverse systems. However, such systems maintain a slow rate of loss whereas standard systems maintain and the various forms of special knowledge allow the gambler to believe that winning is possible. It is not surprising therefore that the safer reverse systems are not so popular.

There is no legal method in roulette of gaining an edge over the house. However, illegal methods are available involving timing the wheel and the use of mathematical models to determine the likely outcome (Thorp 1984). Since problem gambling associated with roulette is unlikely to be based on the use of illegal methods, we shall assume that all systems have an equal expectation of loss for the gambler and concentrate on the question of why the regular roulette gambler continues to return to the table despite overall, increasing losses.

Observation of roulette players in casinos throughout the world will reveal that the regulars are very industrious. Records of the outcomes are maintained through hours of play. Complex calculations are often necessary and roulette may often appear to be hard work to the onlooker. This is not the behaviour of people engaging in an exciting pastime for the thrill of it. It is the behaviour of people focused on the goal of predicting the next spin and of being right sufficiently often to win money from the casino. Sometimes the roulette gambler will win large sums of money from the casino but more often he or she will lose. Perhaps the most convincing explanation for why the roulette gambler persists despite the losses is the range of false beliefs that they hold about the game. Gaboury and Ladouceur (1989) have shown that roulette gamblers, like slot machine gamblers, express beliefs about the game which are false. Many of these beliefs can be categorised as special knowledge of the properties of the roulette wheel. Nearly all of them involve the assumption that the outcome of the spin in any one game depends in part on the outcomes across previous games. Among these beliefs, perhaps the most widespread is the "gambler's fallacy" which occurs when roulette gamblers accept arguments of the following kind. Red and black are equally likely to occur. Therefore, if more reds have occurred in the recent sequence of outcomes then black is more likely on the next spin (to even up the outcomes). Another category of false beliefs held by regular roulette gamblers concerns personal luck. Wagenaar and Keren (1988) have shown that luck through possessions, practices, and personal insight help the gambler make winning choices. Failures are discounted and successes are taken as evidence of the validity of their claims. Long runs of failures can be discounted as errors in determining whether one's luck is in. In this way, roulette gamblers can maintain an illusion of control in a game where they have no control.

Summary

Although roulette is one of the well-known gambling games which comes closest to providing the gambler with a fair bet, it is also one of the games on which large sums of money can be lost quickly. Unlike slot machines, roulette allows gamblers to escalate the betting to a point where their bank roll can be exhausted by a bad run of ordinary proportions. Money management schemes can minimise such risks, but are not seen as attractive by roulette gamblers. These gamblers prefer to "win" by using a range of techniques all of which are based on false assumptions. Roulette players believe that the wheel is predictable and that through personal luck and insight they will win.

The Relative Attractiveness of Gambling Games

In Australia, most forms of gambling are legal in most states. Australia has followed the path of legalisation further perhaps than most other countries, but legalisation is the trend throughout the Western world (Eadington 1987) and the forms of gambling legalised tend to echo similar forms already legalised in other countries. Furthermore, although variations exist from one country to another, the percentage take by the agencies offering gambling to the public is much the same throughout the world for each kind of gambling. Although the house edge in American roulette is twice the size of the edge in European roulette, the percentage taken by casinos in roulette is much smaller than

TABLE 3.6
Percentage take by legal gambling in Australia

Form of gambling	% return	Hoped for win ($)
Casinos—blackjack	99	5[1]
roulette	97	72
Slot machines	85	1000
Totalisator—racing	84	1000[2]
Totalisator—football	75	4000[3]
Instant lotteries	64	25,000
Lotteries	64	100,000
Lotto	60	500,000

Based on Walker 1985, p.146.
[1] Based on basic strategy.
[2] Hoped for "big win", Walker 1988.
[3] Windross 1985.

the percentage taken by totalisators on horse racing throughout the world. Similarly, as large as is the edge in totalisator gambling, it is rarely as large as the house edge in numbers games such as lotteries. Table 3.6 shows the percentage of money wagered which is returned to the gambling public by gambling agencies in Australia (even within Australia there are minor regional variations).

There is an important conclusion to be drawn from Table 3.6. Whatever else we might say, gambling is not a rational economic activity. Each dollar invested by the gambler has a value of less than a dollar. The dollar invested in the slot machine is worth 85 cents and the dollar invested in lotto is worth 60 cents. If financial institutions offered potential investors deals of this type they would soon be out of business. Thus, whatever the explanation for gambling, it will involve psychological principles rather than economic principles.

The heavy involvement of people in the various gambling forms is difficult to understand in purely economic terms. If gaining money was the main reason for gambling, then the vast majority of Australians would be better off buying "Aussie Bonds". One would expect gambling to decline in popularity and finally become the province of a small minority with economically masochistic urges. The fact that gambling remains popular across the years suggests that an answer to the question, "Why do people gamble?", will involve psychological, rather than economic, factors.

(Walker 1985, p.147)

Eadington also draws the same conclusion provided that we accept an objective utility approach to economic rationality. Since all unfair gambles have an expectation of loss, no economically rational person should accept the opportunity to gamble:

No "economic man" would freely and willingly accept a decline in his level of utility, because there is no self-interest in doing so.

(Eadington 1987, p.266)

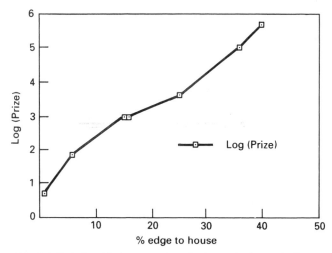

F<small>IG</small>. 3.1 Relationship between size of prize and edge to the house.

However, Table 3.6 reveals an interesting aspect of the psychology of the gambler. The larger the prize that the gambler hopes for, the larger the edge that can be taken by the house. However, there is a regularity about the data in Table 3.6 which is not immediately apparent. Figure 3.1 shows the logarithm of the size of the prize plotted against the edge to the house. The resulting curve is approximately linear, suggesting that attractiveness of different gambles can be quantified and shows regularities that will be explained by any complete theory of gambling.

The curve shown in Figure 3.1 shows us the house edge that gamblers are willing to accept for the chance of winning the prize. However, it does not say anything about the aspects of gambling which will be effective in having the gambler persist with the gambling and invest more than intended. The attractiveness of gambling is only partly about the size of the prize and the edge to the house. It is also partly about all those factors that encourage the gambler to continue despite his or her losses.

If the attractiveness of gambling games is measured by the amount of money or time that gamblers are willing to invest, then a different kind of curve may be obtained. At the one extreme, games of pure chance may be limited in their attractiveness by the fact that there is no opportunity for skill. The gambler must rely on the methods by which personal luck can be used to obtain the prize. Thus, a lottery may be popular in the sense of attracting large numbers of investors but is unlikely to cause the gambler to invest great amounts of time or money. This is not simply because lotteries are drawn hours or days after the ticket is drawn. With scratch lotteries the feedback is immediate and the opportunity exists to buy one ticket after another. But scratch lotteries are rarely associated with problem gambling. There are few ways in which a person can influence the result of the scratch lottery. At the other extreme from the game of pure chance, there are those gambling games in which skilful play can provide a large edge. However, the difficulty in obtaining skill and the fact that money will be lost to more skilful players places limits on the attractiveness of games such as bridge and poker. Thus the most attractive games are likely to be those in which there is a small role for skill but which are primarily determined by chance. The more skill that can be exhibited the better, but that skill must not be sufficiently effective to make the game unattractive to the majority or to the novices who take part. Horse racing is an excellent example of the kind of gambling game which can become a problem for the gambler. There is great potential for showing skill and knowledge but that skill and knowledge is not sufficient for most gamblers to overcome the edge to the house (Solonsch 1990). The level of skill is sufficient for gamblers to be able to say who is or who is not skilled and yet that categorisation does not necessarily reflect who is winning and who is not (Zola 1969). And most importantly, from the perspective of problem gambling, betting on the races provides every opportunity for escalation in the size of bets, chasing losses, and investing more than intended. Similarly, in the area of gambling machines, we would expect the skill based games such as video poker to be more habit forming than the games of pure chance available on standard slot machines. The evidence provided by Hunter (1990) supports this hypothesis.

4

Explanations for Gambling

The Causes of Gambling Behaviour

Theories of gambling are plentiful. However, in many instances, theories believed to be in opposition to one another are actually describing different aspects of the gambling phenomenon. Evidence supporting one theory cannot be interpreted as evidence against the other theory. If the central question is, "Why do people gamble?", then the answer in terms of causes will certainly be complex. The causes of gambling will include the cultural circumstances into which a person is born, the life experiences which define the personality, the history and impact of gambling on the individual, and the current situation with its perceived potentials and rewards for gambling among other alternatives.

When we try to explain why a person gambles, we can be trying to answer one of several different questions. If the question concerns the reasons given for gambling, then our explanation will be in terms of the response to questionnaires and interviews in which gamblers explain why they choose to gamble and, perhaps why they choose one form of gambling over another. However, from some perspectives, the reasons given for gambling are an insufficient explanation of why the person gambles. Nisbett and Wilson, for example, point out a wide range of phenomena in which we show no evidence of knowing the causative factors. When asked for reasons we provide accounts which are often consistent with socially agreed explanations and which explain our actions to our own satisfaction but which ignore crucial causative factors. Thus, if the question concerns the causes of a person gambling, then our explanation may involve factors beyond the individual's awareness and constructs whose range of application is not limited to gambling. Freud's concept of a primary addictive cycle is an example of one such construct. Freud suggested that gambling may be an adult replacement for masturbation (see Chapter 6).

The Reasons Gamblers Give for Their Gambling

The reasons given for gambling are not homogeneous across different forms of gambling. Rather two distinct motivational patterns can be distinguished: one for numbers games such as lotteries, lotto and pools; another for other kinds of gambling such as horse race betting and poker machines. The reasons given by people for taking part in lotteries and similar games can be summarised simply as, "the hope of winning a large sum of money". Other reasons such as the social aspects of gambling, amusement, and excitement are given by only a small minority of persons surveyed. By constrast the reasons given for betting on horses, dogs, football, baseball and the like are more varied. The main reasons given involve excitement and having a good time. Typically, "making money" is given as the main reason for betting (in betting shops and with bookmakers), playing slot machines, and playing casino games by only about one-third of those interviewed (Caldwell 1974; Downes, Davies, David and Stone 1976; Kallick-Kaufmann 1979). Since the majority of gamblers using these forms of gambling lose money over time, it is not surprising that other reasons than making money are given for the activity. If the occasional gambler's motivation is readily understandable, that of the heavy gambler is less easy to comprehend. The monetary losses for nearly all heavy gamblers are likely to be substantial and painful.

Thus, when we seek the explanation for why people gamble, the reasons given will be given little weight. Rather, we shall need to examine their actions in the context of a range of possible causes and seek to eliminate possible explanations by reference to experimental data. It is at this point that the distinction between distal and proximal causes becomes relevant. We shall examine the explanations given for gambling according to where the proposed causes lie in the chain of cause and effect that leads ultimately to the gambling behaviour. Thus we will first examine distal explanations for gambling and then subsequently the proximal causes.

When we consider the causes of a person gambling, it will prove useful to make a distinction between the immediate (proximal) cause of gambling and the more distant (distal) causes that gave rise to the present circumstances (Walker 1990). Psychodynamic conceptions of personality expose a role for gambling which may stretch back to the childhood relations of the gambler with his parents. Explaining gambling in terms of the personality of the individual is an example of distal causation. The proximal cause of gambling will be such that it structures and motivates the gambling behaviour observed. Proximal causes are likely to be either behavioural, as when we link the gambling response to the immediate stimuli and conditioning history of the individual, or cognitive, as when we see the gambling behaviour as the consequence of the positive evaluation of gambling with respect to its alternatives.

Distal Causes of Gambling

Not all people are tempted to gamble. Even in societies where most forms of gambling are legal, there remains a hard core of individuals for whom a bet is anathema. Among the majority who gamble at some time in their lives, many will not be involved in more than the occasional bet. It is not that they are unwilling to have a bet but rather that betting has no attraction for them. Others will buy a lottery ticket regularly but have no interest in extending their gambling to other forms. And finally, there are those for whom gambling becomes a major part of their lives. When we ask about distal factors, we are asking what it is in the history of a person that causes him or her to relate to gambling in a characteristic way.

There is no doubt that the legalisation of new gambling forms increases the amount of gambling (measured by money lost) and the numbers of people who gamble. Beyond legalisation, gender, age, socioeconomic class, ethnicity, and religion, are all related to the incidence of gambling. However, these demographic variables are not sufficient to explain why one person gambles when another does not. People from every cell of the intersection of these variables will be found in the casinos of Reno, Las Vegas and Atlantic City. The missing class of variables are internal. What is it about a person that predisposes him or her to gamble when the opportunity arises.

Personality Based Predispositions to Gamble

Personality traits are one kind of predisposition. They are summary features of the way an individual behaves, in general, across situations. By themselves, they are not explanatory. If the claim is made that a given person gambles because he or she has a high need for achievement, we may still inquire how that personality trait came about. Even worse, some explanations in terms of personality traits are dangerously circular. This person gambles because they are risk-oriented; we know they are risk-oriented because they gamble. In order for personality traits to be of use at all, the presence and level of the trait must be determined independently of the behaviour we seek to explain. The independence of trait from the gambling behaviour is enhanced when a biological basis for the trait can be demonstrated. Sensation-seeking, for example, is correlated with the presence of metabolites of noradrenalin (Roy 1990). If it can be demonstrated that sensation-seeking is also associated with involvement in gambling, fears of circularity in the argument are diminished.

Nevertheless, there is another major problem for trait approaches to the explanation of gambling. This is the issue of causation. If high sensation seekers are more likely to gamble, what is the direction of causation? Does sensation-seeking cause the gambling or do gamblers report being sensation-seekers? If biological differences are found between heavy and light gamblers, was it the biology that caused the gambling or the gambling that caused the differences in biology? Gambling and depression are linked. Naturally, losing at gambling may cause depression. If the biological differences between light and heavy gamblers are related to the presence of depression, then the gambling may have caused both effects.

In order to gain information on causation, longitudinal research is necessary. It is necessary to know whether or not the biological and personality trait differences preceded the onset of gambling. Since gambling typically makes an appearance in primary school, the personality information will have to come from early in the life of the individual. Interestingly, psychoanalytic theories suggest just that. The personality structure of the individual is determined primarily by family relationships in the pre-school years.

Sensation Seeking

Three personality dimensions have been the focus of many of the attempts to isolate the personality characteristics that are associated with heavy gambling: extroversion; locus of control; and sensation-seeking. Of these, perhaps, the strongest case has been made for sensation seeking. Sensation seeking is the "need for varied, novel, and complex sensations and experiences, and the willingness to take physical and social risks for the sake of such experience" (Zuckerman 1979, p.10). According to Zuckermann, we should expect to find that gamblers are higher than non-gamblers on measures of sensation seeking. Table 4.1 summarises the results from studies that have tested this hypothesis.

It can be seen from Table 4.1 that the results are quite variable: Kuley and Jacobs (1988) provide data that support the hypothesised relationship between sensation seeking and gambling, whereas the other studies either find no evidence of a relationship (Anderson and Brown 1984; Ladouceur and Mayrand 1986) or evidence of the opposite relationship (Blaszczynski et al. 1986; Dickerson et al. 1987). Nevertheless, the hypothesis can survive the negative evidence in one of three ways. First of all, those studies providing negative evidence might be rejected on methodological grounds. Thus, Kuley and Jacobs point out that age was not controlled in the Anderson and Brown study. Since sensation

TABLE 4.1
The relationship between sensation-seeking and involvement in gambling

Author(s)	Year	Type of gambler	Status on sensation-seeking
Anderson and Brown	1984	Blackjack players	No difference from non-gamblers
Blaszczynski, Wilson and McConaghy	1986	Pathological gamblers	Lower than norms
Ladouceur and Mayrand	1986	Roulette players	No difference from non-gamblers
Dickerson, Hinchy and Fabre	1987	Horse racing punters	Lower than norms
Kuley and Jacobs	1988	Problem gamblers	Higher than social gamblers

seeking scores decrease with age and since the gamblers in the Anderson and Brown study were older than the control group of non-gamblers, the failure to support the hypothesis might have resulted from this confounding.

Kuley and Jacobs used two criteria to choose their groups of problem gamblers and social gamblers as shown in Table 4.2. It can be seen from Table 4.2 that Kuley and Jacobs have shown that sensation seeking is associated jointly with high frequency gambling and the admission of problems caused by gambling. Strictly speaking we do not know whether sensation seeking causes high frequency gambling (as Zuckerman hypothesised) or whether sensation seeking causes gambling problems. In order to disentangle the two effects, subjects would be required from all four cells. This would almost certainly prove impossible for the problem gambling group since it is extremely unlikely that gamblers who can answer YES to seven or more of the GA questions will have gambled on as few as two days in the last six months. However, the other two cells provide the important comparison between high and low frequency gamblers for who there are no great gambling induced problems. Zuckerman's prediction needs to be tested with this control added.

The second way in which the sensation seeking hypothesis might survive is to realise that sensation seeking and gambling might be interrelated: sensation seeking might predispose a person to gamble but gambling may change the personality of the gambler. For example,

TABLE 4.2
*Criteria for inclusion as a problem or social gambler in Kuley and Jacobs
(1988) study*

	Answer *Yes* to 7 or more of GAs 20 questions	
	Yes	No
Gamble 2 days/week in last 6 months	"Problem"	Not included
Gamble on 2 days or less in last 6 months	Not included	"Social"

heavy gambling may cause financial losses that induce depression. The personality of the heavy gambler may therefore move from a positive sensation seeking mode into a negative and withdrawn mode. Clearly, other similar kinds of arguments might also be advanced to explain why a decrease in sensation seeking scores might occur. All of these arguments would suggest a curvilinear relationship between the extent of gambling and sensation seeking scores. Non-gamblers would be lower on sensation seeking; moderate gamblers would be higher; but heavy gamblers with gambling problems would score lower on sensation seeking. Such a curvilinear hypothesis fits the data better, although the studies by Anderson and Brown (1984) and Ladouceur and Mayrand (1986) are still inconsistent. Also, by moving to an interactive model, we have given weight to the argument that the gambling may cause the scores on sensation seeking (rationalisation of behaviour) rather than the reverse.

Finally, the hypothesis may survive if it is argued that it is not the frequency of gambling that is related to sensation seeking but the betting behaviour itself. Gamblers who are high on sensation seeking would be expected to make bigger bets and to prefer longer odds. Evidence in favour of this hypothesis comes from several studies. Anderson and Brown found that regular blackjack players who were high on sensation seeking made bigger bets in a casino blackjack game. Similar results have been reported by Kuhlman (1976) and Wolfgang and Zenker (1982).

Thus, it is too early to dismiss sensation seeking as having no relationship to gambling. At this time, the requirement is for models of gambling which might incorporate sensation seeking in a way that makes sense of the results to date. Brown, in particular, has developed such a model and this will be considered later in this chapter.

Extroversion

Although the popularity of the personality traits of introversion and extroversion began, perhaps, with the work of Jung (1923), the important work in developing the theoretical constructs and measuring the dimensions was carried out by Eysenck (1947, 1952, 1975). While the two dimensions were described first by use of factor analysis of questionnaire data, Eysenck has subsequently underpinned introversion and extroversion psychophysiologically. Introverts are easily aroused and are generally more cortically aroused than extroverts. In terms of learning, introverts condition rapidly and extinguish slowly. This difference in psychophysiology gives rise to the well-known personality differences of introverts and extroverts. Introverts prefer being alone, working in quiet surroundings, and respond to alcohol by becoming more outgoing. They are more moral, more inhibited, and more influenced by punishment. By contrast, extroverts are happier, more

TABLE 4.3
The relationship between extroversion and involvement in gambling

Author(s)	Year	Type of gambler	Status on extroversion
Moran	1970	Pathological gamblers	No different from norms
Seager	1970	Compulsive gamblers	High on extroversion
Koller	1972	Slot machine addicts	Low on extroversion
Wong	1980	Gamblers Anonymous	High on extroversion
McConaghy, Armstrong, Blaszczynski and Allcock	1983	Pathological gamblers	No different from norms
Blaszczynski, Wilson and McConaghy	1986	Pathological gamblers	Low on extroversion
Ladouceur and Mayrand	1986	Roulette players	No different from non-gamblers

sociable, crave excitement, enjoy noisy, active environments, and are put to sleep by alcohol. They are less aware of social rules, more other-directed, more likely to be impulsive and act on the spur of the moment. Importantly, they are more influenced by rewards than punishment.

Given these differences, is it the introvert or the extrovert that we should expect to be drawn to gambling? The characteristics presented suggest that it is the extrovert that should enjoy gambling the more. The extrovert craves excitement and there is adequate evidence to suggest that, to the gambler, the gambling is exciting (Dickerson 1984). Furthermore, since the extrovert is more influenced by the rewards, the steady trickle of rewards in repetitive games such as slot machines and horse betting should be sufficient to keep the extrovert involved. The introvert will focus on the losses and can be expected to leave the game early. Thus gambling can meet a need in the extrovert that is not present in the introvert. The introvert craves a stable and predictable environment and shuns a life full of chance and risk. Thus we would not expect to see introverts involved in gambling. Since they are risk averse it is more likely that they will take out insurance!

When we examine the evidence on the relationship between extroversion and gambling (see Table 4.3) we are bound to feel disappointed. There is no consistency between the expectations we have formulated and the evidence that exists.

However, before abandoning the hypothesis, it is important to note that the studies listed (with the exception of Ladouceur and Mayrand) have all examined subjects from a very narrow segment of the gambling population. Pathological and compulsive gamblers are a very small proportion of the gambling population. The problem that was present in the interpretation of the sensation seeking data is more strongly involved here. We do not know how pathological gambling effects the personality structure or how it may affect the way in which gamblers fill out questionnaires. It is possible, for example, that it is the extrovert who is

TABLE 4.4
The relationship between locus of control and involvement in gambling

Author(s)	Year	Type of gambler	Status on locus of control
Moran	1970	Pathological	High on external locus of control
Devinney	1978	Heavy	High on external locus of control
Wong	1980	Gamblers Anonymous	High on external locus of control
Glass	1982	Pathological and social	No different from non-gamblers
Jablonski	1985	Sports betting, lotto	No differences between groups
Kusyszyn and Rutter	1985	Heavy and light	No different from non-gamblers
Ladouceur and Mayrand	1986	Roulette players	No different from non-gamblers
Hong and Chiu	1988	Match Six players	High on external locus of control

attracted to gambling. Since the majority of studies are examining gamblers at the end of their gambling careers, they cannot clarify which people are attracted to gambling in the first place.

Locus of Control

Locus of control is one of the personality dimensions which is most heavily used in research. The central idea is that reinforcement which is perceived to be under the control of the individual will increase the habit strength of the reinforced behaviour, whereas reinforcement which is perceived to be independent of the individual will not increase habit strength. Rotter, with whose name internal-external locus of control has become associated, defined external locus of control as follows:

When a reinforcement is perceived by the subject as following some action of his own but not being entirely contingent upon his action, the, in our culture, it is typically perceived as the result of luck, chance, fate, as under the control of powerful others, or as unpredictable because of the great complexity of the forces surrounding him. When the event is interpreted in this way by an individual, we have labelled this a belief in *external control*.

(Rotter 1966, p.1)

With regard to gambling, it seems clear that an internal locus of control would predispose the individual to avoid gambling whereas an external locus of control would be congruent with the activity. The research available weakly supports this hypothesis. In none of the studies in Table 4.4 is it found that gamblers have a higher internal locus of control than non-gamblers. However, in only four out of the eight studies listed is it found that the gamblers are significantly higher on external locus of control.

The problem is that even if it is shown that gamblers have a more external locus of control, we do not know whether the external locus of control preceded the gambling or whether the gambling preceded the external locus of control. It seems likely that if large amounts of time are spent gambling, then the gambler is likely to discover how little power he or she has in determining the outcome; with experience, gamblers would learn that they have little or no control over the outcome, especially in the case of lotteries and slot machines.

Other Personality Variables

Table 4.5 shows that a range of personality traits and dimensions have been measured in various studies of gamblers. Dickerson (1984) has pointed out that few conclusions can be drawn from such diverse studies. The gamblers measured range from occasional gamblers through to members of Gamblers Anonymous; their stages of life range from

TABLE 4.5
The relationship between other personality traits and involvement in gambling

Author(s)	Year	Type of gambler	Status on personality trait
McGlothlin	1954	Female poker players (cf. general population)	More emotionally stable Better adjustment at home Better social adjustment
Morris	1957	College gamblers (cf. college non-gamblers)	More secure Less responsible More dominant More masculine No difference on happiness
Roston	1965	Gamblers Anonymous (cf. neurotic patients)	More rebellious More active More socially active More expansive Less able to profit from experience
Moravec and Munley	1983	Pathological gamblers (cf. population norms)	Bright normal intelligence More depressed High on psychopathy No difference on other MMPI High on achievement High on dominance High on heterosexuality High on exhibition High on autonomy Low on order Low on endurance Low on deference
Kusyszyn and Rutter	1985	Heavy gamblers (cf. light gamblers, non-gamblers and lottery players)	Higher on risk-taking than lottery players No differences between groups on anxiety Depression Hostility Aggression Defensiveness Familial discord
Graham and Lowenfeld	1986	Pathological gamblers (cf. alcoholics)	Better educated Similar profiles on the MMPI

early adulthood to middle and old age; the tests used vary even for the same trait; the comparisons are made sometimes with population norms for the test, sometimes with nongamblers, and sometimes with other patient groups. Thus it would be surprising if any uniformity in the results was to be found.

Nevertheless, when the results for ordinary gamblers (those not receiving treatment for gambling problems) are examined, a clear trend for positive results emerges. McGlothlin (1954), Morris (1957) and Kusyszyn and Rutter (1985) all report that the main differences are favourable to gamblers. Although the majority of differences between groups in the Kusyszyn and Rutter study are insignificant, these authors report another finding of comfort to regular gamblers. For heavy gamblers, the number of years spent gambling was *positively* correlated with a number of personality traits: long term gamblers were more likely to have high self-esteem ($r = 0.33$), more likely to favour taking risks ($r = 0.35$), less likely to be anxious ($r = -0.42$), and less likely to be depressed ($r = -0.46$). Given that pathological gamblers also appear to be more intelligent than the general population, there would seem to be some considerable solace for gamblers in these results.

Summary

The results of studies which attempt to describe the personality traits of people who are attracted to gambling are disappointing. The studies are generally open to various methodological criticisms. Most importantly, very few studies compare high frequency gamblers with low frequency gamblers where other relevant variables are controlled. Thus, even if the results of the various studies were in agreement, strong conclusions about the personality profile of the typical gambler could not be reached. In fact the studies reviewed are not in agreement. But the failure to find agreement does not mean that there are no personality traits which distinguish the high frequency gambler from the low frequency gambler; the heterogeneity of the results may represent the heterogeneity of samples and measuring instruments rather than anything else. What little agreement exists suggests a difference in locus of control, with high frequency gamblers being more external than low frequency gamblers. However, if such a relationship is a reality, then it is just as likely that the gambling causes the trait as that the trait causes the gambling.

Psychoanalysis and the Origins of Gambling

Psychoanalytic explanations for gambling have at the core two explanatory mechanisms: first, that all behaviour is motivated by the gratification of instinctual drives; and secondly, that the dynamics of mental illness can be traced back to the first relationships in the early years of development. Any behaviour which appears to be irrational from a conscious appraisal of the facts will be understood in terms of the psychodynamic structure by which that behaviour fulfils instinctual drives in the individual. Gambling is such a behaviour.

Unfortunately, psychoanalysts do not agree about which aspects of the early relationships are significant in predisposing a person to gamble. The oral (Maze 1987), anal (Fuller 1974), Oedipal (Bergler 1957) and phallic (Freud 1928) phases have all been implicated in the development of the gambler. Fuller (1974) and Trompf (1987) go further in drawing parallels between gambling and religion. In this section we will examine one psychoanalytic account (oral fixation, Maze) in detail. In Chapter 6 we will examine Freud's idea that gambling and childhood masturbation are linked and in Chapter 7 we will consider the explanation for pathological gambling given by Bergler who has used psychoanalysis as a therapy. In each case the main problem associated with psychoanalytic theories is the failure to provide evidence which either supports or refutes the theories.

Lady Luck is a Gambler's Mother

Certainly the infantile character of addictive gamblers seems to be revealed in their mental processes. They show what Bergler calls infantile megalomania or what Freud referred to as the belief in the omnipotence of thought. Essentially, this means the belief that wishing can affect the course of physical events—the fall of the dice, the resting place of the roulette wheel, and so on.

(Maze 1987, p.210)

Early in life the child is effectively omnipotent. Although it has few desires, all of its desires are realised. Unfortunately, as the child grows older it comes to realise that adults in its world control the gratification of desires. It is the mother who is omnipotent, at least where the supply of breast milk is concerned. Weaning in most children is to some extent resisted. The child is orally frustrated during weaning. Since the love of the mother is experienced by the child as the unconditional meeting of its needs, weaning is the point at which the mother's love is most clearly defective in the child's experience. Worse is to come. As the child grows older, it becomes clear that the gratification of any or all of its desires is in the hands of the parents and that they will supply food, comfort, stimulation and so on, only on condition that the child gives up naughty behaviour. The parents place pressure on the child to face reality and to "grow up" by giving up "childish" behaviour. All of this is difficult for the child to accept and the child will spend effort in trying to restore its omnipotence. However, all of the attempts of the child to reinstate the parents as unfailing sources of gratification fail. At this point the child begins to feel anger at the parents who are perceived as unloving. For some children this becomes a spoiled child syndrome in which the child makes impossible demands (spoiled child) on the parents which the parents then refuse (punishing parents). The child then feel righteous anger at the parents for their failure to love. This is the psychodynamic structure that unfolds in the child and becomes the basis of problem gambling in the adult.

Winning at gambling is the representation of the freely given milk from the mother's breast. The gambler continually gambles in the hope of reinstating the unconditional supply of gratification that was present in the early omnipotence phase. Regression to omnipotent thinking can be seen in the irrational actions of the gambler (superstitious behaviour) and the associated magical thinking by which the gambler seeks to influence the outcome (the mother). Unfortunately, the gambling will eventually produce losses, the equivalent of the mother failing to love sufficiently. At this point the gambler will feel righteously angry that his or her desires have not been met. According to Maze, "it is this feeling of *justified rage* which is rewarding". The child is trying to punish the mother for her failure to be sufficiently loving. Thus the instinctual drive that is gratified by gambling is aggression which in the case of gambling will be directed at the mother-surrogate: the gambling machines, the gambling structure, the representatives of the gambling industry, and the creditors. Since problem gamblers are often depressed, we can assume that some of the aggression directed outwards at the gambling (the mother) is also directed inwards. In childhood, the child becomes angry at the parent and fears the parent's response. This fear induces severe self-punishment and it is this that is the origin of the depression in the adult gambler.

One problem for psychoanalytic accounts, such as that provided by Maze, concerns how it is that individual differences arise such that one person becomes a problem gambler whereas another person does not. According to Freud, the early childhood relations described occur in the life of every child. How is it then that only some (small) fraction of people become problem gamblers?

There seem to be two answers immediately available to this question. First of all, gambling is only one among many possible representations of the basic dynamic structure. Alcoholism and petty stealing, for example, appear to be likely alternatives. Secondly, Maze makes the point that children are not equivalent in their oral enjoyment of the breast. Whereas, one child may spontaneously give up the breast in favour of other enjoyable foods supplied by the mother, another child will have to be traumatically removed from the breast. This biologically based difference in response to the breast is assumed to be another source of differences in response to gambling. However, Trompf (1987) suggests that breast trauma is too common for it to be the basic mechanism behind heavy gambling. The critical age for the development of the psychological basis of gambling problems is much later, perhaps at the age of ten or eleven years of age according to Trompf.

The Secundus Complex

The most well-known psychoanalytic theory of gambling (Bergler 1957) assumes that the psychological basis of the heavy gambling arises from Oedipal conflict. Bergler's account is presented in Chapter 7 in connection with the theoretical basis of psychoanalysis as a means of treating pathological gambling. The Oedipal conflict and its resolution has been one of the major constructs of psychoanalytic theory. It is possible that the concept of "making a killing" at gambling allows an immediate connection to be made between gambling and the Oedipal conflict.

It has been suggested by many writers that the origin of the urge to gamble to excess will be found in the family dynamics operating in the gambler's childhood (for example, Jacobs 1986; Gray 1990; Lorenz 1990). The argument is typically that the child grows up feeling unloved. The low self esteem of such a person is a source of pain and unhappiness that continues into adulthood. Gambling is an exciting and absorbing activity that enables the gambler to escape the negative feelings of everyday life. From a psychoanalytic perspective, we might take the further step of saying that the gambling replaces the mother as a source of love for the gambler. At this point it becomes clear that the central construct in all of these accounts is the attempt to gain or reinstate the love of the mother through the activity of gambling.

Trompf (1987) has provided an alternative analogy to the Oedipal conflict and an alternative construct to the love of the mother in explaining the genesis of heavy gambling. Trompf describes the myth of the "silent philosopher" as follows.

The material, which had a curiously determinative impact on the whole course of mediaeval scholastic method, concerns the neo-Pythagorean silent philosopher (of the second century AD), who earlier in his life returned home as an unknown stranger to Athens. Having been taught as a child by "primitives" (the ancient Scots!) that women were dangerous and not to be trusted, Secundus journeyed back home as a young man, his travels entailing extreme rigorism and deprivation. On arriving at the family house quite unrecognized, he used money to persuade his own mother (who did not perceive him to be her very own son) to go to bed with him. The act, however, was a test; the returning son did nothing but lie upon her breasts—all night. When in the morning his mother sought some answer to this enigma, Secundus revealed his true identity. In horror his mother fell dead (or committed suicide, as one version has it); and in consequent sorrow Secundus chose to remain forever silent.

(Trompf 1986)

The first point to note about this story is that its historical truth is unimportant. Rather, Trompf believes that the story is a "psychological" truth about individuals. It refers to the idea that children are continually testing their world to determine its nature. In the normal course of events the child learns the social rules of his or her society from an extended period of childhood testing and ultimately develops a stable ethical perspective. This socialised ethical perspective enables the adult to act responsibly. However, the development of an ethical perspective and social responsibility breaks down in the avid gambler. The gambler becomes fixated in the pre-ethical testing phase of life. The reason for this will be found in the child's relations to significant others and especially to the parents. One of the main ways, according to Trompf, in which the child will fail to develop an ethical perspective, is the inconsistency of the parents in rewarding and punishing the child. If the testing behaviour is sometimes punished and sometimes rewarded, the child cannot form a stable perspective on the consequences of actions. The ethical consciousness of the child is disengaged from its behaviour. Secundus fails to see the ethical implications of the test that he makes of his mother. He is locked in to the testing mode since he has not learned whether or not his mother can be trusted.

By analogy, the gambler is also locked in to the testing mode. Every gamble re-creates the uncertainty that was present in childhood. The gambler seeks the means by which to predict outcomes and continues to be frustrated in the search. The fact that it is money which the gambler plays for makes it appear that he or she is engaged in a responsible, adult activity. However, gambling is a game and the gambler is still the child testing the outcomes within that game.

According to Trompf, the value of Gamblers Anonymous in the treatment of gambling problems is that it provides the ethical perspective which the gambler has failed to obtain from the parents. Gamblers Anonymous makes the gambler aware of the social and moral consequences of continued gambling (the suicide of the mother and the destruction of self). Trompf found support for his alternative account in the stories of members of Gamblers Anonymous. Interviews with members of Gamblers Anonymous revealed the presence of family dynamics of the kind he has described. Unfortunately, however, Trompf did not interview a control group of individuals who are heavily involved in some non-gambling activity. Thus, it is possible that the hypothesised perceived inconsistency of parents that is antecedent to avid gambling is generally present in adults and thus not a specific cause of gambling at all.

Summary

Psychoanalytic accounts of gambling attempt to specify the psychological function of the gambling for the individual. The basis for gambling occurs in childhood and typically involves defective relations between the parents and the child. According to different accounts, the gambling may be the means by which the child re-creates the love of the mother, the means by which the child is punished by the father for seeking the love of the mother, or the means by which the child is testing reality. The problem for all psychoanalytic accounts is one of generating testable hypotheses and providing evidence for their validity.

Access to Gambling

The theories of gambling considered in this chapter are psychological. They seek to explain why it is that some individuals become heavily involved in gambling whereas others do not. There are many other factors involved beyond the psychology of the individual and these have not been discussed so far. In particular, the demographic features of gamblers are known and provide a context within which psychologically oriented theories should operate.

First of all there are gender based differences in involvement in gambling. Women are over-represented in some forms of gambling in some countries and under-represented in other forms. Thus female gamblers are more likely to be found gambling on slot machines and at bingo than they are to be found in betting shops and at the races. The suggestion that female gamblers avoid games of skill should be rejected, since blackjack, for example, attracts both men and women. The more likely explanation is that the involvement of women in any given form of gambling depends upon their access to that form of gambling historically. Access is determined often, not by the law but by social rules and customs. Thus, betting shops may attract smaller numbers of women because for long periods of time the betting shop was perceived as the man's province.

Gambling is not equally attractive to people independently of socio-economic class. In Chapter 3 it was pointed out that the less affluent working class is over-represented in numbers games. There are social and economic explanations for the greater attraction of the less affluent to gambling. However, it should not be concluded that gambling is always a working class activity. Whether or not it is so depends on the social and historic origins of the gambling in a given culture. Thus, in Great Britain horse racing and racecourse gambling were organised from Newmarket by *The Jockey Club* which was largely an aristocratic institution (O'Hara 1990). Although racing now attracts gamblers from all walks of life in Britain, it remains a predominantly upper-middle class form of gambling (Downes et al. 1976). By contrast, horse racing in Australia was organised by the working class and farming communities in small towns and remains a predominantly working class form of gambling (O'Hara 1990). Similarly, casino gambling in Great Britain was legalised on a very restrictive basis (Club membership) and has remained a predominantly middle class activity whereas, in the United States, casino gambling was legalised in two states initially and set up as a holiday and recreational activity for the masses (Eadington 1990).

Age is another factor predisposing certain groups in society to different forms of gambling. Downes et al. characterised heavy gamblers in Britain as young, single, skilled working class men from a low income background. However, although perhaps valid as a generalisation, there are exceptions as well. Thus, in general, lotteries are attractive to an older segment of the population than are casino games. However, the attractiveness of different gambling forms to differently aged groups may be determined by access. Thus casinos are relatively new in many parts of the world and may be perceived as an adventure for the young but as a matter of anxiety for some of the older residents in a community. Similarly, the siting of the gambling is important. Video poker machines in Nevada are equally attractive to both men and women (Hunter 1990) but in Australia the machines are licensed for use in hotels. Since hotel bars are socially and historically a male province in Australia, we should expect to find that poker machine gambling is and will remain in the short period a predominantly male activity.

These examples of demographic differences in the involvement in gambling illustrate the general point that who it is who becomes a gambler is determined not simply by the psychology of the individual but by the relative availability of different forms of gambling to different segments of the population.

Summary

When we ask about the reason why one person becomes heavily involved in gambling but another does not, we should be careful not to expect a full explanation in terms of any one factor. What has been said often about many other behaviours is also true for gambling: that a range of historical, social, situational, and developmental factors will combine to predispose any given person to gambling. Furthermore, distal variables of the kind considered (personality, character, and demography) cannot be a complete explanation for gambling no matter how complex their interaction. What is missing from such explanations are the details of the individual factors which immediately precede the gambling. In one sense, it is these proximal factors which are the real cause of the gambling, since it is these factors that immediately precede the gambling itself. Clearly, the causal chain passes from distal to proximal causes, but no account of the psychology of gambling will be complete without the specification of the proximal causes.

Proximal Causes of Gambling

Proximal causes of behaviour refer to the immediate antecedents. Thus the proximal causes of gambling will be found in the individual and his or her relation to the gambling environment at the time. However, there are two senses in which we can ask about the immediate causes of gambling. First of all, we can ask why the gambler decided to initiate the gambling; that is, what caused the gambling session to begin? Secondly, having begun to gamble, we can ask why, at any point in the session, the gambler does not stop. These two facets will not necessarily involve the same kind of explanation. For example, we could imagine that cognitive factors may play an important role in causing the start of gambling and behavioural reinforcement causing persistence within the gambling session. In this section we shall examine a range of proximal causes for the initiation of gambling and, in the next section, possible causes for persistence once the gambling has started. Of course, the same causative factor may be involved in both initiation and persistence.

Need-State Models

A need-state model asserts that gambling is a behaviour which is carried out to fulfil some need that a person has. For example, one person may gamble because he is generally depressed and gambling relieves the depression; another person may gamble because she is bored and gambling relieves the boredom. In one sense, need-state models are necessarily true; all gamblers have reasons for gambling and all reasons can be reconstrued as needs. One gambler gambles in order to win money—he has a need for money; another gambles to gain status and prestige—she has a need for status and prestige; yet another gambles to escape family and work—that person has a need to be alone and without responsibilities. Considered in this way, need-state models are circular and uninformative. Need-state models have been proposed in a variety of discussions of gambling (McCormick 1988; Jacobs 1986). The need-states that have been identified as creating an attraction to gambling include chronic hypo-arousal and chronic depression.

Hypo-arousal as a Need-State Satisfied by Gambling

It is claimed that some individuals become gamblers because they are under-aroused (bored) and gambling increases their arousal (excitement) to a pleasant degree.

What these gamblers do verbalize is a sense of frequent boredom—a strong, enduring need for almost constant excitement and stimulation. . . . Gambling satiates the need-state for these pathological gamblers.

(McCormick 1988, p.262)

This lifelong persistent state of either hypo- or hyper-arousal is believed to predispose the individual to respond only to a rather narrow "window" of stress-reducing, but potentially addictive substances or experiences.

(Jacobs 1986, p.17)

Since it is the state of hypo-arousal that predisposes the individual to gambling and ensures that the gambling will persist at a high frequency despite losses, we have a straightforward expectation concerning heavy gamblers, problem gamblers and pathological gamblers. No matter what other conditions must be met before the chronically hypo-aroused individual becomes a heavy gambler, we can be sure that heavy gamblers as a group will exhibit lower resting states of arousal. Unfortunately, there appears to be relatively little information concerning long-term differences in physiological arousal between light and heavy gamblers. Furthermore, the little information available does not support the central assumption of the need-state model. Dickerson and Adcock (1987) compared high frequency (three times per week or more often) slot machine players with low frequency slot machine players and found no differences in heart rate between the groups when resting or when shown a slot machine. In another study, Dickerson, Hinchy, Cunningham and Legg-England (1990) compared high frequency players (once per week or more often) with medium and low frequency players on self-report measures of mood and again found no differences in the measures.

Given the centrality of the arousal variable to the need-state model of gambling, the results of research are disappointingly sparse and discouragingly negative. However, on the positive side, the retrospective accounts of members of Gamblers Anonymous suggest that in many cases withdrawal symptoms involving mood are experienced (Wray and Dickerson 1981). Furthermore, "restlessness and irritability if unable to gamble" was made a criterion for the diagnosis of pathological gambling (DSM IIIR 1987). Such mood changes are consistent with a need-state model.

Chronic Depression as a Need-State Satisfied by Gambling

Depression is frequently associated with heavy gambling (McCormick, Russo, Ramirez and Taber 1984; Graham and Lowenfeld 1986; Lorenz and Yaffee 1986). This depression might be seen as resulting from failure at gambling and the large monetary losses sustained by the gambler. However, the need-state model asserts that the depression precedes the gambling and that the gambling becomes the means by which the individual copes with the long-term depressive condition.

. . . for a significant number of these gamblers the depression is a lifelong pattern which may precede their gambling.

(McCormick 1988, p.260)

Many serious gamblers say that gambling does much more for them than provide recreation, sociability and excitement. They say they use it as a way to find relief from anxiety, tension, worry, depression.

(Custer and Milt 1985, p.36)

According to McCormick (1988), cognitive style may be the crucial variable related to heavy involvement in gambling. Abramson, Seligman and Teasdale (1978) identified explanatory style as a variable associated with learned helplessness and depression in humans. When people are unable to control events they search for the cause of their failure. Three attributional dimensions are relevant: internal-external: one can attribute helplessness internally (I couldn't do anything) or externally (no one could do anything); global-specific: global attributions apply across a wide range of entities (I'm hopeless at everything) whereas specific attributions are limited (I'm hopeless at this thing); stable-unstable: stable attributions apply to a lengthy period of time (I've never been able to do it) whereas unstable attributions apply for one or two occasions (I couldn't do it that time). The most damaging helplessness is that which is attributed internally, is global in its effects and stable over time. Positive and negative effects occur for everyone on a day-by-day basis. How we attribute the causes of these different events can be the basis of both happiness and sadness. When one believes that desirable outcomes are unlikely, expects undesirable outcomes to occur, and sees no way to change this situation, helplessness and depression will result.

Peterson, Seligman and Vaillant (1988) have demonstrated that the pessimistic explanatory style is associated with mental illness. In a thirty-five year longitudinal study they found that Second World War veterans with pessimistic explanatory style were subsequently more likely to suffer ill health of both a physical and mental kind. Thus it is possible that the pessimistic cognitive style (labelled *depressenogenic* by McCormick) is a cause of depression and the subsequent gambling activity is a coping mechanism by which the individual dispels the depression.

Unfortunately, there is no evidence supporting depression as a cause of heavy gambling. Retrospective studies on gamblers in treatment, such as those completed by Taber and his associates (McCormick et al. 1984; Taber, McCormick and Ramirez 1987), are unable to disentangle the temporal order of the depression and the gambling. What is necessary are the results from longitudinal studies which compare the frequency of heavy gambling among individuals with and without depressive tendencies. There are no such studies.

If heavy gambling is a means of coping with depression which results from a pessimistic cognitive style, then we should expect to find evidence of this negativity in the actual expectations of gamblers with respect to their gambling. However, such expectations are at variance with the observations of Bergler (1957) who pointed out that pathological gamblers are in fact inappropriately optimistic.

Reversal Theory

Reversal theory as it applies to gambling is a variant within the general category of arousal theories (Anderson and Brown 1987). It is assumed that arousal is interpreted within one of two states: the telic and the paratelic. When gambling, a person may switch from one state to the other and this reversal of state is used to explain why a person starts, continues or ceases to gamble.

A telic state is one in which the individual is goal-directed, whereas a paratelic state is one in which the individual is concerned with pleasure.

A telic state is defined as one in which the individual is primarily oriented towards some essential goal or goals. A paratelic state, in contrast, is defined as one in which the individual is primarily oriented towards some aspect of his continuing behaviour and its related sensations.

(Anderson and Brown 1987, p.180)

With respect to gambling, a person may gamble in order to make money (telic state) or may gamble for the pleasurable excitement it affords (paratelic state). Within the gambling session, both motives may be found but they will prevail at different times. One person may begin with the intent of winning money but later will play for the sheer excitement of the activity, whereas another person may be attracted by the excitement but, after losing, may focus on recouping the money lost.

According to Anderson and Brown, arousal will be interpreted differently depending on whether the individual is in a telic or paratelic state.

In telic states people are future-oriented, planful, concentrating on foci outside themselves, enjoying the pleasure of goal anticipation, meaningfully employed and prefer to remain in a state of low intensity and low arousal. In paratelic states people are present-oriented, spontaneous, sufficient unto themselves, enjoying the pleasure of immediate sensation and prefer states of high intensity and arousal.

(Anderson and Brown 1987, p.180)

High arousal is interpreted negatively in the telic state (as anxiety) but positively in the paratelic state (as excitement). By contrast, low arousal is interpreted positively in the telic state (as relaxation) but negatively in the paratelic state (as boredom). These relations are shown in Figure 4.1.

According to Anderson and Brown, reversal theory helps us understand gambling behaviour in several ways. First of all, we can infer who it is who will be attracted to gambling and to high stakes while playing. It is the person who is habitually in a paratelic state who will be more

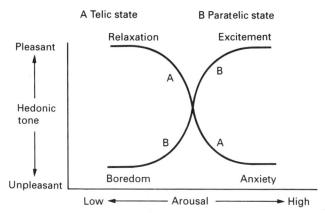

FIG. 4.1 Relations between arousal and hedonic tone for telic and paratelic
states. Based on Anderson and Brown 1987, p.181.

attracted to gambling because he or she is the one who will find the
excitement of gambling pleasurable. The person who is habitually in a
telic state will find that the gambling situation provokes anxiety. Furthermore, the habitually paratelic person will make larger bets in order to
increase excitement whereas the habitually telic person will make small
bets to minimize anxiety. Secondly, people may seek out gambling for
quite different reasons, depending on whether they are in a telic or
paratelic state: a person in a telic state and high arousal (busy day at
work) may gamble in order to induce a switch to a paratelic state in which
the high arousal will be experienced as pleasurable excitement; but a
person in a paratelic state and low arousal (boredom) may gamble in
order to relieve the boredom.

During play, reversals may occur depending on whether the player is
winning or losing. Winning is associated with transition to the paratelic
state (pleasurable excitement), whereas losing may induce a shift to the
telic state (unpleasant anxiety). Thus the losing gambler may become
concerned with the goal of winning back the money that has been lost.
Many gamblers may quit at this point because the gambling has become
unpleasant. Although reversals to the telic state are more likely to be
associated with losing, they may also occur when the gambler is winning.
In this case, the gambler may perceive that at a certain point he or she
will have sufficient funds to buy a car, take a holiday, or acquire some
other luxury. This may account for some gamblers not quitting while
ahead.

Anderson and Brown also suggest that reversal theory can help us
understand pathological gambling. The pathological gambler gambles
frequently and heavily over a long period of time. Most of the time he is
losing, which induces a telic state wherein he typically chases his losses.

During this losing phase, he suffers distressing levels of anxiety. On the occasions when he wins, the telic state reverses to the paratelic and the anxiety is converted to very pleasurable sensations. Over time, the pathological gambler has learned that persistence through the period of anxiety is often rewarded. Thus, where the normal gambler may leave the situation because of the anxiety, the pathological gambler persists with the gambling despite the anxiety.

Unfortunately, for this theory, no results have been published yet which show that regular gamblers are habitually paratelically oriented. The best supporting evidence is a significant correlation between paratelic dominance and the average size of bet. However, correlations of this kind tell us little about the direction of causation.

Reversal theory is another mechanistic theory in which behaviour is caused by physiological differences linked to conditions of reinforcement. Mechanistic models sometimes provide important insights into the origin and maintenance of human behaviour. However, reversal theory is unlikely to provide such insights because it is fundamentally mistaken about the nature of gambling. Anderson and Brown do not seem aware that gambling behaviour and the paratelic state are logically inconsistent.

A telic state is characterised by goal-directedness. The concept of a goal derives from its usage in games. In playing games, behaviour is necessarily directed towards achieving the goals of the game, otherwise one is not playing the game. Every move of the chess player is directed towards the goal of mating the opponent; it must be so or one is not playing chess. Similarly, in gambling games, behaviour is necessarily directed towards the goals of the game. For example, in blackjack, the player endeavours to have his cards sum to a number which is closer to 21 than the sum of the bank's cards; in roulette, one endeavours to choose the number, the dozen, the colour, or whatever which will be the same as the outcome of the roulette wheel; and, in horse-racing, one endeavours to select the winning horse. Therefore, gambling games are always goal-directed and the gambler is always in a telic state while gambling.

Who will be attracted to gambling, the habitually telic individual or the habitually paratelic individual? This is a difficult question! According to Anderson and Brown it will be both individuals but for different reasons: the paratelic to dispel boredom, the telic to win money. However, it is likely that habitually paratelic individuals will be attracted to quite different gambling games from the habitually telic. The telic individual should prefer the games described in Chapter 2, since these offer the best chance of realising the goal of making money. Paratelic individuals should be attracted to games offering excitement. Unfortunately, there is little evidence comparing the intrinsic excitement of different types of gambling. However, we can speculate that casino games such as craps and two-up will be preferred over slot machines and blackjack and that attendance at the races will be preferred over televised races viewed at home. Until such evidence is available, we must suspend judgement of the value of reversal theory.

The Theory of Reasoned Action

Factors such as demographics, socioeconomic, personality, information processing biases, and motivation are reviewed as only indirectly affecting behavior. Their effect on the intention to gamble is reflected in their influence on the attitudes and normative beliefs toward gambling.

(Cummings and Corney 1987, p.197)

Fishbein and Ajzen (1975) proposed a causal theory of behaviour in which the key variables are intentions, attitudes and subjective norms. The only internal cause for behaviour is the intention to behave. Thus the intention to buy a lottery ticket causes the action of buying the ticket provided that external causes do not intervene (for example, all the tickets have been sold). The application of the theory of reasoned action to gambling behaviour has been investigated by Cummings and Corney (1987).

Intentions to behave are jointly caused by attitudes to the object of the behaviour and subjective norms concerning the behaviour. Thus my intention to buy the lottery ticket is caused by the fact that I would like to buy a ticket (the attitude) and the knowledge that my family expects me to buy a ticket (the subjective norm). Clearly, norms and attitudes about gambling are not necessarily consistent. Thus if my family makes it clear that I should not waste money on a lottery ticket, this will oppose my desire for a ticket and curb my intention to buy one. In a general sense, as a corollary, we can expect much more gambling when a community legalises gambling since the subjective norms have changed.

The attitude to a behaviour is the person's evaluation of the behaviour: how much it is liked or disliked. Since many beliefs will be held about a given behaviour and its consequences, the attitude will always be a composite of the evaluative component of the salient beliefs. My beliefs about buying a lottery ticket may include: you've got to be in it to win it; it's my turn to win something; I feel lucky today; and, I can afford the $1 it will cost. Such beliefs add up to being strongly in favour of buying a ticket. Of course, the salient beliefs concerning a piece of behaviour are not always consistent. The regular slot machine player may well feel ambivalent about the next session because of a mixed set of positive and negative beliefs about the possible consequences. Whether the resultant attitude to playing the machines is positive or negative will depend on the sum of the values of each of the associated beliefs weighted by the likelihood that the belief will be borne out. Interestingly, even if the resultant attitude is negative, "I don't want to play the machines tonight", the player may still be found in front of his or her favourite slot machine. This would happen if the importance of spending time with one's friends playing the machines (a subjective norm) outweighed the personal desire not to play (the attitude).

Subjective norms are beliefs concerning the moral attitudes to the behaviour of individuals and institutions which are of importance to the individual. Some people may never gamble because gambling is inconsistent with religious principles. Other people give up gambling when they marry because of the negative attitude to gambling held by the spouse. In general, the strength of the subjective norm component will be the sum of the attitudes of the significant others moderated by the individual's willingness to comply.

The influence of distal variables can be understood by their impact on the intention to gamble and are mediated by the attitude to gambling and subjective norms. For example, orientation to risk-taking can be regarded as a personality dimension. It is associated with the need for achievement, change and dominance. In turn, orientation to risk-taking determines a person's beliefs about the consequences of gambling and thus feeds into the attitude to gambling. Again, risk-taking may be valued by one's friends and thus the same personality dimension also determines the positivity of the subjective norm.

Cummings and Corney's adaptation of the theory of reasoned action makes sense of the apparently important role played by irrational thinking about gambling. The belief that one can influence a slot machine to make a pay-out is irrational. However, such a belief will feed into the attitude to gambling in a direct way. Furthermore, the higher the subjective probability that one can influence the outcome the more positive will be the attitudinal component and the stronger will be the intention to gamble.

The difficulties faced by the theory of reasoned action are of two kinds. There are general criticisms of the adequacy of the theory as an explanatory model (Maze 1973; Maze 1983; Summers, Borland and Walker 1989) and there are questions concerning the limitations of the theory in the extent to which it explains the full range of gambling behaviour. With respect to the theory itself, criticisms are directed at the concept of an attitude as an evaluation (attitudes are prescriptions or moral beliefs) and at the relationship between intention and behaviour (intentions have no causal significance). Here we will concentrate on the limitations of the theory as it is applied to gambling.

There is no doubt that the subjective norms for an individual gambler can be extremely negative (Custer and Milt 1985). If family, friends, the bank manager and the boss are all urging the gambler to stop, then either the attitude to gambling must be extremely strong and positive or the weight given to the subjective norm must be low. However, case studies of compulsive gamblers suggest that the attitude to gambling is often ambivalent or even negative (see Freud's analysis of Dostoevsky) and the weight given to the subjective norms is high. Why does the person continue to gamble? Again, even with gambling at everyday levels, the theory may produce the wrong answer. Consider, for example, a man who dislikes gambling and whose significant others believe that he should not gamble. Both the attitude and the subjective norm are negative. Are there any conditions under which this man will gamble? What will happen if he hates his wife? Might he not gamble precisely because his wife thinks he should not? These extreme examples are intended to make the point that the motivation of the gambler is an important variable in understanding whether or not gambling will take place. More generally, we can imagine two gamblers whose attitudes and subjective norms are positive and equal in strength. Will they gamble and will they gamble to the same extent? If one gambles for the associated social interaction whereas the other gambles for money, the first will not gamble if his or her friends are not present, whereas the second will not be influenced in the same way and may possibly gamble for longer precisely because the friends are absent.

Summary

The proximal causes of gambling are those that immediately precede the gambling. From one perspective, gambling follows from the intention to gamble which in turn follows from positive attitudes to gambling and the expectation that one will gamble. Distal causes may be seen as acting on the beliefs and attitudes of the individual and thus influencing the intention to gamble. However, intentions have a dubious status as causes and behavioural theories of gambling avoid the use of such cognitive constructs. Behavioural theories suggest that the individual begins gambling because in the past gambling has been reinforced. The main reinforcer is often assumed to be arousal or excitement rather than money. According to some theories, gambling is a means of manipulating hedonic tone. It can be seen that such theories avoid one philosophical problem only to introduce another, agency. Similarly, some theories assume that gambling is sought as a means of reducing states of need. Such theories introduce further problems in the notion of needs as causes.

Persistence at Gambling

The categories of explanation considered so far concern why a person chooses to gamble. However, there is a different question which may involve a different kind of answer. The question concerns why the person makes the next gamble in a session, why the person continues to gamble having already started. The explanation we give will be in terms of the factors that determine how and why the gambler makes the next bet. Dickerson (1990) discusses a similar distinction when he points out that the causes of a person beginning a gambling session may be quite different from the causes of a person continuing a gambling session which is in progress. One set of causes explain why the person starts the gambling session whereas the other set of causes explain why he or she does not end the gambling session. The possible causes of a gamble within a session are quite limited. The causes can be cognitive or behavioural and little else. Cognitive causes refer to the gambler's goals and the means perceived by the gambler as facilitating the reaching of those goals. Behavioural causes refer to stimulus control over behaviour. According to a behavioural analysis, gambling behaviour, similar to all other behaviour, is a conditioned response. The gambling behaviour is explained without recourse to cognitive factors.

Thus, the question of why people gamble can be analysed into two components: (1) why does the person start gambling? and (2) once gambling, why doesn't the person stop? The previous sections have reviewed explanations of why people choose to gamble. In this section we review accounts of why gamblers persist with the gambling.

Gambling as Conditioned Behaviour

Learning theory would seem to be particularly applicable to the explanation of gambling behaviour. This expectation follows from the striking resemblance between pigeons pecking discs and rats pressing levers on the one hand and humans pulling the handles of slot machines on the other hand. Since modern learning theory is grounded in the performance of simple responses and their reinforcement among rats and pigeons, it is to be expected that, if the laws of learning are general, then the generalisation to human behaviour will be straightforward when the use of gambling machines is considered. This expectation is complicated by the fact that there are two major strands to modern learning theory: instrumental learning and classical conditioning. Unfortunately, explaining the acquisition of behaviour (even among rats and pigeons) often involves deciding which strand of learning theory gives the best or most comprehensive account of the phenomena. That is as much the case with respect to gambling as it is with any other human behaviour. Thus, we will consider the contributions of learning theory in two sections corresponding to the two major strands listed.

Instrumental Learning

Perhaps the most striking feature of gambling is its goal directed nature. The explicit goal of all gambling is the acquisition of money. However, we can talk about goal directed behaviour either with or without reference to cognitions. From a cognitive perspective, we can state that gamblers stake money with the specific intention of winning more money. By contrast, from a behavioural perspective, intentions do not have a causal status.

The acquisition of money is an acquired drive. Gambling behaviour is reinforced by drive reduction. Thus, the gambler's behaviour will be selectively reinforced by gambling "wins". Furthermore, it is not simply the action of staking money that is reinforced but all of the behaviours which precede and ultimately lead to the placing of the bet. Also, the main reinforcer, the acquisition of money after a win, may be supplemented by the pleasant reaction to anticipatory responses prior to the result of the bet. That is, the pleasurable tension prior to the result of the bet may also act as a reinforcement for the preceding behaviour. Brown (1986) suggests that arousal or excitement may be the major reinforcement for gambling. The fact that money is lost in the long run does not extinguish the behaviour because the gambling behaviour is maintained by one of the most powerful reinforcement schedules, random reinforcement according to a constant probability. Skinner states that,

The efficacy of such schedules in generating high rates has long been known to the proprietors of gambling establishments. . . . Winning depends upon placing a bet and in the long run upon the number of bets placed, but no particular payoff can be predicted. The ratio is varied by any one of several "random" systems. The pathological gambler exemplifies the result. Like the pigeon with its five responses per second for many hours, he is the victim of an unpredictable contingency of reinforcement. The long-term net gain or loss is almost irrelevant in accounting for the effectiveness of the schedule.

(Skinner 1953)

Given an instrumental conditioning account, a range of predictions can be made about the persistence of gambling behaviour. For example, the gambling behaviour should be responsive to the delay between the behaviour and the reinforcement and to the magnitude and rate of reinforcement. Long sequences of unreinforced responses (that is, long losing sequences) should lead to extinction and rate of gambling should be reduced by punishment. Early losses may extinguish the gambling response, whereas early wins should strengthen the response. Persistence should also depend on the schedule of reinforcement.

Such expectations appear to apply best to continuous forms of gambling where the cycle of gambling behaviour and reinforcement (the outcome of the gamble) is repeated frequently within a session. Slot machines have been cited frequently as the paradigm example of operant conditioning controlling the behaviour of human beings. However, other forms of gambling, such as roulette and craps, would appear to fall into the category of gambling games to which conditioning theories are particularly well suited. There is some evidence for the instrumental conditioning approach in the accounts given by regular gamblers. Dickerson (1974) found that 72% of betting shop gamblers who attend and gamble frequently reported having early luck, whereas only 15% of the occasional betting shop gamblers reported early luck.

Unfortunately, the available evidence does not provide unreserved support for the instrumental conditioning approach. In the case of slot machines, the magnitude of the reinforcement and the rate of responding do not appear to be related in a straightforward way. Whereas the theory leads to the expectation of increased rates of response with increased magnitudes of reinforcement, the evidence suggests a curvilinear relationship: increased rates of responding with smaller reinforcements and decreased rates following larger reinforcements (Dickerson 1990). Again, the majority of slot machine responses are not "unreinforced" but are punished by the loss of a credit. As the length of a session increases, so the cumulative punishment increases. According to the theory, we should expect a suppression of the response strength and a lowered rate of responding as a consequence. Well-practised players (regulars) do not show any decrease in the rate of response. In roulette, the gambler may choose between alternative bets such as "rouge" and "noir". If the bet is placed on red and red wins, the behaviour of betting on red has been reinforced and its response strength should increase. Alternatively, if red loses, the response strength for betting on red should decrease. Thus the theory leads to the expectation that roulette players are more likely to bet on the same alternative again if it wins than if it loses. However, evidence provided by Cohen (1972) suggests that roulette players are more likely to bet on the same colour if it loses ($p = 0.75$) than if it wins ($p = 0.5$). This result is an example of the gambler's fallacy that equal numbers of red and black should be expected in any given period.

It is clear that instrumental conditioning is not supported by the detailed analyses indicated. Nevertheless, the general proposition that the steady flow of "wins" from persistent play maintains the activity of gambling is generally supported. However, persistence under these conditions can also be understood at a cognitive level. The challenge to conditioning theory is first to explain gambling phenomena such as the gambler's fallacy. Until such phenomena are understood in terms of reinforcement, cognitive accounts are likely to prevail.

Classical Conditioning

It is easy to see why classical conditioning leads to the expectation that repeated gambling will be pleasurable. A successful gamble is one in which the outcome of the bet is rewarding: the gambler wins money, tokens or credits. The acquisition of money or its equivalent gives pleasure. The behaviours which preceded the pleasure of winning become conditioned with repeated gambling so that the preliminary behaviours leading to the placing of a bet produce a conditioned response of pleasure. Furthermore, once the bet has been placed, any intervening stimuli, such as listening to a racing commentary or watching the slot machine wheels spin, would be expected to become discriminative stimuli for the pleasure of winning.

Brown (1986) has suggested that arousal is central to understanding initiation and persistence at gambling. There is no doubt that gamblers experience excitement during the course of gambling (Anderson and Brown 1984) and Brown speculates that this excitement may be the major reinforcer in gambling. Excitement is to be understood as the subjective state corresponding to high arousal so that the theory is actually an account of the relationship between gambling and arousal. According to Brown, every person has an optimum level of arousal which he or she strives to maintain. Different environments provide different levels of arousal. For some individuals whose typical level of arousal is lower than the optimum, gambling will provide a means of raising the level of arousal. Thus gambling will be rewarding to the individual who will seek continuing involvement. Similarly, some individuals may have biologically based optimum levels of arousal which are relatively high. Such individuals will be high on sensation seeking and, like the individuals from environments with low levels of stimulation, may find a ready solution to their biologically based deficit in the activity of gambling.

Brown refers to this account as neo-Pavlovian. However, it is not immediately clear in what way Pavlovian principles are involved. The central concept is arousal, although Brown is not clear whether the arousal concerned is cortical, somatic or autonomic. The basic assumption is that gambling raises the level of arousal and that an increase in arousal will be experienced as pleasurable by someone whose arousal level is lower than optimum. This assumption should not be granted as automatically true. For example, confrontation with a venomous snake is an arousing experience which is aversive for the majority of people whatever their prior state of arousal. It is clear that arousing stimuli may be aversive. Thus, we must ask why it is that gambling is experienced as pleasurable. One explanation for the pleasurable excitement associated with gambling is the uncertainty phenomenon itself. Uncertainty is experienced as aversive (Lovibond 1968). Gambling not only produces uncertainty but also resolves the uncertainty. Thus the outcome of gambling is a negative reinforcement which functions alongside the positive reinforcement provided by the successful gambles.

One of the predictions from such a model which is supported by observation is the occurrence of superstitious behaviour. Gambling provides reinforcement on a constant probability basis. Thus, every so often the gambler will be rewarded by a winning outcome. Whatever behaviour immediately preceded the outcome will be conditioned to the gambling behaviour. If the gambler was holding a cent coin at the point at which the successful outcome became known, he or she is more likely to hold a similar coin in future. Successful gambles will "stamp in" this superstitious behaviour.

A Composite of Mood, Arousal and Cognitions

Arousal plays a central role in many accounts of gambling (Carlton and Manowitz 1988; Dickerson 1984; Rule, Nutter and Fischer 1971). It is assumed that people persist where possible with exciting activities. For some people gambling is exciting. The more exciting the gambling, the more a person will persist with the activity. If subjective excitement is translated as positively labelled physiological arousal, then such arousal could act as a positive reinforcement for the activity. Thus, gambling will persist until the conditioned arousal habituates, or until other factors intervene.

Dickerson and Adcock (1987) have made arousal the central variable in a theoretical model of persistence at gambling which also includes the influence of mood states and the influence of the illusion of control a cognitive factor. According to Dickerson and Adcock, the arousal of regular gamblers during the gambling activity will be higher than that for occasional gamblers. This higher level of arousal will ensure that regular gamblers, as a group, continue gambling for longer than occasional gamblers, as a group, other things being equal. Disturbed mood states retard the rate at which arousal habituates and thus the gambling will be prolonged. In the model, the illusion of control does not directly affect arousal but interacts with mood state so that an elevated mood allows the illusion of control to appear in gamblers who were initially depressed. Figure 4.2 shows a schematic version of the model.

According to Figure 4.2, arousal and the illusion of control jointly determine persistence in gambling. Illusion of control, as a variable, is discussed in more detail in Chapter 5. It is sufficient here to regard illusion of control as the belief of the player that he or she has more influence over the outcome of the gamble than, in fact is the case. In the case of slot machines, since no control over the machine is possible (excluding fruit machines, video poker and the like), any belief that the outcome can be influenced will count as illusion of control.

In the figure, regular players are shown as playing for a longer period of time because the level of arousal increases more at the start and the illusion of control is stronger. Regular players with a disturbed mood are shown as persisting even longer than if there was no prior disturbed

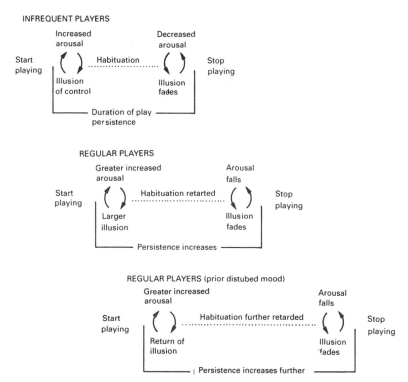

FIG. 4.2 A theoretical model of persistent gambling (based on Dickerson and Adcock, 1986, p.7).

mood. This last construct introduces a source of confusion into the model. The disturbed mood that Dickerson and Adcock consider is depression. Citing evidence from other studies, they claim that the illusion of control is not present in depressed subjects but may occur in those subjects when the depressed mood lifts.

> In brief, although depressed subjects do not show the illusion, if they are subjected to a mood induction manipulation raising their mood level to "normal," then they do subsequently show the illusion.
>
> (Dickerson and Adcock 1987, p.6)

The difficulty is that, to the extent that the gambler is depressed at the beginning of play, the illusion of control is not present. If arousal is equal across players, then the regular non-depressed gambler should persist longer than the regular depressed gambler. And even if the depression lifts and the illusion of control returns, the total would not be expected to exceed the total for the initially non-depressed gambler. The figure taken from Dickerson and Adcock actually shows the regular non-depressed player as having the "larger increased arousal".

Since both arousal and illusion of control are hypothesised to be related to persistence, it is not clear why the arousal variable is given the central role in the description of the model. Nevertheless, the results of the initial experiments conducted by Dickerson and Adcock, to test the model, support the dominant role given to arousal. The mean change in the arousal level of regular slot machine players over the first three minutes of gambling was higher than that for occasional slot machine players. By contrast, the measure of illusion of control showed no such effect. Unfortunately, illusion of control was measured by players rating how successful they think they will be on the machines in that session. The socially desirable response would be to say that they expect to lose, they don't expect success. This is the socially desirable response because it is generally agreed that success on the machines is a matter of luck and most people who play them will lose. Interestingly, although they found no evidence of the influence of illusion of control in their data, the authors are aware that their measure is, perhaps, failing to tap the feeling of control which may be present.

> Nonetheless the concept of the illusion of control remains pertinent to an understanding of persistent gambling. Very real differences between the behavior of regular and naive players was observed in Study 2 which could only be based on personal attributions of control over play. Naive players take the first machine they see and rarely change. Regular players take some time to choose; they consider the form of payout, cash or credits, lever or button control, position in the machine array, past experience, the feel of the handle when pulled, etc.
>
> (Dickerson and Adcock 1987, p.13)

Finally, Dickerson, in his recent work, has not found the data which is necessary to support the model. If arousal is the important variable mediating persistence in gambling, then a positive correlation between arousal change and play-by-play gambling behaviour should be evident. Dickerson and his coworkers (Dickerson, Hinchy, Schaefer, Whitworth and Fabre 1988) have developed a methodology which allows continuous recording of heart rate while a subject is playing the slot machines and without intruding on the play. Specifically, he concludes on the basis of detailed play-by-play analysis that neither arousal change nor illusion of control are related in any direct way to persistence on slot machines.

Summary

Persistence at gambling involves continuing from one gamble to the next. Why does the gambler persist? Behavioural theories point to the importance of conditioning. Instrumental conditioning occurs when the gambling response is reinforced. Studies with animals have shown that constant probability schedules of reinforcement of the kind that operate in gambling venues are very powerful in maintaining behaviour. Gambling behaviours also cause excitement which may be rewarding in itself. Such accounts have no role for cognitions. However, it is likely that both the mood states of the gambler and beliefs about the gambling are also determinants of persistence at gambling.

A General Theory of Gambling

The preceding sections summarise some of the main explanations given for gambling. It is clear that a whole range of factors may interact to predispose a person to involvement in gambling. The main categories of distal causes can be set out, but the weight to be given to each remains a matter for empirical investigation. Here, the factors are set out in approximate temporal order of their impact on the individual and with some attempt to specify the power of each to determine the individual's response to the opportunity to gamble. The choice of categories is to some extent arbitrary and alternative lists can be found in Dickerson (1984), Brown (1986) and Rosecrance (1988).

Culture

The opportunity to gamble clearly depends on the culture in which the individual lives. The culture affects the opportunity to gamble in three main ways: the extent to which different types of gambling are available within the culture historically; the attitudes and customs of the culture which encourage or discourage involvement in available forms of gambling; and the laws and regulations of the culture which determine the kinds of gambling for which involvement will be punished. Availability of gambling is a priori a prerequisite for gambling to occur. Aboriginal Australians did not gamble prior to colonisation by the white man because there were no gambling games (Caldwell et al. 1985). Furthermore, the introduction and legalisation of new forms of gambling increases the amount of gambling in a community (Haig 1985). The "gambling dollar" is to some extent elastic: the more forms of gambling, the more money invested and the greater the number of investors. Cultural attitudes are very important too. Thus religious differences in attitudes to gambling are associated with real differences in the extent of gambling (Grichting 1986). Furthermore, positive attitudes to gambling within a culture encourage gambling. It is no surprise that the Australian culture, in which the non-gambler is negatively stereotyped as a "wowser", has very high levels of involvement in gambling. Thus historical and cultural factors can be expected to carry heavy weight in the determination of whether or not any given individual gambles.

Reference Groups

A reference group for an individual is that group of people with whom the individual identifies, whether or not he or she is a member of the group. The attitudes towards gambling of salient reference groups may play an important role in determining whether or not the individual gambles. Gender differences in gambling involvement are unlikely to be based on differences in ability to gamble but rather on the attitudinal differences of gender based reference groups. Traditional sex roles in the family specify that the man will be the "bread winner" whereas the woman keeps house. Despite the futility of the enterprise, gambling can be legitimised as means of acquiring money consistent with the man's sex role, whereas a woman's place is in the home. With attitudes of this kind prevalent within a society it is not surprising to find that male reference groups, but not female reference groups, encourage gambling (Zola 1963; Henslin 1967; Zurcher 1970; Rosecrance 1986). Work groups may be another important reference group which encourages or discourages gambling. Work groups may provide social pressure to gamble (Hardy 1958) and the kind of work in which the individual is engaged may provide appropriate leisure time for gambling (Rosecrance 1986).

Many cultural and subcultural factors influence the individual indirectly through the agency of reference groups. Thus, socioeconomic status differences in level of gambling involvement are reported frequently. However, socioeconomic status should not be thought of as a characteristic of the individual but rather of the reference groups to which the individual belongs. Thus, through business contacts the affluent middle class are more likely to become involved in buying and selling stocks and shares, whereas the working class are more likely to be found at sporting events and thus betting on sporting results. The ethos of mateship and the pub mentality of working class Australians is more likely to bring the working class man in contact with video poker machines in Australia. Similarly, racial and ethnic differences are likely to have their impact through the reference groups to which members belong. It is clear that reference groups can act both as an encouragement to gamble or as an inhibitor of gambling and will have an important contribution in the overall gambling equation.

Social Learning

Social learning refers to the processes of observation and imitation by which one person can learn from the actions of another. Even the most simple and straightforward gambling games require some training. The slot machine is among the most simple of games, yet the novice gambler must learn not only how to play the machine but also the social rules that apply. For example, many machines do not pay out in coins following a win but store "credits". The novice gambler must learn how to convert credits to money. Similarly, following a large win some machines do not pay out in money but the win must be collected in another way. Finally, to gamble on slot machines with comfort, the novice gambler must learn the social rules surrounding their use. For example, the novice gambler must be able to identify the "markers" which determine that a machine is not currently available.

Social learning takes place primarily within reference groups and thus should not be regarded as a factor which is additional to and independent of reference groups. In particular, the family, which is a primary reference group for nearly everyone, has been identified as an important training ground for gambling (Cornish 1978). Children learn about the excitement of gambling by watching the reactions of their parents (vicarious reinforcement). Furthermore, parents often involve their children in their gambling activities by asking their advice and giving them a role in the actual gambling itself by filling out coupons, carrying the money, or looking after the tickets (response priming). In many Western countries there is extensive advertising of gambling: the venues, the means, and, most importantly, the prize. Thus television may teach the viewer where to go to a casino, how exciting is a day at the races, and what one can do with the big lottery prize. In this way the appropriate gambling behaviours are communicated and the salience of the payoff is increased. Thus, social learning appears to be one of the important processes which gives individuals the capacity to gamble and encouragement to take part.

Personality

The factors outlined so far could be grouped together as external influences on the individual which predispose or inhibit involvement in gambling. They are situational factors. A large literature is available which suggests that situational factors account for much of the variance in behaviour. With respect to gambling, we can reasonably ask whether the situational factors are sufficient to explain who will become involved in gambling and who will not, or whether some predisposition of the individual must also be included in the equation to account for each person's level of involvement. From a behaviourist perspective this is not a real issue. Personality traits and dimensions are regarded as the summary of the situational influences that have exerted control over the individual's behaviour. Thus, the child may acquire an internal locus of control (personality factor) through reward and punishment controlled by the parent (a situational factor). The personality factor is simply a shorthand way of expressing the influence of situational factors. Of course, this is not the case if the personality factors are grounded biologically as is the case with introversion and extroversion (Eysenck 1970) and sensation seeking (Zuckerman 1983).

The evidence at this time suggests a role for personality factors. However, the failure to reliably demonstrate the involvement of any given factor casts doubt on the weight that such factors will receive in the overall equation. Similarly, the role for other personality traits which are not biologically based is not clear. A case can be made for the motivating role of need for power, need for achievement, and the need for recognition. However, there is no convincing demonstration of the role of these factors. This does not necessarily mean that such personality traits do not have a central role, however. It may simply reflect the inadequate way in which such motivational factors are assessed.

Numerous authors, including the psychoanalytic school, have stressed the importance of family dynamics. These authors argue that a poor or defective home life and less than ideal relations between the child and its parents can produce an adult with character defects. It is argued that such an adult will exhibit those defects as an adult or will search for some way of compensating for those defects. Either way, gambling may be the means or the balm that is appropriate for such an individual. At this time there is little basis for assessing these arguments and it is these factors which research will show ultimately as being either really important in the genesis of gambling or having little or no impact at all.

Crises and Stress

Gambling can provide an escape from stress in the way that any other absorbing activity can. Life crises should not be thought of as predisposing an individual to become involved in gambling but rather as intensifying a pre-existing involvement. Various life crises have been implicated in this way, including death in the family (Lorenz 1990) and marital disharmony (Pokorney 1972). Treatment agencies have identified escape as a primary motivation for excessive involvement in gambling (Custer and Milt 1985; Hand 1990). Gambling fulfils multiple functions for such an individual: removing the individual from the source of stress; focusing attention away from the source of stress; and providing a means of avoiding social responsibility. According to Cornish (1978), one of the side effects of this heavy involvement in gambling may be to provide sufficient time for the gambling behaviour to come under the control of the reinforcement schedules that are operating within the gambling game. Thus, this factor can be seen as contributing to the depth of involvement in gambling for some individuals and as possibly having a contributory role in the development of gambling problems.

Leisure Time

In the same way that gambling is restricted by the number of gambling outlets available to the individual, so gambling is also restricted by the number of opportunities that the individual has to gamble. Thus it is not surprising that being young, single and unemployed are associated with level of involvement in gambling. Jacobs (1986) has suggested that as developed countries move further into the technological age, leisure time will increase and thus involvement in gambling will increase as well. Similarly, various studies have demonstrated an increase in gambling among those who have retired (Rosecrance 1986; Brenner and Brenner 1988). Thus gambling involvement depends in part on the extent to which leisure time is available to the individual. However, gambling as a form of recreation must compete with the growing number of alternative leisure pursuits.

Social Rewards

Gambling does not take place in isolation. It is possible for the individual to opt out of social involvement as in the case where the horse racing gambler makes his or her bets from home or the slot machine player chooses to play a machine away from the others. However, unless special action of this kind is taken, the regular gambler is surrounded by other regular players who have the same goals and similar knowledge. It is not surprising that frequency of contact under these conditions produces friendships and a gambling community of like-minded members. Such a community is rewarding to its members. The importance of gambling groups in maintaining the involvement of the individual in gambling has been described in careful observational studies of gambling groups. Zurcher (1970) described poker as a game which provides a basis for special relationships and knowledge of the participants. Zola (1963) showed how knowledge of the horses and their chances was the basis for status in a bar room gambling group. Rosecrance (1986) found that race talk was the basis for social relationships at the racetrack. Goffman (1967) and Oldman (1978), who both worked as casino croupiers, report that gamblers are ordinary people engaged in seemingly rational enterprises. Goffman argued that the main reward for gambling was recognition by others in the group of their courage and strength in the face of great risks. Thus, the social dimension is likely to be an important factor in maintaining involvement in gambling over long periods of time.

Psychophysiological Arousal Needs

This factor has been described as a central cause of gambling by a wide range of writers (for example: Dickerson 1984; Brown 1986; Jacobs 1986). The idea is that some individuals have a need to increase their level of arousal. The deficit in arousal may be biologically based or situationally induced. Gambling is exciting and is thus attractive to such individuals as the means of increasing arousal and thus feeling more comfortable. Evidence for a biological deficit in arousal is not available. The idea that individuals gamble for the excitement that is missing in their everyday life is an interesting one. Brown takes this idea further when he suggests that other individuals may gamble as a means of relaxation or as a means of transforming the telic state involved in work to the paratelic state involved in play.

The idea is interesting because it links the motivation to gamble with the motivation for taking stimulant drugs. However, there are many aspects of this claim that are not clear. No one has clarified whether the arousal which is involved is cortical arousal, somatic arousal or autonomic arousal. What is clear is that, whatever the underlying variable, the outward manifestation is felt excitement. Gambling is exciting and thus rewarding. The problem with such an account is that regular gamblers frequently gamble without any show of emotion (Caldwell 1974). There is excitement when the race is called or when the big prize is won, but for most of the time the serious gambler shows in posture and face the antithesis of excitement. The avid slot machine player continues stoically with the task over long periods of time and in the face of a mounting cost in coins. The blackjack player takes the good fortune and the bad with equanimity. Poker and bridge players show intensity and strain as the contest ebbs and flows. There is not the level of excitement that one would expect if excitement was the central factor attracting individuals to gambling. But excitement and arousal are not the same. The crucial test is in terms of arousal. There is substantial evidence that gambling is arousing at least in the early stages of a session (Anderson and Brown 1984; Leary and Dickerson 1985). What has not been demonstrated is that arousal continues to be a factor as the session develops. In fact, what evidence there is suggests that arousal does not have an important role in causing gamblers to persist through long sessions (Dickerson 1990).

Cognitions

The cognitive factor refers to the beliefs that the gambler holds about the gambling: beliefs about the nature of the gambling, strategies for play and the interpretation of results. Since gambling is set up as a venture in which the gambler should expect to lose money, the accurate beliefs, which an individual ought to hold in a rational appraisal of gambling activities, involve the fact that that anyone who gambles should expect to lose; there are no successful strategies but perhaps there are levels of inadequacy among unsuccessful strategies; and the results confirm these beliefs. Gambling would not be popular if gamblers engaged in a rational appraisal of the activity. According to cognitive theory, the cognitions of gamblers involve invalid beliefs such as: that gambling involves skill or special knowledge; that the individual can influence the outcome of the gamble; that good luck is a personal characteristic; and, that the results of their own gambles demonstrate the validity of these beliefs. It is the central thesis of this book that cognitions are the most important factor in explaining why people gamble. Although cognitive factors have been described by many writers, there does not appear to have been any attempt to integrate the diverse array of factors into a unified cognitive theory of gambling. In the next chapter we will attempt to specify one way in which the cognitive factors give rise to increasing involvement in gambling.

5

A Sociocognitive Theory of Gambling Involvement

What accounts for "normal" gambling? Why the high volume of betting around the world? What brings tourists to Nevada? Nobody really knows.

(Skolnick 1978, p.22)

Our analysis of different forms of gambling has shown that gambling is not a homogeneous category of human behaviour (see also Abt, Smith and Christiansen 1985). Piling the different games together and believing that involvement in any one is just like involvement in any other is analogous to piling chalk and cheese together and believing that the rat will eat it all. Believing that the avid poker player will enjoy an evening at keno is like believing that the hungry rat will enjoy eating chalk. It will happen occasionally, but we would be foolish to believe that the exception has any generality.

Advance in science often involves taking a pile of heterogeneous observations and applying a new perspective so that the collection becomes understood in terms of a new and simple formulation (Kelly 1955). Can we find a simple formulation which will explain the attraction of gambling to some people but not all and also explain the loyalty of the gambler to one chosen form of gambling? We are talking here about ordinary involvement in gambling and not about compulsive gambling. However, it would be a satisfying bonus if such a simple formulation would also make sense out of the excessive gambling that becomes a problem for the gambler, his or her friends, and society in general.

The Elements of Gambling

Gambling is about risk and money. Gambling may involve an exchange of goods or services rather than money but money represents goods and services. Throughout history men have gambled and lost lands and dwellings, servants and slaves, wives and their jewels, but we can assume that, had the money been readily available, it is the money that would have been wagered first. Thus, we lose no generality in asserting that a necessary condition of gambling is that it is an activity in which money is wagered against the chance of obtaining more money. Since this condition is also characteristic of business enterprises in general, we must add another condition: that the activity is not directed at producing goods or providing services but is simply a redistribution of money. Although a casino wagers money against the gamblers, it can also be seen as providing services and paying wages. The casino is not a gambler for this reason. It might be objected that the casino is not a gambler, in any case, because it is betting on a certainty: the casino arranges its games so that it has an edge. However, professional gamblers also have an edge and it would not be consistent with our definition to say that professional gamblers are not gamblers at all.

Thus, gambling is an activity which involves a simple redistribution of money, does not involve the production of goods or provision of services, and in which the gambler risks losing a certain sum of money against the chance of winning more money. Two flies up a wall epitomises the gambling enterprise. One child says to the other, "I bet you five cents the left one reaches the top first." That is the essence of gambling and all else is the acculturation of gambling.

Two flies up a wall is a fair gamble for two children on a wet afternoon, but it is an uneven contest if you are betting on the left fly against an entomologist who has examined the flies closely and finds that the left one is a crippled female laden with eggs. And it is not a fair contest if you are betting against an unscrupulous person who has placed a dab of honey in front of the left fly. Legalised gambling in modern life has some of the characteristics of betting on the wrong fly against an unscrupulous entomologist. The bookmaker sets his market so that he can expect to make a tidy profit; the totalisator takes its percentage before paying out the winning bets; lotteries support education and health care; slot machines are money spinners; casinos take a percentage of the pot and always choose to be banker at blackjack.

So we have a choice in analysing gambling involvement. We can base our analysis on fair gambles such as two flies up a wall or unfair gambles such as are available throughout the world of legalised gambling. If we choose to analyse the attraction of fair gambles, then we might attempt to generalise to unfair gambles by arguing that people mistakenly confuse the two. However, although not wholly accurate in assessing the take by gambling agencies, the gambling public is in no doubt that the opportunities offered by legalised gambling are not fair (Rosecrance 1988; Walker 1988). Alternatively, if we can understand the willingness of people to make unfair gambles, then we should have little difficulty in understanding the attraction of fair gambles. Thus, we shall plunge straight into an analysis of the attraction of all those unfair gambles that abound in Western societies.

The Challenge of Gambling

The first assumption we make is that gambling offers a challenge to many people. It is the same kind of challenge that people have found in a kaleidoscope of different tasks through the ages. Some people climb mountains, explore caves, run marathons, engage in activities that challenge their resourcefulness and strength of purpose. Other people grow roses for exhibition in shows, carve boats inside bottles, strive to complete the *Times* crossword and engage in activities that demand both persistence and ability. There is no denying that large numbers of people in every country enjoy the challenge of difficult activities. For many people who gamble, the activity is more than a diversion; it is a challenge to their resourcefulness, persistence and strength of purpose. It is also not simply a challenge like completing the *Times* crosswords, but also offers the lure of a financial bonanza to the successful. Thus, we might expect to find either or both of two motivations behind the activities of the regular gambler: the prime motive may be to beat the system or it may be to accumulate substantial wealth. In either case winning money is the index of success.

Individual Differences in Attraction to Gambling

For many people, gambling is not a challenge and never will be a challenge. The reason for this is that, at a core level, they believe gambling offers nothing of value. For some among these, gambling is simply wrong. According to Inglis, the sinfulness of gambling is a Protestant claim:

On gambling there was never a common front. Evangelical Protestant church leaders said that it was essentially sinful; Catholic moral theologians said that it was not. In Australia, Methodists, Presbyterians, Congregationalists, Baptists and some Anglicans grew up learning that gambling was bad; Catholics grew up learning that it was harmless in itself and only bad in excess.

(Inglis 1985, p.12)

Even if a person does not believe that gambling is wrong, they might nevertheless not find the activity at all challenging. Gambling is not challenging if one simply accepts that the gambles offered are unfair and that the task of gaining an edge is either impossible or simply beyond one's capacity. Again, the attractions of gambling may not be apparent to a person who has already committed their resources to another, more challenging project. The mountain climber has little incentive to study the racing form. Yet again, if money and its acquisition has little appeal to a person, then we would not expect to find that person interested in gambling.

It is not difficult to understand why some people will not gamble at all within one year or the next. Similarly, it is not difficult to understand why many people who do gamble, only do so occasionally. In many countries, people who would not normally gamble, will nevertheless have a bet on a horse race: on the Grand National in Britain, the Kentucky Derby in the United States, or the Melbourne Cup in Australia. We can assume that such occasional gamblers are not responding to the challenge of gambling but to the norms of their culture. Many people occasionally buy a lottery ticket or visit the local casino. They do not view gambling as a challenge. A lottery ticket is a chance of winning a large sum of money at little cost and the casino is a world of glitter and novelty. For these occasional gamblers, the challenge of beating the system may not be perceived at all. Some writers on the subject of gambling (Bergler 1957; Cohen 1972) assert that occasional gamblers are not gamblers at all.

> Is the movie-goer who used to play "screeno" or "bingo" a gambler? Is the man who risks five dollars betting on the gubernatorial election a gambler? Or the *Times* reader who, in a joking mood, bets that the editorial page in the next edition will be numbered 22 or 28? The answer in each case is "no."
>
> (Bergler 1957, p.2)

While it is manifestly false to say that the occasional bet is not gambling, the essential point remains true: that the occasional gambler has not accepted the challenge, has not made a commitment to beating the system, and has no real concern over losing. In this regard, an important distinction can be made between gambling as entertainment and gambling as a source of wealth (Eadington 1987). For the occasional gambler, the entertainment afforded by gambling is the primary motivation. Of course, the wealth acquired by winning will be a source of elation, but for the occasional gambler, the loss of money will be written off as part of the entertainment. Indeed, many gamblers set aside the amount of money they expect to lose while gambling: they budget for a loss (Downes et al. 1976).

According to the sociocognitive theory, the regular gambler is quite different in this regard. No one can mistake the intent of the committed gambler. Numerous writers have commented on the deep commitment to the task of winning that is evidenced in regular gambling.

> The gambler is apparently the last optimist; he is a creature totally unmoved by experience. His belief in ultimate success cannot be shattered by financial loss, however great. He did not win today? So what? Tomorrow will be lucky. He's lost again? It doesn't prove a thing; someday he's bound to win.
>
> (Bergler 1957, p.3)

By contrast with the entertainment commitment of the occasional gambler, the serious gambler is committed to winning. Money lost is not written off as part of the entertainment but is considered as a temporary setback or investment which will be made good (Cohen 1972). Again, it must be realised that we are not talking about hard and fast categories of gamblers here, but are simply acknowledging that much low frequency or sporadic gambling is not motivated by a commitment to beating the system. At the same time, certain kinds of gambling are motivated primarily by the hope of winning a large sum of money (for example, lotteries) and yet the participants are not necessarily serious gamblers. The primary distinction we are making is based on whether or not a gambler has accepted the challenge of gambling and thus has set about devising means of beating the system and making a fortune. Lotto and roulette are number games based purely on chance. Do not ask whether the players hope to win but observe the way they make their choices. The serious lotto player calculates the potentially winning numbers and the serious roulette player frowns in concentration over the exact location to place his or her bet.

Gambling involvement can be regarded as the passage of people through a filter system. Any given person begins by being uninvolved in gambling. However, a large proportion of the initially uninvolved people will gamble at some point and most people in any society will remain relatively low frequency gamblers. Since their gambling is primarily a response to social pressures and incentives, it would not be improper to call such people social gamblers. However, the use of labels such as "social gambler" carries with it the risk of believing that there are types of gamblers: social, problem, excitement, escapist and compulsive. Indeed, some gambling specialists believe that there are such categories (for example, Custer and Milt 1985). The implication that is often drawn from such typologies is that the compulsive gambler is a different type of person from the social gambler; that one is sensibly engaged in a leisure activity whereas the other is out of control; that one is adjusted whereas the other is maladjusted; and that one is healthy whereas the other is sick. Given such a typology, it is appropriate to construct diagnostic criteria, appropriate to search for the underlying disability, appropriate to search for cures, and appropriate to specify abstinence from gambling as a goal. However, the existence of such a typology is an assumption. According to the sociocognitive theory, it is an unnecessary assumption. Sociocognitive theory assumes that, in principle, any person could develop a problem with gambling and the theory attempts to specify the kinds of processes (social and cognitive) which lead a person into increasing involvement in gambling. However, it should be noted that the assumption that there are types of gamblers, such as social and compulsive, is also open to various kinds of empirical testing and the implications of such tests will be discussed in the next chapter when we address the fit given by different theories of gambling to

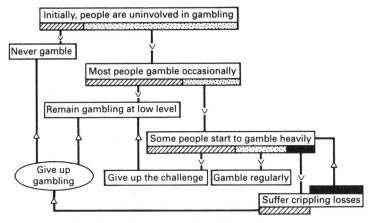

FIG. 5.1 A filter system of gambling involvement.

the data available. For the present argument, it is sufficient to understand that low frequency gambling covers a range of gambling involvement from a very low level of involvement, such as buying a raffle ticket at a friend's request, through to moderate levels of involvement, such as spending an hour or so on the poker machines when the family visits the local club.

For most low frequency gamblers, the role of gambling in their lives will remain incidental and relatively unimportant. However, some proportion of those people who begin by having an occasional gamble will appreciate the challenge that a given form of gambling presents. These gamblers will return again and again in an effort to master the challenge. They become regular gamblers and gambling becomes an important and consuming activity in their lives. Some among them will "burn their fingers" and will realise that the challenge is too great. They will return to occasional levels of gambling. Others will remain gambling regularly and heavily for the rest of their lives. And some percentage of them will throw all their resources into the challenge and fail. They will be called "compulsive gamblers". This filtration of people through gambling involvement is depicted graphically in Figure 5.1.

The important thing to notice about Figure 5.1 is that the boxes do not represent categories of persons in any clear sense. The boundaries are fuzzy and people may be found cycling through different levels of involvement over time. In particular, the diagram does not have a box that contains "compulsive" gamblers. This should not be taken as meaning that there are no compulsive, pathologically addicted gamblers, but rather that we are dealing here with involvement level rather than causation. Subsequently, we shall examine closely the applicability of the various labels, such as "compulsive", that have been given to heavy gamblers from time to time. However, now the immediate challenge is to understand why people make the transition from occasional, socially-driven gambling to a heavy commitment to gambling for its own sake.

Core Beliefs of the Regular Gambler

I think everyone in the racing game is trying to solve the same problem. It's like a gigantic jigsaw puzzle in which you have to put all the pieces together.

(Scott 1987, p.197)

The resilient hope, robust overconfidence, and dogged persistence of many gamblers often exact significant financial and psychological costs.

(Gilovich and Douglas 1986, p.229)

Three core beliefs are assumed to lie behind and motivate the active involvement of a person in gambling (Walker 1985, pp. 153–157):

1. That through persistence, knowledge and skill it is possible for a person to make money through gambling.
2. While many will fail in the attempt, the gambler believes that he or she, unlike those others, has the resources needed to win.
3. That persistence in applying oneself to the task will ultimately be rewarded.

These beliefs function as a set of core constructs which are continuously tested by the gambling activity. Invalidation of these constructs will be a negative experience for the gambler who can be expected to use a range of techniques to deny or modify the evidence. The first belief is not without some foundation. Through persistence, knowledge and skill, professional gamblers do win money at bridge (Walker 1987), poker (Hayano 1984), blackjack (Spanier 1987) and racing (Scott 1978), and may also win through unorthodox methods at roulette (Thorp 1985). The existence of professional and successful gamblers is a significant factor influencing many people to become heavily involved in gambling. Furthermore, rumours of gambling successes are endemic in every type of gambling. Newspapers publish stories of successful gamblers. Lotto is played out on television. And the professional gambler has a comfortable home overlooking the water. For any person attracted by gambling, the signs are all in place that the resourceful and persistent can win.

It is not sufficient to know that a person can succeed in making money at gambling. Even the most religiously anti-gambling person is forced to admit that the lotteries produce winners. The necessary ingredient to convert an occasional gambler into one that accepts the challenge of gambling is a belief in one's own ability to succeed. Concerning this belief, we can predict that one contributing factor will be early success. Imagine that you have a bet on the Grand National. After reading the form and the tips of the experts, after watching the pre-race analyses and stories on television, and after talking with one's mates, you choose your horse and make a moderate sized bet. Most of us have done this and most of us have lost our money. But, for some people, the horse will win and a not inconsiderable sum of money will be acquired. In another scenario, you happily agree to accompany your friends to a casino. Not wishing to be left out, you buy a "how to play" guide on casino games and choose blackjack as your specialty. After some practice, you have a fair idea of basic strategy. On the night, you play your cards moderately well and win a large sum of money. Experiences such as these may lead you to mistakenly believe that gambling is your game. More effort and more success may convince you that your fortune is within your grasp. In this way, early success can foster the belief that you have the resources to beat the system and win at gambling.

The importance of early success as a precursor to heavy gambling is well recognised (Custer and Milt 1985; Greene 1982; Moran 1970; Shubin 1977). Custer and Milt (1985, p.134) state that, "It is generally those who win early and consistently in their gambling career who become the compulsive gamblers." The gambler who suffers substantial losses early can be expected to become discouraged and give up the challenge. The empirical evidence supports this point of view. For example, in one analysis of 50 pathological gamblers, 20 out of the 50 reported that they had had a large win early in their gambling career (Moran 1970).

Whether or not gamblers are successful early in their careers, an important factor leading to heavier levels of involvement in gambling is the belief in one's own capacity to win (Eadington 1987). This was nicely demonstrated in a study of 1,022 gamblers who used one particular casino in Atlantic City (Lowenhar and Boykin 1985). In three separate studies, Lowenhar and Boykin examined the size of expected wins and losses. They hypothesised that gamblers' expected wins would be greater than their expected losses (in dollars).

Although the data in Table 5.1 do not uniformly support the hypothesis, the important aspect of the data can be seen in the comparison of high frequency, heavy betters with the other groups. These heavy gamblers differ from other groups by expecting much larger wins than losses. This is consistent with the second core assumption of the sociocognitive theory: that while many will lose, the committed gambler believes that he or she will win.

Not every heavy gambler has a history of early successes in their chosen form of gambling. Although the majority of potentially serious

TABLE 5.1
Perceptions of wins and losses by gamblers at an Atlantic City casino

| | Gambling frequency per year | | |
	1–3	4–19	20+
Light gamblers			
Study 1	+31	+5	+36
Study 2	+15	+27	+5
Study 3	+24	+15	+17
Moderate gamblers			
Study 1	+59	−49	+60
Study 2	+40	+273	−73
Study 3	+25	+43	+24
Heavy gamblers			
Study 1	−923	−511	+180
Study 2	−156	+1,418	+3,020
Study 3	−495	−256	+226

Note that the data are the differences between expected wins and expected losses. The actual numbers are (dollars * constant) to preserve the confidentiality of the data. A negative sign indicates that this group of gamblers expected bigger losses than wins.

gamblers may be disheartened by losses, for some people early losses may spur them to try harder. We have all met people for whom the greater the difficulty of a task, the greater also is its attraction. For these people, no effort is too great provided that success is eventually achieved. To hear that it is impossible to win at gambling is just the incentive necessary to persuade such a person to expend an extraordinary effort to overcome the odds.

Gambling is not a stable activity. The more one gambles, the more one becomes aware of the vicious oscillation of fortune (Rosecrance 1985). Money won will be lost. Desperate losses will be made good.

Any man who calls himself a gambler has experienced the thrill of dizzying winning streaks and suffered through the despair of protracted losing streaks. His ability to cope with these streaks—to maximize his profits during the good times and minimize his losses during the bad times—largely determines his ultimate success or failure.

(Beyer 1978, p.12)

Because gambling is unfair economically, the serious gambler is likely to sustain many more losses than he will relish wins. The losses will be sufficient to convince some people that they are engaged in folly. But for others, the losses will be considered as temporary. For these people, the conviction that they have the knowledge necessary to win is all that is needed. Clearly, if you have an edge, then you must persist until the profits have accrued. No matter that ten thousand dollars have been lost: it would be foolish to stop when success is guaranteed in return for perseverance. Losses must be expected and victory will never be won with a weak will.

The name given to such beliefs and the accompanying logic is *irrational thinking* (Ladouceur and Gaboury 1988). The sociocognitive theory of gambling involvement is based on the premise that gambling is maintained by irrational thinking.

The Role of Irrational Thinking in Gambling

All numbers games are structured around chance, so that the same kind of irrational thinking used by lottery ticket buyers applies to all such games. Lotteries are particularly useful for the study of irrational thinking because there appears to be no other numbers game in which the player has so little control over his or her entry. The logic of the lottery ticket buyer runs something like this:

1. Someone must win the lottery.
2. Past experience shows me that I am not an unlucky person.
3. I have a chance of winning.

The problem with these beliefs is that (2) and (3) are mistaken, not as they are written but as they are interpreted by the ticket holder. First of all, luckiness is attributed historically but has no relevance as a basis for anticipation. Secondly, the chance that you have of winning is outside your range of experience. Lotteries offer chances that are very much smaller than those offered in raffles. One must imagine 150,000 people: much more than the attendance at the FA Cup final; much more than the attendance at any football match of any kind anywhere in the world. Picking the winning ticket is like picking the person called Robin Hood at the FA Cup: unthinkably remote. Subjectively, the most accurate meaning that a person can reasonably give to the lottery ticket they hold is that they have no hope of winning.

Nevertheless, even in lotteries, further irrational thinking can take place. The player may choose any ticket from within a book of tickets and can choose to go to one kiosk rather than another (Downes et al. 1976). Many lottery investors report buying their tickets from one kiosk or newsagent rather than others because that agent is believed to be "lucky". We have already seen that a belief in luck is irrational: it is not that a person or agent has not been lucky in the past, but only that such an ascription, even if true, can have no relevance for the future (Maze 1983). Similarly, the belief that any method of choosing a ticket has an advantage over any other method is fallacious.

It can be seen that there are two components to irrational thinking as it applies to lottery investors. The first component consists of those beliefs and the associated reasoning that result in the overestimation of the chance of winning, *independently of any action taken by the gambler*. The second component consists of those beliefs and associated reasoning that lead the lottery investor to conclude that he or she has more control over the outcome than is in fact the case. We will refer to these two components of irrational thinking as *belief in luck* and the *illusion of control*. The belief in luck can be assumed to be present not only in lottery ticket buyers but in all players of numbers games. It has been recognised as a major component of gambling by many observers (Li and Smith 1974; Wagenaar 1988). By comparison, the illusion of control is encouraged more by some games than others. In the lottery, control over your number is minimal whereas in lotto and keno the numbers are chosen by you. Thus lotto and keno give a greater opportunity for the illusion of control over the outcome.

Illusion of Control and Gambling Behaviour

Imagine that you entered in the local raffle by paying $1 for your ticket. The ticket seller writes your name and address on the stub, tears off the top ticket and gives it to you. Later on the ticket vendor returns and tells you that unfortunately the raffle is sold out and several people have missed out. They are keen to obtain a ticket and are willing to pay extra to buy your ticket. How much would you ask for the ticket? In one study using this approach, the average selling price was $1–95 (Langer 1975). Of course it makes little difference which ticket the new owner obtains: one ticket is as good as another, isn't it? Not so! In another condition of the same experiment, the entrants in the raffle were allowed to choose their own tickets. When asked for how much they would be willing to sell their tickets, the average price was an astounding $8–75. People have more confidence in the ticket they select for themselves than the one which they are given.

The illusion of control has been demonstrated experimentally in roulette (Letarte, Ladouceur and Mayrand 1985). Letarte, Ladouceur and Mayrand found that roulette players who believed that strategies of play may influence the outcome of a game also believed that their method of play in an actual game influenced the outcome in 44% of instances. By contrast, players who believed that chance is the main factor in roulette reported much less influence over outcomes (14%).

The illusion of control is heightened in lotto and keno because the player has control over the numbers that are entered. All numbers are equal in terms of winning the game although Allcock has pointed out that careful choice of numbers can minimise the number of others with who you might have to share the prize in lotto (see Chapter 3). However, many players believe that they are able to choose lucky numbers and are thus able to increase their personal chance of winning the big prize. The question we must answer concerns how it is possible for a person to maintain faith in their special numbers or their luck despite failure week after week. Part of the answer may lie in near misses. Lottery ticket owners take note of the fact that certain digits in their own number are the same as those in the winning number. Players are especially aware of having the same digits in the same positions as the winning number and may become highly elated when they find that they have "missed" the winning number by some small amount. Objectively, all misses are equally valued and no one ticket is any nearer than another to winning the prize. However, "near misses" may convince the lottery players that they have a real, significant or meaningful chance of winning a lottery in the future. Similar observations have been made of slot machine players (Strickland and Grote 1967; Scarne 1975). Scarne pointed out that the player sees not only the unsuccessful sequence of symbols but also the sequence of symbols one removed (the line before and the line after). Thus the slot machine player also observes "near misses". Strickland and Grote went further and demonstrated that by having more winning symbols on the first reel to stop and least winning symbols on the last reel to stop, players could be induced to persist longer in playing a machine. This feature became standard in slot machines and is effective presumably because it induces the belief that full success is imminent. However, not all attempts to investigate the influence of "near misses" have been successful (Reid 1985). Reid reports a series of experiments in which an attempt was made to repeat the findings of Grote and Strickland. Although subjects in the "near miss" condition persisted at a slot machine game longer than those who were in the "early lose" condition, the differences were not statistically significant. Despite the negative results reported by Reid, everyday observation suggests that near misses in chance events are not treated in the same way as clear misses. Lottery ticket buyers frequently report the extent by which they "missed" a prize. Imagine that the winning number in a lottery was 865304 and consider how you would feel if your ticket was variously 361204, 965304, or 865305 (Kahneman and Tversky 1982). Objectively, all three tickets are equally failures, but undoubtedly the third number would cause the most pain.

In gambling games containing an element of skill, such as selecting winners in horse races, the impact of near misses on the gambling may be greater. If your horse finishes second in a photo finish you will undoubtedly feel disappointed. However, from the point of view of evaluating your system of choosing horses, a photo second may be just as valuable as selecting the winner. A few metres more or a few metres less and your selection might have been correct. Thus, we can predict that "near misses" in the racing game will be interpreted positively by gamblers and induce greater persistence with their methods.

Biased Evaluation of Outcomes

Successful outcomes tend to be readily accepted as reflections of one's gambling skill or the soundness of one's system, whereas unsuccessful outcomes are often explained away and discounted.

(Gilovich 1983, p.1111)

The illusion of control may be maintained by another aspect of self deception: biased evaluation of outcomes. One of the most powerful explanatory mechanisms to arise from attribution theory is the notion of self-serving bias (Ross and Sicoly 1979). Successful outcomes are attributed to factors internal to the person such as skill and effort, whereas failures are attributed to factors beyond personal control such as obstructions and bad luck. Football teams claim ability and prowess when they win, but point to poor refereeing when they lose (Lau and Russell 1980). In the area of gambling, the role of biased evaluation of outcomes has been demonstrated for sports betting in particular (Gilovich 1983) but also for games of chance in general (Gilovich and Douglas 1986).

Imagine that you regularly bet on basketball matches. This week UCLA are playing Louisville and the outcome is expected to be close. Having examined closely the form of the two teams, the team selections, and after noting the playing conditions, you reach the conclusion that UCLA should win and therefore you bet accordingly. It is a close match which has Louisville in front by one point with seconds left to play. Suddenly, one of the UCLA players, Vandeweghe, intercepts a pass and has a simple shot for the basket which he misses. It is a shot which he would expect with confidence to make. So your bet was lost, but did you make the right bet in the first place? Gilovich (1983) has shown that flukes of this kind have little impact on your evaluation of the outcome. You would argue that, but for the fluke missed shot, the better team (UCLA) would have won. However, the Louisville supporter actually made the correct bet. The outcome justifies the bet and the good fortune that allowed Louisville to win is discounted. If we ask who would receive your bet in a rematch between the two teams, you would most likely bet again on UCLA. Gilovich asked football betters which team they would back in a re-match after a fluke victory. Provided that we limit the question to those for whom sports betting is an important part of their lives, we find the incredible result that 100% of betters will pick the same team, the one that they bet on initially, to win the re-match.

The result of the first match has no impact on the selection for the second. We can understand why the UCLA supporter does not change. The really interesting aspect is that the fluke success has no impact on the Louisville supporter. A win, no matter if it is a fluke, is taken as overt evidence of the correctness of the bet. Furthermore, Gilovich was able to show that sports betters spend less time discussing their wins and recall their losses more than their wins three weeks later. This evidence is consistent with the claim that biased evaluation of outcomes may be the basis for persistence at some forms of gambling despite losses. Wins are taken as evidence of skill in selection (thereby discounting chance factors) whereas losses are given more thought and chance factors emphasised in explaining the losses. This biased evaluation of outcomes will allow the losing gambler to continue to believe in his or her ability to beat the system despite the monetary losses. However, such a mechanism would appear to be limited in its applicability to gambling in which there is a certain amount of skill. It would not seem to be the case that biased evaluation of outcomes would be relevant to games of pure chance such as lotteries, keno, bingo and roulette. Thus, the work of Gilovich and Douglas (1986) with a game of *bing* is of great interest.

In the game of bing, two players compete against each other. Each player has a card with 12 squares (four columns × three rows). Each player selects twelve different numbers between 1 and 24 but excluding 11 and 22 for the twelve cells on the card. The players take turns to press one of five keys each of which generates a different random number between 1 and 24. If that number is on the player's card, then that cell is filled in. The first player to fill in all twelve cells is the winner. If the number generated in a turn is 11 or 22, then the player is allowed to fill in any two squares. The whole game is presented and scored on a computer screen which allows the experimenter control over the outcome. Far from being random numbers generated by the computers, the numbers are actually chosen so that the winner does so by a clear margin or else flukes a win. In the case of the fluke win, the ultimate winner has six squares (half the card) to complete when the other player requires only one more cell to win. In the next five turns, the player requiring six more squares gets two doubles and the remaining two singles, thus winning the contest. The players bet on winning with the experimenter. Two games are played and we examine the impact of a fluke win or loss in the first game on the size of the bet in the next game.

Gilovich and Douglas found that both church sponsored bingo players and university students exhibited evidence of a biased evaluation of the outcome of the first game. Players who won on the first game increased their bets on the second game whether or not the result of the first game was a fluke. Furthermore, players who lost in a fluke result also increased their bets. Only players who lost convincingly reduced their bets. Thus, similarly to the evidence from sports betting, fluke results have no impact on winners or losers. Biased evaluation of the fluke outcome allows both the winners and the losers to maintain their belief in the likelihood that they will win.

The results of the studies by Gilovich and Douglas provide evidence for the operation among gamblers of a powerful explanatory principle that has been investigated in the context of attributional research. Self-serving bias refers to the fact that people are motivated to take personal responsibility for their successes but to blame the situation for their failures. For example, Ross and Sicoly (1979) asked husbands and wives how often each was responsible for doing different household chores. "Who puts out the rubbish for collection?" On that item husbands and wives both claimed to do the chore 70% of the time! In the same way, gamblers may be motivated to attribute their successes to their skill and knowledge rather than to good fortune. Interestingly, Gilovich found the effect was stronger for committed gamblers than for those who did not take their betting seriously.

While Gilovich and Douglas showed that biased evaluations of outcomes can occur in games of chance, it is likely that a third mechanism is even more powerful in promoting persistence despite losses. Specifically, regular gamblers may become *entrapped* by the structure of their chosen form of gambling.

Entrapment in Gambling Games

After this, no matter where he went, no matter how he tried, he could not win. His continuous losses were devastating—not least to his self-esteem. As a mathematician he could not understand it. He re-analysed his game and checked his calculations. Everything was correct. Yet he had now lost thirty sessions in a row. . . . He was not playing an even game, he actually had the advantage. So how on earth could this happen? It simply wasn't credible.

(Spanier 1987, p.28)

Gamblers inevitably find themselves losing. It is in this situation that they must choose between persisting with their strategy or cutting their losses. It is like waiting at the bus-stop for the bus when you could easily have walked the distance involved. After waiting the time it would have taken to walk the distance, you are still standing at the stop. Should you start walking and cut your losses or continue to wait in the hope that the bus will surely arrive soon? The gambler, like the traveller, is entrapped by the situation. The decision to stick with the losing strategy entraps the victim further and further.

The phenomenon of entrapment has been defined, by Brockner and Rubin (1985, p.5), as "a decision making process whereby individuals escalate their commitment to a previously chosen, though failing, course of action in order to justify or 'make good on' prior investments". The research on entrapment has concentrated on the use of games played in the laboratory by students. However, these games appear to capture the essential features of everyday entrapment. The counter game, developed by Brockner and Rubin, has many features in common with gambling games such as lotteries and provides and, at the same time, shows how powerful entrapment can be.

Subjects are placed in front of an electronically controlled counter and told that the counter will increase by units of one at a rate of approximately one unit per second. They are also told that a computer has randomly generated a winning number, such that when that number appears on the counter a buzzer will sound, indicating that they have "hit the jackpot". There are two forms of the game: in the 400-game, the jackpot is worth $2, whereas in the 500-game, the jackpot is worth $3. Here we will describe the 500-game (the 400-game is the same in every aspect of structure). Subjects are given $5 in payment for participation and instructed that they will have to pay 1 cent for each unit expired on the counter in order to purchase the jackpot. For example, if the winning number is 50, subjects will have to pay 50 cents, and will receive the $3 jackpot in return. Thus, provided that the winning number is less than 300, subjects stand to earn additional money by participating. In all versions of the counter game subjects are led to believe that it is likely but by no means certain that the winning number will be reached if they let the counter increase long enough. (This characteristic is consistent with the defining element of entrapping situations mentioned earlier—that the probability of goal attainment is uncertain.) The winning number could be greater than 300, in which case it would cost more than $3 to win the $3 jackpot. Moreover, the subjects are instructed that it is entirely possible, though not likely, that the winning number may never be reached. For example, in several studies subjects were informed that the winning number was between 1 and 600. They were told that if the counter reached 500 and the winning number had not been reached, the experimenter would stop the proceedings and require them to pay $5 for the 500 unit "bought" on the counter. Of course, in this instance they received no money in return. Thus, regardless of when (or whether) the winning number was reached, participants had to pay 1 cent for each unit expired on the counter.

Subjects were told that if they attempted to win the jackpot, they were free to quit at any point. They merely had to inform the experimenter that they no longer wished to let the counter increase. By quitting, subjects could retain a portion of their initial stake. For example, if a person quit at 100, he or she paid the experimenter $1 and left with $4. In reality there was no winning number. Thus, once having decided to try to win the jackpot, subjects either allowed the counter to increase until they quit, or until the counter reached 500. To increase the credibility of the existence of a "winning number", the experimenter had subjects complete a practice trial, during which the winning number was pre-set at 25.

Do subjects play this game and do they become entrapped? The majority of subjects decide to play the game (Brockner, Shaw and Rubin 1979). A small percentage of subjects (14%) choose not to play and a similar percentage (12%) play until they have entirely lost their payment for taking part. The amazing thing about this game is that anyone plays it at all. The game, as described, has a value of -0.5 cent. The most that can be won is $2.99, but the most that can be lost is $3.00. That means that if you played the game repeatedly, you should expect to lose in the long run; it is no different, in this regard, to all the unfair gambling games played by the gambling public. The rational action to take in the counter game is to avoid the game, take the pay and leave. Once having begun the game, the expected pay-off becomes increasingly negative with each increment to the counter. Thus, the argument in favour of cutting one's losses increases with time (ignoring the wretched trickery of the experimenter!) and yet more than 10% of the players stay until their money is entirely lost. If a game with such a small jackpot produces entrapment, how much more strongly will a game with a large jackpot entrap the unwary?

In gambling games, perhaps the clearest example of entrapment comes in games of the lotto or keno variety. In Australia, lotto is the most preferred game among a long list of gambling games. In one version of the game, the player must select six correct numbers from forty-four. Which six numbers should be chosen? Systems exist for choosing the numbers; strategies for maximising the pay-off have been announced (Allcock and Dickerson 1986); and it is probably the case that the vast majority of players believe that certain numbers have a greater chance of being drawn than other numbers. Many players believe in the special properties of telephone numbers, street addresses, birth dates, among other important figures. Let us assume that you are a player of lotto and that the birth of each of your three children was a lucky event. Their birth dates are: March 15th, April 1st, and December 31st. This yields six numbers (3, 15, 4, 1, 12, 31) with the important property of being associated with lucky events. Thus, your numbers are favoured to win. Each week you buy a ticket with your lucky numbers. Very quickly you become entrapped. After five years, you may well have reached the situation where you cannot take a holiday unless you know that your coupon will be entered in your absence. How would you feel if, on the one week you did not enter a coupon, your numbers hit the jackpot? Far worse than leaving the bus-stop and moments later watching the bus roar by.

All gambling is entrapping, provided that you believe that, with persistence, you will win. Regular horse players are heavily entrapped by their methods and systems. Blackjack players are entrapped by basic strategy and the lure of counting. Slot machine players know how to avoid the "hungry" machines. Lotto players have magical insight winning combinations. All that is necessary is persistence. But persis ence produces losses which increase the importance of remaining in the game until those losses are recouped. The greater the losses the greater the entrapment.

Summary

Potentially heavy gamblers are attracted by the challenge of gambling. They believe that they have the ability and resources to win where others fail. They maintain and increase their involvement in gambling by engaging in irrational thinking. The irrational thinking is characterised by three well-known social psychological processes: (1) the illusion of control—that there is more skill in the game than is objectively the case; (2) biased evaluation of outcomes—the wins are evidence of ability whereas the losses are discounted as evidence of failure; and, (3) entrapment—an escalating commitment to a decision strategy that has already failed.

Sociocognitive Theory and Development of Gambling Problems

The heavy gambler is at risk continually. The risk is that a sufficiently long run of bad luck will annihilate his resources. Heavy gamblers frequently borrow from one another and from their family and friends. This money is paid back in part or in whole, after a big win or after a run of favourable collects. However, a bad run may extend over many months and a massive debt may be accrued. This is the core of a gambling problem. All of the major difficulties that affect the lives of gamblers, their family and their friends can be attributed to the money lost at gambling. The large losses undermine the gambler's self-concept and self-esteem. The same losses place the family at risk and may jeopardise the gambler's employment.

Why does the heavy gambler continue despite the massive losses? Because he believes he will win in the long run. It is only a matter of fine-tuning the basis for selections and persevering until the edge that one has allows one to recoup the losses. How does the gambler keep going in the face of massive losses? By borrowing from anyone who will lend. It is essential to borrow because the big win may occur very soon and it is imperative to continue until one's luck changes. What will happen as the bad losing streak continues? We should expect to see several changes in the behaviour of the gambler:

(1) Chasing losses. Losses are not forgotten. Losses occur primarily due to chance misfortune and other unknown influences. Essentially, the system or method of gambling works in spite of bad breaks.

be quickly eliminated by raising the stakes, since
_teed by the system. If $100 have been lost in the first
_r mind! The selection in the fifth has every prospect
_ a larger bet of, say, $100 will wipe out the earlier
_t the gambler ahead. It is the notion of having the
_at makes accelerated betting seem good sense.

(2) C__ _____ mood. The continuing losses will cause depression. Biased eva_uation of outcomes can maintain an optimistic perspective over short periods of loss. However, it is unreasonable to expect that such a mechanism can cope with the obvious failure of the gambler's stratagems over long periods. Continuing losses become overwhelming evidence that the gambler's ability, knowledge and strategies are inadequate. The core role constructs concerning being a successful gambler and having the resources necessary to win are invalidated. Furthermore, repeated losses can be expected to have an impact on the family, and the central people in a gambler's life are likely to be unforgiving for the losses and their consequences. It is not surprising that the gambler becomes increasingly depressed as his resources for gambling dwindle to nothing.

(3) Withdrawal and secretiveness. The gambler is absorbed by a seemingly insoluble problem. His strategies are failing and his finances are chaotic. He desperately waits for the turn in fortune. He cannot tell anybody how much he has lost—he can barely believe it himself. If he can keep the lid on his losses, he may yet survive if his fortunes change. It is imperative that the significant people in his life do not learn the true state of affairs; they would surely move to stop him, there would be no chance of making good, and they would force him to accept that he is a failure. No one must know just how far down he is.

(4) Lying and deceit. It cannot be wise, in meeting the challenge of gambling, to allow others to know how much you invest or how often you bet. The proof of your prowess is the fact that you make money. However, every gambler knows that fortunes fluctuate; that even the professionals have losing sequences. Outsiders may not understand that heavy losses on any given day do not mean that the gambling is a failure. In order to avoid that kind of interpretation being given to one's less successful attempts, it is better to camouflage and understate one's gambling. You cannot afford to be truthful concerning the actual number of times in a week that you go gambling because of the explanations that will then be required. Similarly, you cannot be truthful about how much is wagered, how much is lost, or even where the money has come from. Outsiders do not understand that to be successful at gambling requires dedication and access to large sums of money.

(5) Irritation and anger. Losing runs absorb the gambler's attention. As the losses escalate, every bet becomes crucial. Nothing must interfere with the outcome. Hence, the intrusions of family are not merely annoying, they may be the final straw that tips the balance against the gambler. They do not understand the precarious nature of gambling.

(6) Foolish financial transactions. In order to persist until the systems and methods provide the wins which are expected, money is necessary. The salary is used and then the savings. Later, assets must be sold. Then money is borrowed from friends, family and anyone else who will stand the loan. Ultimately, money is borrowed at exorbitant interest or stolen by whatever means is available. Most of these financial dealings are foolhardy but must be undertaken in order to give the system and methods time to work. Then the loans can be repaid. These foolish transactions simply add to the burdens already carried by the gambler and therefore feed into the negative affect already described.

The attributes described follow in a straightforward way from the irrational beliefs held by serious gamblers. In many cases these attributes are the visible evidence which outsiders point to as indicating problem gambling. Interestingly, every attribute has been observed and reported in studies of compulsive gamblers. We will review this evidence in the next chapter.

Impact on the Spouse and Family

Gambling and other activities such as competitive sports, hobbies, and pastimes generate difficulties in the home life of the individual by two major means: the time spent away from the family and the financial costs to the family. The major care giver in the Western nuclear family is, typically, the mother. In the traditional family structure, the mother cares for home and family whereas the father is the main provider of income. Nevertheless, even in traditional homes, the father will have duties. Furthermore, there is movement to more egalitarian family structures in which the mother also has an income. In these modern families the major share of the home duties and child care are the responsibility of the mother, but the father is expected to play a significant role. Thus, the absence of the father for extended periods, for whatever reason, can be expected to create problems at home and adversely affect the satisfaction of the mother. Gambling is no different in this regard from any other time-consuming activity. There will be "gambling widows" just as there are "golf widows", "cricket widows", and "fishing widows". The more time during which the man is absent, the greater will be the impact on the family.

Golf is an expensive hobby. Golf clubs and other golfing paraphernalia cost large amounts. Instruction is expensive. Fees are exorbitant. But the amount of money spent on their hobby by the aspiring player pales by comparison with the sums lost by problem gamblers. The reason why gambling has an enormous impact on the family is not the time spent away from the family but the misuse of the financial resources of the family that are needed for survival. Up to a point the money lost by the gambler has little effect on the family. Indeed, the losses may be so well hidden that the wife of the gambler has little idea about whether money is being lost at all. However, the ability to hide the losses changes when the house money is borrowed or the car is sold. We can predict that, from this point on, the losses suffered by the gambler will be a source of great distress for all those involved.

Compulsive or Pathological Gambling

Severe financial losses caused by gambling will force the gambler to seek help. Having used up all available sources of money, he will be forced to admit that his gambling has been a failure. At this point he is a broken man. He will be classified as a compulsive or pathological gambler. He will be motivated to accept the label and the implication that he is ill because the label and illness mean that he is not fully responsible for all the damage that he has done. The treatment agency, whether it is Gamblers Anonymous or a gambling clinic, is motivated to apply the label because the gambling disease is their *raison d'etre*. The psychiatrist can set about curing the compulsion or excising the pathology.

From the point of view of the sociocognitive theory, the problem gambler is neither sick nor compulsive. There is no pathology, only the damage caused by financial loss. There is no addiction, only false beliefs and irrational thinking. Pathological gamblers are typically casino gamblers or racing gamblers, not lottery players or bingo players. The reason for this is simple: racing and casino play make it possible to lose large sums of money over relatively short periods of time. The lotto player may be so entrapped by his game that he cannot concentrate on anything else until his ticket is bought and his lucky numbers are entered. But he will never be classified as a compulsive gambler because his gambling is not financially dangerous. Similarly, the professional gambler may be just as "compelled" to gamble as the person with a problem, but he will never be classified compulsive because he wins money in the enterprise.

6

Problem Gambling and Its Explanation

The Prevalence of Problem Gambling

How many problem gamblers are there? Clearly, the answer is likely to vary from country to country. Australians are heavy gamblers, whereas gambling in Communist countries is likely to be much less frequent because of government policies inhibiting gambling. In Western Europe, gambling rates vary markedly from country to country (Haig 1985) and in the United States of America the legal forms of gambling vary widely from one state to another. This large variation from place to place in opportunities to gamble makes it essential that estimates of prevalence be interpreted carefully according to where the research was conducted. Prevalence of problem gambling is likely to be highly correlated with opportunity to gamble.

The prior question, which we must answer before we can address the question of prevalence, concerns what is meant by the term *problem gambling*. To whom is the gambling a problem and what characteristics of the gambling define the problem? We will use the term *problem gambling* very loosely to represent the class of gambling problems which includes compulsive gambling, pathological gambling, excessive gambling and gambling addiction. These different terms are examined in more detail throughout this chapter. Here, we will simply note that each of the labels has less precision than we require to make a reliable estimate of the prevalence of the gambling behaviour so defined.

Excessive Gambling

Excessive gambling is a term which is more popular in Britain and Australia than in America. It implies that the gambler is gambling more often and losing more money than he or she would like. It does not imply that the gambler is mentally ill, but only that the gambler is finding his or her gambling too costly in some personal sense.

Excessive Gambling in Britain: Derek Cornish's Data

In Britain, estimates of the prevalence of excessive gambling have been derived from data collected in 1976 by Gallup. The Gallup poll estimated the frequency with which people took part in a variety of gambling activities. However, different forms of gambling are not equivalent when frequency of participation is the criterion for excessive gambling. A person who buys a lottery ticket once a week is highly unlikely to regard him or herself as gambling excessively but a person who goes to an off-course betting house once a week may well consider his or her gambling to be excessive. There are several reasons for this difference: punting on horses and dogs typically involves larger sums of money being invested and a betting shop allows for a high frequency of bets in one visit to the betting shop. Of course, a person could buy large numbers of lottery tickets in one visit but typically does not (Moran 1975) for reasons we examined in Chapter 3. Thus, in using frequency of betting as a criterion for excessive gambling, it is important to eliminate those forms of gambling which do not allow a rapid sequence of bet and outcome repeated in a single visit. Excessive gambling is nearly always associated with those games which allow rapid and repeated staking in a single session: betting, both on and off the course; slot and video machines; and casino games (Dickerson 1984; Orford 1985).

When we eliminate games such as lotteries and football pools which are not conducive to excessive gambling, then we are left with those forms of gambling which have been termed *continuous* since they allow for repeated staking (Dickerson 1984). The next step in estimating the prevalence of excessive gambling involves deciding on a frequency criterion for what will be counted as excessive. It is obvious that the rate of excessive gambling which we calculate will depend on this criterion: a criterion of once a week or more will produce a high rate of excessive gambling whereas a criterion of five times a week or more will produce a lower rate of excessive gambling. Cornish used the Gallup figures for continuous forms of gambling and a criterion of once a week or more to estimate the frequency of excessive gambling in the United Kingdom (Cornish 1978). As you might expect, Cornish came to the conclusion that excessive gambling is prevalent in Britain. About 4% of adults in Britain are excessive gamblers. This figure is composed of 2% for off-course betters and 2% for other forms of gambling. Thus off-course betting produces the highest prevalence of excessive gambling according to Cornish.

Unfortunately, the estimates of Cornish are likely to fail to satisfy us for two related reasons. First of all, gambling once a week in the betting shop, while clearly being a serious pastime, is hardly a level of gambling which would merit the use of the term *excessive* unless coupled with another criterion such as excessive losses. The golfer who plays eighteen holes once a week and the bridge player who takes part in the duplicate game once a week are unlikely to be labelled excessively interested in their activities. Secondly, the term *excessive* means 'more than it should be'. It is a moral concept (Maze 1973). An excessive amount of gambling means more gambling than there *should* have been. The concept *excessive* differs from other concepts such as *heavy*. Heavy gambling implies more gambling than light or occasional gambling, more gambling than the average and more gambling than some arbitrary criteria involving frequency of gambling, time spent gambling and amount wagered. But it does not imply more gambling than there should have been just as a heavy weight does not imply more weight than there should have been. By using the term excessive gambling we imply that the activity has passed some criterion of what is right and proper. But whose judgement is involved in what is right and proper? When society makes that judgement, through the American Psychiatric Association and the diagnostic manual DSM III, excessive gambling is called *pathological*. We will examine the prevalence of pathological gambling in the next section. Here, we will reserve for the individual gambler the judgement of what is excessive. Excessive gambling means not only that the gambler is a heavy gambler but also that the gambler is gambling more than he or she thinks that one should. This meaning is consistent with the conceptual analysis of Orford and the empirical analyses of Dickerson.

Excessive Gambling in Australia: Mark Dickerson's Analysis

Legalised gambling is the norm in Australia and betting shops, known as TABs (Totalisator Agency Boards), can be found in every state. By contrast, slot machines (known as poker machines) are legal in two areas alone: New South Wales and the Australian Capital Territory. The research conducted by Dickerson took place in the A.C.T. (Dickerson and Hinchy 1988).

It is possible to assess the frequency of gambling among the general public by means of polls such as those conducted by Gallup but, as we have seen, it is not possible to derive an estimate of the prevalence of excessive gambling from such data alone. It is necessary to examine additional information which will measure whether the gambling exceeds the level at which the gambler thinks it should be. It follows that it is necessary to interview the gambler or to use a survey questionnaire. The prevalence of excessive gambling can be estimated by combining information from these two sources. In a two-stage process, the frequency of gambling in the community is estimated first and then the frequency of excessive gambling is estimated in a limited population of high frequency gamblers. If 10% of the adult population visits a TAB betting shop once a week or more often and if 10% of betters in TABs gamble excessively, then the prevalence of excessive gambling in TABs can be calculated to be 1%. This two-stage process can be repeated for other forms of gambling and the results combined to give an overall estimate of the prevalence of excessive gambling.

A survey of people on the streets in the A.C.T. in 1983 indicated that about 5% of the population bet regularly in the TABs (McNair Anderson 1983) where regularly means once a week or more frequently. More recently, telephone interviews with a representative sample of 497 inhabitants of Canberra (the major city in the A.C.T.) found that only 2.6% of the sample bet at the TABs once a week or more frequently. Thus, we may assume that the regulars in TAB shops make up between 2.6% and 5% of the A.C.T. population.

In the second stage of the process, Dickerson and Hinchy interviewed 172 members of the general public who had just placed a bet in a TAB. The interviews were kept short so that they would not interfere with the gambling activity of the participants. Each of the people interviewed was given a longer questionnaire to complete at home and return through the post. Among the questions were several which could be used to set up criteria for excessive gambling. Four levels of criteria for excessive gambling were constructed as follows (from Dickerson and Hinchy 1988, p.141):

Level 1 Betting once or more a week *and* reporting either or both
        a. losing more than can afford six or more times.
        b. losing more than planned on four or five of the last five sessions.
Level 2 Satisfying level 1 criteria and at least *one* of the following questionnaire items:
        c. Usually or always chases losses.
        d. Yes, betting causes debts.
        e. Yes, I want to stop or cut back.
        f. Yes, I have tried stopping.
Level 3 Satisfying level 1 criteria and at least *two* of c-f.
Level 4 Satisfying level 1 criteria and at least *three* of c-f.

It can be seen that the proportion of gamblers whose gambling is excessive will decrease as we move from level 1 to level 4 criteria. Based on the assumption that between 2.6% and 5.0% of the general public bet in TAB shops once a week or more often, Table 6.1 shows the estimated prevalence of excessive gambling according to the four levels of criteria.

The prevalence of excessive gambling in betting shops in the A.C.T., based on the criteria selected, appears to be between 0.1% and 1.0% of the adult population (about 170 to 1,700 persons, 90% of whom are

TABLE 6.1
*Estimated prevalence of increasing levels of excessive gambling in betting shops in the Australian Capital Territory**

Levels of excessive gambling	N	% of sample meeting the criteria	% in the general population who bet once/week or more	
Bet once/week or more	149	100	5	2.6
Level 1	30	20.2	1.01	0.51
Level 2	7	10.3	0.51	0.21
Level 3	4	5.9	0.29	0.15
Level 4	2	2.9	0.15	0.08

* Based on figures from Dickerson and Hinchy (1988) and Caldwell et al. (1988).

male). However, off-course betting is only one form of continuous gambling. The other major form of continuous gambling in the A.C.T. is slot machines (known as poker machines in Australia and as fruit machines in Britain). Unfortunately, Dickerson and Hinchy did not include the questions relevant to criteria c-f in their survey of slot machine players and so the estimates of excessive gambling based on the level 2, 3 and 4 criteria cannot be calculated. For the level 1 criteria, we can estimate the prevalence of excessive gambling as follows. According to the McNair Anderson survey of slot machine playing in Sydney, 2% of the adult population play the machines once a week or more frequently (McNair Anderson 1983b). Among those playing the machines once a week or more, 36% satisfy the level 1 criteria (Dickerson and Hinchy 1988). Thus we can estimate that 0.74% (0.36 of 2%) of the adult population gamble excessively on slot machines using the level 1 criteria.

The overall prevalence of excessive gambling involves combining the estimates for off-course betting with those for slot machines. Dickerson and Hinchy make a series of assumptions at this point. First of all they assume that those who gamble excessively in the TABs are a different population from those who gamble excessively on the slot machines. This assumption is probably fairly accurate. Dickerson and Hinchy report that only 5.8% of the TAB punters sampled have ever played slot machines and, conversely, only 12.5% of the slot machine players sampled have ever been into a TAB shop. The overlap in terms of joint excessive gambling can reasonably be assumed to be close to zero. A second assumption is that excessive gambling on other forms of gambling can be excluded. This assumption may well be false. Certainly, numbers games such as lotteries, which are non-continuous forms of gambling, are unlikely to contribute significantly to the overall level of excessive gambling. However, there are other forms of continuous gambling which have been excluded. Both bingo (also called "housie"), instant

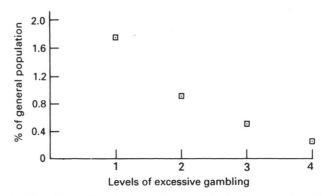

FIG. 6.1 Prevalence of levels of excessive gambling in the general population for off-course betters and slot machine players.

lotteries (also called "scratchies"), and video draw poker machines are very popular and may lead to excess in terms of the levels defined. To the extent that excess is associated with these different forms of gambling, the estimates provided by Dickerson and Hinchy may underestimate the true prevalence of excessive gambling. Finally, Dickerson and Hinchy assume that excessive gambling rates for slot machines will parallel those for the TABs for the level 2, 3 and 4 criteria. Little can be said about this assumption other than to warn that its accuracy is unknown.

Given these assumptions, overall excessive gambling can be estimated for the A.C.T. for each of the four criteria proposed. The estimates shown in Figure 6.1 are based on the larger TAB figure of 5% attending the betting shops once a week or more frequently.

Dickerson's analysis clearly shows that the prevalence of excessive gambling depends on the criteria by which excessiveness is judged: the more strict the criteria, the lower the estimated prevalence. This leaves the problem of judging which criterion should be used in our assessment. Let us examine the criteria again, but this time we shall ask whether the characteristics described select gamblers whose gambling has *consistently* gone beyond what they can afford and is *currently* causing them pain.

The level 1 criteria pick out regular gamblers who sometimes lose more than they can afford and who currently have been losing more than they planned. Are these punters gambling excessively? Are they betting more than they think they should? The fact of the matter is that every regular punter knows that there will be bad runs where it is hard to bring the winners in. Even the best punters acknowledge the inevitability of these losing streaks.

Every week, I make my own calculations and I quietly observe that there's every chance of a complete wipe-out. There's every chance that every one of my horses will go down. On the weeks that I have some success, I'm most amazed, a little elated, and a great deal relieved. I'll have my bad runs but I believe in cycles.

(Matthews 1987, p.194)

Regular punters will typically have many occasions, over a period of years, in which they lose more than they can afford. Similarly, a losing streak will inevitably involve losing more than planned: few punters go to the betting shop planning to lose every dollar in their pocket. We are speculating now about what a regular punter will consider excessive, but I think it is a very good bet that the regular punter expects to rough through losing streaks.

The characteristics c-f which define excessive gambling in levels 2, 3 and 4 are very similar to the characteristics which are used to define pathological gambling. Chasing losses is a dangerous pursuit involving wagering larger and larger sums in order to recoup previous losses. Gamblers who have hit rock bottom always admit to chasing losses and the gambling experts warn against the practice. However, we must note that the assertion "every busted gambler chased his or her losses" does not imply the assertion "every gambler who chases losses will go bust". Chasing losses may be dangerous, but it does not imply that the gambler is consistently betting excessively. It is likely that many regular punters chase their losses as the race meeting comes to an end. After all, "double or nothing" is a practice we learned as children and is a concept which may be central in the gambler's thinking.

The three remaining characteristics are more indicative of excess. If the gambler admits that the betting causes debts, then it is likely that he or she will also agree that more is being wagered than ought to be. If the gambler agrees that he or she wants to stop or cut back, then it is implied that more has been wagered than is desired. Similarly, a gambler who has tried unsuccessfully to stop gambling is one who presumably believes that the level of gambling at that time was too high. However, we must recognise that a losing streak is very painful for the regular gambler and it would seem highly likely that *at some time* the regular gambler will have gone into debt, will have wanted to stop or cut back, and will have tried to stop gambling. We can correctly infer that, *at that time,* the gambler was gambling excessively. What remains unclear is whether such a gambler should have his or her gambling labelled excessive as a general feature or whether we should simply state that from time to time regular gamblers may feel that their gambling has become excessive.

How many gamblers are consistently excessive in their gambling? The answer to that question cannot be derived from Dickerson and Hinchy's data. However, we can predict that a consistently excessive gambler will sooner or later run out of resources. Perhaps our best estimate of the prevalence of excessive gambling will come from an analysis of gamblers in treatment and gamblers facing bankruptcy in the courts. We will examine these figures under the heading of *compulsive gambling*.

Pathological Gambling

Most attempts to estimate the prevalence of pathological gambling in the general population are based on the use of the South Oaks Gambling Screen which consists of 20 items (see Table 6.2). The items were devised

TABLE 6.2
The South Oaks Gambling Screen (SOGS)*

1. Please indicate which of the following types of gambling you have done in your lifetime. For each type, mark one answer: "not at all", "less than once a week", or "once a week or more".
    Play cards for money
    Bet on horses, dogs or other animals (at OTB, the track or with a bookie)
    Bet on sports (parlay cards, with bookie, or at Jai Alai)
    Played dice games (including craps, over and under or other dice games) for money
    Went to a casino (legal or otherwise)
    Played the numbers or bet on lotteries
    Played bingo
    Played the stock and/or commodities market
    Played slot machines, poker machines or other gambling machines
    Bowled, shot pool, played golf or some other game of skill for money
2. What is the largest amount of money you have ever gambled with on any one day?
3. Do (did) your parents have a gambling problem?
4. When you gamble, how often do you go back another day to win back the money you lost?
5. Have you ever claimed to be winning money gambling but weren't really? In fact, you lost?
6. Do you feel you have ever had a problem with gambling?
7. Did you ever gamble more than you intended to?
8. Have people criticised your gambling?
9. Have you ever felt guilty about the way you gamble or what happens when you gamble?
10. Have you ever felt like you would like to stop gambling but didn't think you could?
11. Have you ever hidden betting slips, lottery tickets, gambling money, or other signs of gambling from your spouse, children or other important people in your life?
12. Have you ever argued with people you live with over how you handle money?
13. (*If you answered yes to question 12*): Have money arguments ever centred on your gambling?
14. Have you ever borrowed from someone and not paid them back as a result of your gambling?
15. Have you ever lost time from work (or school) due to gambling?
16. If you borrowed money to gamble or to pay gambling debts, who or where did you borrow from?

* Based on Lesieur and Blume (1987, pp.1187–1188). The scoring key is provided in the Lesieur and Blume paper.

TABLE 6.3
Estimates of the prevalence of pathological gambling

Author(s) and years	Country and State	Sample size	Problem gamblers %	Pathological gamblers %
Volberg and Steadman (1988)	US, New York	1,000	3.9	1.4
Volberg and Steadman (1989)	US, Maryland	1,000	4.1	1.4
	US, New Jersey	1,000	4.4	1.7
Ladouceur (1990)	Canada, Quebec	1,002	2.6	1.2
Cayuela (1990)	Spain, Catalonia	1,230	2.5	n/a[1]

Note: Cayuela provides only one estimate for "potential gambling pathology".

by Lesieur and Blume (1987) who based the construction of the items on DSM III. A score of three or four classifies the respondent as a problem gambler, whereas a score of five or more classifies the respondent as a probable pathological gambler.

If we assume that all probable pathological gamblers are actually pathological gamblers, then the SOGS can be used to provide estimates of the prevalence of pathological gambling. Prevalence estimates based on the SOGS are available for the United States, Canada and Spain (Table 6.3).

Volberg (1990) reported the combined results for six states of America and was able to specify the groups in her samples who were over-represented in the combined problem or pathological gambling categories (here referred to as problem gamblers). Men are more likely to be problem gamblers than women, since only 43% of the sample were men, but 70% of the problem gamblers were men. Those under the age of 30 years (26% of sample) are more likely to be problem gamblers (37%). Non-whites (18% of sample) are over-represented in the problem gambling group (36%). Finally, people who report gambling "very often" in the last year (5%) are more likely to be problem gamblers (34%). One final result reported by Volberg is of considerable interest. Even though 30% of the problem gamblers are women, it is significantly less likely that a female problem gambler will enter treatment than a man. The entry rate of women into treatment programmes for pathological gambling is only about 13%. This may mean that women are less likely than men to seek help for gambling problems or that the gambling problems of women are not as severe as those for men.

Unfortunately, there are several problems with the methodology used by Volberg and others where a questionnaire is administered to a random sample of the population. These problems are so severe that great caution must be exercised in quoting the rates obtained.

The Problem of Non-response

Non-response is a problem in all general surveys. However, if the cause of non-response is unrelated to the issue under investigation, accurate estimates may still be obtained with reduced samples. However, if the cause of non-response is related to the issue under investigation, then there is a grave danger of unreliable estimates. This appears to be the case in the estimation of prevalence rates for pathological gambling. In Volberg's studies across six states of America, response rates ranged from 65% (New Jersey) to 76% (Iowa) using a telephone interview method. The problem for Volberg is twofold. First of all, gamblers who have large debts and long-standing unpaid accounts are more likely than other people to have had their telephone cut off. To the extent that this is true, pathological gamblers will be under-represented in the sample. Secondly, pathological gamblers are known to be deceitful concerning their involvement in gambling (Custer and Milt 1985). In fact, denial is one of the diagnostic characteristics listed in DSM IV for pathological gambling. Again this factor would lead to lower estimates of the prevalence of pathological gambling. Thus the general effect of the non-response rate in Volberg's studies is likely to have been to lower the obtained prevalence rates.

The Problem of Baseline Rates

The SOGS gambling questionnaire was designed to detect problem gamblers and probable pathological gamblers. It was validated on two groups of individuals: 536 non-problem gamblers and 226 problem gamblers. The efficiency of the SOGS in detecting the problem gamblers was 0.93. This means that 19 individuals were classified as problem gamblers when they actually belonged to the non-gambling group, a false positive rate of 7%. The problem arises when the SOGS is used to detect problem gamblers in the general population. Based on Volberg's own data, we know that the rate of problem gambling in the general adult population of the United States is approximately 4%. Thus, 96% of adults are not problem gamblers. When the 7% false positives is transferred to a study of the general population, approximately 7 in every hundred will be incorrectly classified as problem gamblers, whereas only 4% are correctly classified as problem gamblers. Thus the error rate in the classification of problem gamblers is about two in every three. It follows that an obtained rate of 4% yields a best estimate corrected rate of about 1.5% for problem gamblers. Furthermore, an even larger reduction of the estimates for pathological gamblers would be expected since the baseline rate of pathological gambling in the community is lower than that for problem gambling. We may conclude therefore that the problem of baseline rates leads to an over-estimation of the prevalence of pathological gambling by a large amount.

The Validity of the SOGS Items

The SOGS was based on the conception of pathological gambling set out in DSM III. We shall see that perspectives on pathological gambling changed radically when DSM III was revised in 1987 (see below). It is possible that the SOGS does not accurately identify pathological gambling as defined in DSM IV. More generally, there is concern that the criteria for pathological gambling in both DSM III and DSM IV are too weak; that everyday gamblers with everyday financial problems, who are not reasonably designated "abnormal", will be detected by the SOGS as "pathological gamblers". Evidence for this concern comes from data obtained by Dickerson (1990) in the Australian Capital Territory. Dickerson asked regular punters at betting shops and racecourses to fill in the SOGS and found that 37% of these punters were classified as problem gamblers and a further 30% were classified as probable pathological gamblers. It would seem unlikely that the SOGS was correctly identifying two-thirds of regular punters as problem gamblers and one-third as pathological gamblers. One aspect of the SOGS which may contribute to the low validity of these estimates is that the time frame for the questions is not specified. The respondent indicates if he or she has had problems at any time in the past. When regular gamblers are interviewed, it is likely that they can recall "bad runs" where severe financial problems caused a whole range of other problems such as those investigated by the SOGS. If we are interested in the current rate of pathological gambling, then questions must specify a shorter and current time frame in which the questions should be answered.

Conclusion

It is clear that the determination of prevalence rates for gambling problems is fraught with difficulty. One source of this difficulty is that the questionnaires being used have unknown validity and we have no good way of determining their validity. This is not true in other areas of research. For example, in research on AIDS, questionnaires are also used with similar problems to those experienced in gambling research. However, in the case of AIDS, the efficiency of the questionnaires in detecting the disease can be established by reference to another test, "The Western Blot", which is an accurate test for AIDS but not widely used because of its expense. Pathological gambling has no equivalent standard test. In view of the problems in establishing prevalence rates based on direct screening of the general population, alternative methodologies should be sought. The best alternative at this time appears to be a two-stage process of determination such as that used by Dickerson.

The Impact of Heavy Gambling on the Family and Society

The individual is part of the family which, in turn, is part of the society, and so we must ask why it is of value to analyse separately the impact of heavy gambling on each. Heavy losses may depress the gambler to the extent that he or she withdraws from the family and takes days off from work: the effects of the gambling on the individual, the family, and society are thus inter-related. However, if we take such a holistic view, we may not realise that the impact of gambling is also modified by the different relations between the gambler, the gambling and the larger units of society. It is the gambler who is closely involved with every move in the gambling game, not the family or the employer. We may hope to trace the cumulative effect of the gambling on the individual on a blow-by-blow basis, but it will make no sense to evaluate the impact on the family or the employer in the same way. The deteriorating sexual relationship between the gambler and spouse is an effect which we would not expect to find in the deteriorating relationship between the gambler and employer, although the cause of the deterioration in each case may be the same. Thus we will examine the impact of gambling on the family and on society in two different sections, but we must not lose sight of the connections between these areas.

Stress and Strain in the Family

Everyday living places stresses on families. In materialist consumer societies, especially societies based on the nuclear family, financial stress is a background factor for most families. Houses must be bought and maintained, mortgages repaid, and the day-to-day costs of living met. Beyond the economic stresses, there are social stresses involved in coping with changing relationships and circumstances. Heavy gambling typically increases the economic and social stresses on the family and we can predict that the strain will show in the decreased happiness and well-being of the members of the family. However, it is important to realise that gambling is only one among many activities which create financial and social stress. Many hobbies are expensive and time-consuming; high level sporting involvement always consumes large amounts of time and frequently also costs large amounts of money. Similarly, excessive involvement in work or recreations such as gardening cost time if not money. Thus, heavy gambling is but one among many activities which may increase the stress on the family.

When we search for the origins of the problems which arise in families as a consequence of gambling, we shall be trying to discriminate among causes. We might expect to reach one among several conclusions. First of all, it may be the case that the family problems are a direct consequence of the increased financial stress caused by gambling losses. Secondly, it may be the case that the problems result partly from the decreased economic resources of the family but also partly from the decreased time that the gambler spends with the family. Finally, the problems may have existed before the period of heavy gambling began and thus the gambling can be seen both as a consequence and a convenient scapegoat for the general malaise of the family.

In order to differentiate between these explanations of the impact of heavy gambling on the family, carefully controlled studies are necessary. For example, in seeking to determine whether it is time lost or money lost which is the important factor associated with family problems, we might conduct two different kinds of comparisons. The first comparison would involve gambling families with different characteristics. In order to test whether it is the financial stress which is important, we might compare the happiness and well-being of families where the gambler wins money with those where the gambler loses money. Perhaps surprisingly, there are gamblers who succeed in winning (Kaplan 1988) and for whom gambling may be their profession (Allcock 1985; Hayano 1982; Scott 1987; Walker 1987). Racing, bridge and poker all support professional gamblers. Thus, if gambling losses form the main factor accounting for family problems, then the families of successful gamblers will not report the same problems or the same magnitudes of problems as the families of heavy losers. A similar kind of comparison may not be possible when we try to evaluate the importance of absence from the family as a factor. Whereas heavy losses may be incurred in short periods of time, as when the stock market crashes, heavy losses over an extended period of time are unlikely unless there is also an equally heavy investment of time. Nevertheless, an approximation to the ideal comparison might be obtained by comparing measures of family strain for families where the gambler gambles regularly once a week and families where the gambler gambles several times per week. Amount lost as a percentage of expendable income would have to be controlled by matching or used as a control through statistical means.

A second kind of comparison involves families with and without a gambling problem. If the length of time for which the gambler is absent from the family is the source of problems, then similar problems should be found in other families where one of the parents is absent for a similar period of time but with some other activity than gambling. For example, the gambling man may be absent on Friday night and throughout Saturday which causes his wife to feel lonely, frustrated and fatigued. If another husband is a "workaholic" rather than a gambler and is absent also on Friday nights and throughout Saturday, then the same strain might be expected in the wife. By comparison with families where the husband remains home, the impact of absence can be assessed.

Concerning the possibility of family problems pre-dating the gambling problems, a different kind of methodological issue arises. Data obtained from families with a gambling problem necessarily must be retrospective data which is open to all the questions of validity we raised in Chapter 1. The best data for this issue will come from longitudinal studies where the relationship of current family problems can be compared for families with and without a gambling problem and before and after the onset of heavy gambling.

Unfortunately, it appears that no studies with any of the design features we have specified have been published. We are left with a small number of studies which simply describe the kinds of problems which can be found in families where there is a gambling problem. In nearly all of the cases studied, the gambler is a man and the strain is measured in his spouse. There appears to be no data describing the effects on the children in such families.

Furtive Dollars: Decreasing Resources in the Home of the Heavy Gambler

One of the most interesting studies of the wives of heavy gamblers was conducted in New Zealand (Syme 1987). The *New Zealand Women's Weekly* agreed to help Syme contact wives, whose husbands gambled, by placing a footnote at the end of an article about gambling addiction. The footnote asked readers to contact Syme if they would like to help with his research. Questionnaires were mailed to those who responded to the request. Syme's analysis is based on twenty completed questionnaires dealing with horse racing as the mode of gambling. Fifteen out of twenty of the gamblers were reported as placing bets daily. Thus it is reasonable to assume that the sample is primarily or entirely made up of responses from the wives of heavy gamblers.

Seventeen out of twenty wives resented the gambling activity of their husbands. A large part of this resentment appears to have been directed at the squandering of financial resources. Syme (1987, p.281) states that, "For at least seventeen of the sample a clear pattern emerged. These women found themselves in a situation where they knew that the amount of money being bet on horses was increasing over time yet found themselves powerless to do anything about the situation." The extent to which decreasing financial resources are at the centre of the wife's concerns can be observed in the descriptions given to Syme by the women concerned. One such description which appears to be typical is shown below:

Case Study

The amount of money my husband bets is $10–$100 per week out of $192 unemployment money. My husband has only shared his winnings with me a few times and this money has gone towards buying household needs. I try to put some money aside so that I will always have something to pay an unexpected bill with. Because of his unrealistic approach to life, he is very hard to talk to. His conversations are mostly about horses and racing and I can't make him understand that we need money to live on. I try to help by keeping a vegetable garden and cut costs by second hand clothes. He has become a compulsive liar and I and others cannot believe anything he says. He tells others that he owns lots of things he hasn't got, that he owns stocks and bonds and that he is going to buy a house soon. My husband would never admit that he was a compulsive gambler, but things came to a head before Christmas. He was convicted of the theft of several thousand dollars which he gambled. He then sold our vehicle and lost the money so he sold some of our bits and pieces from the house and wrote out dud cheques. We ended up with nothing for Christmas except for a little bit I had put aside that he did not know about. I could not afford to buy any proper food for over a month.

(Syme 1987, p.281)

Disrupted Lives: Studies of the Impact of Gambling on Members of Gam Anon

The main information about the families of heavy gamblers comes from Gam Anon, a voluntary fellowship of men and women who are relatives of compulsive gamblers. The vast majority of members are wives. In the descriptions that follow, we will assume that the heavy gambler is a man and that impact on the family refers to impact on the wife and children of the gambler. However, it must be remembered that gambling problems also occur in women and that men may join and do join Gam Anon.

Perhaps the most extensive studies of members of Gam Anon have been conducted by Valerie Lorenz and her colleagues in the United States of America (Lorenz 1987; Lorenz and Shuttlesworth 1983; Lorenz and Yaffee 1988). In the first of two separate studies, Lorenz surveyed 144 members of Gam Anon attending the 1977 National Conclave for Compulsive Gamblers held in Chicago. 98% of the respondents were women and 94% were married to the gambler.

The state of the spouse can be seen in the data shown in Table 6.4. Wives are beset by financial concerns, usually have to borrow money to get by, typically have a negative view of the gambler, and feel generally emotionally disturbed.

The loss of financial resources as a cause of problems is echoed by the stories of individual Gam Anon members. For example, Don (1987, p.289), a member of Gam Anon, states that, "Over a period of time the

TABLE 6.4
Problems of spouses in their relationships with compulsive gamblers

Description of problem	Percentage agreement
Financial problems	
Financial problems directly related to gambling	99
Given personal savings to the gambler	65
Borrowed money from family/friends to give to gambler	56
Relationship problems	
Emotional, verbal and physical abuse by gambler	43
Gambler loses interest in sex	50
Wife threatens separation or divorce	78
Personal problems	
Emotionally ill as a result of their experiences	84
Excessive drinking, smoking, eating, spending, etc.	50
Attempted suicide	12
The gambler is characterised as	
a liar	93
dishonest	89
irresponsible	89
uncommunicative	88
insincere	82
impulsive	80
emotionally ill	100

Lorenz and Shuttlesworth 1983.

pursuance of compulsive gambling will cause financial hardship to many persons besides the gambler; in brief, family members, the employer and the debtor."

It may seem surprising that so many of the wives have stayed with their husbands (94%), when the conditions for the relationship are so adverse. However, it must be remembered that this is a self-selected group of women who have chosen membership of Gam Anon as a means of coping with the gambling problems of their partners. Presumably, many more women may have divorced their husbands, left Gam Anon (if they ever joined), and started a new life free from the problems caused by gambling. Gam Anon may be a very biased sample of spouses: those that care enough to stay and confront the problem.

In her second study, Lorenz focused her attention on the personal and relationship difficulties experienced by the spouses of compulsive gamblers. The Gam Anon members were attending three GA conferences in the United States and altogether 215 respondents, all of them women, completed and returned the questionnaire. As would be expected, the majority were married to or living with the gambler (94%). The questions focussed on illness and feelings of the spouse and relationships within the family. The results are summarised in Tables 6.5–6.8.

TABLE 6.5
Illnesses suffered by spouses of pathological gamblers during the desperation phase (N = 215)

Illness	Percentage "Yes"
Chronic or severe headaches	41
Irritable bowels, constipation, diarrhoea	37
Feeling faint, dizzy, having cold, clammy hands, excessive perspiring	27
Hypertension, shortness of breath, rapid breathing or other irregularity	23
Backaches	18
Asthma	14
High blood pressure	11
Bleeding or other menstrual irregularities	5
No physical symptoms	20

Lorenz and Yaffee 1988, p.16.

TABLE 6.6
Most frequent, constant feelings experienced by spouses of pathological gamblers during the desperation phase (N = 215)

Feeling	Percentage "Yes"
Angry and/or resentful	74
Depressed	47
Isolated from the gambler, feeling lonely or alone	44
Guilty and responsible for causing or contributing to the gambling	30
Confused	27
Suicidal	14
Being ineffective as a parent	13
Feeling helpless, hopeless, or like a beggar	5

Lorenz and Yaffee 1988, p.16.

TABLE 6.7
Sexual satisfaction as reported by the spouses of pathological gamblers (N = 198)

Sexual relationship	During desperation phase %	After abstinence %
Satisfactory for both	32	67
Satisfactory for gambler only	23	14
Satisfactory for spouse only	2	4
Unsatisfactory for both	43	15

Lorenz and Yaffee 1988, p.20.

TABLE 6.8
Family relationships of pathological gamblers

Relationship behaviour	Percentage agree
Gambler spends enough time with children	48
Children understanding to gambling father	54
Children loving to gambling father	26
Children empathic towards the gambling father and his problems	13
Children confused	14
Children indifferent to gambling father	9
Children equally close to mother and father	53
Children close only to mother	44

Lorenz and Yaffee 1988, p.20.

Conclusion

It is clear from the work of Lorenz and others that the problems brought about by gambling are not limited to the gambler and are not simply financial. The spouse of the gambler is usually angry and resentful and frequently physically ill. The sexual relationship between the couple suffers. The children do not receive proper care by both parents. And any trust in the relationship of the gambler to his or her family is destroyed. However, what is not clear from the research is the extent to which the link between gambling and problems in the family is simply the financial losses suffered by the gambler. It is possible to explain the impact of gambling on the family without recourse to the assumption that the family itself is pathological or that the gambler is abnormal or diseased. Such an explanation was presented in the previous chapter.

Compulsive Gambling

Until the twentieth century, excessive gambling was regarded as a character defect. Excessive involvement with wine, women and gambling were examples of vices that claimed weak-willed men (Inglis 1985). The initial change from "gambling as sin" to "gambling as sick'" was associated with the development of the psychoanalytic perspective on human nature. Early analysis suggested that over-indulgence in activities such as gambling and drinking (alcohol) should be regarded as examples of mania. Later, heavy gambling came to be regarded as a compulsion and the term "compulsive gambler" is one which is readily understood and widely used in Western society (Caltabiano 1989). However, in the last decade it has become clear to the medical community that heavy gambling does not have the characteristics of a classical compulsive neurosis (Dickerson 1984; Maze 1987). Compulsions are banes in life. Obsessive-compulsive hand-washing for example is not something that the patient wants to do or looks forward to, but rather

TABLE 6.9
The twenty questions of Gamblers Anonymous

1.	Do you lose time from work because of gambling?
2.	Is gambling making your home life unhappy?
3.	Is gambling affecting your reputation?
4.	Have you ever felt remorse after gambling?
5.	Do you ever gamble to get money with which to pay debts or to otherwise solve financial difficulties?
6.	Does gambling ever cause a decrease in your ambition or efficiency?
7.	After losing, do you feel you must return as soon as possible to win back your losses?
8.	After you win, do you have a strong urge to return to win money?
9.	Do you often gamble until your last dollar is gone?
10.	Do you ever borrow to finance your gambling?
11.	Have you ever sold any real or personal property to finance gambling?
12.	Are you reluctant to use "gambling money" for normal expenditures?
13.	Does gambling make you careless of the welfare of your family?
14.	Do you ever gamble longer than you have planned?
15.	Do you ever gamble to escape worry and trouble?
16.	Have you ever committed or considered committing an illegal act to finance gambling?
17.	Does gambling cause you to have difficulty in sleeping?
18.	Do arguments, disappointments, or frustrations cause you to gamble?
19.	Do you have an urge to celebrate any good fortune by a few hours of gambling?
20.	Have you ever considered self-destruction as a result of your gambling?

From Custer and Milt 1985, pp.255–257.

something that has to be done despite the negative feelings generated. Excessive gamblers do not fit this model (Oldman 1978). The gambler looks forward to the venture, plans and organises for the next round, and is generally excited by the prospect of gambling (Lesieur 1990). Thus, medical opinion has shifted away from regarding excessive gambling as compulsive and towards the more general view that it is pathological.

However, a specific meaning to the term "compulsive gambling" has been provided by Gamblers Anonymous. Since Gamblers Anonymous is the major means by which gamblers in need of help can receive it, the point of view of the organisation is worthy of further consideration. Gamblers Anonymous has devised a 20-item questionnaire (Table 6.9) which asks about the details of a person's gambling. Answering "yes" to seven or more of the questions is sufficient for categorisation as a compulsive gambler.

The Gamblers Anonymous view of compulsive gambling is an example of a medical model. Compulsive gambling is regarded as a disease or illness which is progressive in nature. Gambling will ruin the life of the compulsive gambler unless the gambler can abstain from the activity. Furthermore, a person is never cured of compulsive gambling but, at best, reaches a state of being in which he or she is able to control the urge to gamble. When members tell their stories, they always begin by stating, "I am a compulsive gambler but I haven't had a bet today." In this way each member accepts the core belief of Gamblers Anonymous that "once a gambler always a gambler". Ruin is always only one bet away. For this reason, complete abstention from gambling is necessary if the compulsive gambler is to survive and build a happy and productive life.

The term "compulsive gambling" has been abandoned by most agencies now, although it is still used by Gamblers Anonymous and is still widely accepted as descriptively accurate by the general population. Early research attempted to show that there are different categories of gamblers. Typically, one such category was the compulsive gambler. Thus, Morehead (1950) and Wykes (1964) concluded that the four main types of gamblers were: gambling house owners, skilled gamblers, cheats and compulsive gamblers. Scimecca (1970) found seven groups of gamblers including a category of compulsive gamblers and more recently Kusyszyn (1980) has suggested sixteen categories of which one is the compulsive gambler. What was meant by "compulsive gambler" is roughly the same as is now described by the term "pathological gambler" and many authors treat the terms as synonymous. Thus, in 1988, the *Journal of Gambling Behavior* published a special issue on compulsive gambling which contained a set of papers which, in most cases, discussed pathological gambling. Furthermore, the *Journal of Gambling Behavior* was sponsored by the National Council on Compulsive Gambling. When the journal changed its name to the *Journal of Gambling Studies* in 1990, the co-sponsor changed its name to the National Council on Problem Gambling.

Research on "compulsive gambling" has now begun to focus attention on what is meant by the term when used by the general population. One kind of research investigates people's stereotypes of compulsive gamblers (Caltabiano 1988). Caltabiano presented people in Queensland, Australia, with descriptions of a compulsive gambler who was either male or female and was either Australian, British or Italian. Australian compulsive gamblers were perceived as better adjusted than Italian or British compulsive gamblers. Female compulsive gamblers were perceived more negatively than male compulsive gamblers based on social distance scores. It is possible that female compulsive gamblers are viewed more negatively because of greater conflict between gambling and the female sex role.

Another kind of research investigates how compulsive gamblers are viewed in relation to people with other excessive behaviour problems (Shaffer and Gambino 1989). Shaffer and Gambino asked subjects, mainly college graduates, whether or not the names of 80 different activities represented "diseases". These 80 names included gambling. Names such as "AIDS" and "syphilis" were rated as diseases by 94% of subjects, whereas "sex", "eating", "computer use" and "jogging" were rated as diseases by less than 10% of the sample. "Gambling" was judged to be a disease by 57.6% of the judges. Shaffer and Gambino draw the conclusion that gambling is perceived to be similar to excessive behaviour patterns such as workaholism rather than to drug abuse. Similar results have been reported by Orford and McCartney (1990). With a sample of the general population in Exeter, England, Orford and McCartney found that excessive gambling was perceived as being done because it was enjoyable and the gambler was morally weak rather than that the gambler was addicted to the activity in the way a person may be addicted to alcohol. Thus, the studies of both Shaffer and Gambino and Orford and McCartney indicate that the general public draws a distinction between the kind of behaviour, and the nature of the explanation, involved in compulsive gambling on the one hand and drug addiction on the other. As we shall see later, medical opinion favours the opposite point of view.

Is "Pathological Gambling" Pathological?

Heavy gambling leads to financial problems. In the general community, gamblers who continue to gamble heavily despite major losses are often labelled as "compulsive gamblers". As we have seen, such a term is probably inappropriate for most gamblers with gambling problems. In the last decade it has become clear to the medical community that heavy gambling does not have the characteristics of a classical compulsive neurosis (Dickerson 1984; Maze 1987). Consequently, there has been a widespread move, especially among psychiatrists, to see excessive gambling in a different perspective. There has been a clear trend for medical opinion to shift from the concept of problem gambling as a disorder of impulse control (compulsive gambling) to problem gambling as an addiction. In DSM III (1980), the diagnostic manual of the American Psychiatric Association, pathological gambling was described in terms of impulse control and listed with other impulsive behaviours such as kleptomania, whereas in the revised edition, DSM IIIR (1987), pathological gambling is defined in terms of criteria which are very similar to those for alcohol and drug dependence (see Table 6.11). The next edition of the diagnostic manual, DSM IV (1991), continued with the core idea that pathological gambling is similar to psychoactive substance dependency. The criteria for a diagnosis of pathological gambling set out in DSM IV are listed in Table 6.10.

Using the DSM IV criteria, gamblers with problems can be diagnosed as pathological gamblers. At this time, little is known about the efficiency with which these criteria correctly identify gambling pathology. However, a prior issue concerns the question of whether gambling

TABLE 6.10
DSM IV criteria for pathological gambling

Pathological gambling is diagnosed when *four* or more of the following characteristics are present

1. Progression and preoccupation: reliving past gambling experiences, studying a system, planning the next gambling venture, or thinking of ways to get money

2. Tolerance: need to gamble with more and more money to achieve the desired excitement

3. Withdrawal: became restless or irritable when attempting to cut down or stop gambling

4. Escape: gamble in order to escape from personal problems

5. Chasing: after losing money gambling, often returned another day in order to get even

6. Denial: denied losing money through gambling

7. Illegal activity: committed an illegal act to obtain money for gambling

8. Jeopardising family or career: jeopardising or loss of a significant relationship, marriage, education, job or career

9. Bail out: needed another individual to provide money to relieve a desperate financial situation produced by gambling

From Lesieur and Rosenthal 1990.

problems of the kind suffered by inveterate gamblers are, ever, properly called pathological. Pathology refers to the presence of disease or abnormality and implies that there is an identifiably separate group of gamblers who are different from other gamblers. Quite clearly DSM IV cannot provide an answer to this question since a criterion approach is being used. It would seem merely a matter of statistical properties that determines that the criterion is four and not some other number. DSM IV does not pretend to specify a complete set of characteristics that unfailingly identify pathological gamblers. If there is an underlying pathology, it must be determined independently of DSM IV. Such a pathology might be demonstrated at the level of physiology.

A disease model of heavy gambling (that is, pathological gambling) demands a biological and physiological basis. The central question in understanding an individual predisposition to pathological gambling concerns the actual mechanism that is different in such a gambler. In the case of alcohol consumption, there is evidence suggesting that the routes by which alcohol affects the neurotransmitters in the brains of abusers are different from those for non-abusers (Carlson 1990). Whether or not these differences are confirmed and whether or not they can be extended to other addictive drugs, the possibility of such individual differences allows for a pathological or disease model for drug addiction. Clearly, a similar basis for a disease model of problem gambling cannot exist, since gambling does not affect the neurotransmitters directly. Hence, theorising about pathological gambling has involved the search for biologically based differences that would be responsive to some aspect of the gambling behaviour of the individual. The excitement of gambling has been the key construct in making this connection.

One theory of individual differences in susceptibility is that some individuals are chronically under-aroused. Stimulants such as amphetamines and exciting activities such as gambling raise the arousal level to a point where the individual is functioning normally (Jacobs 1986). Another theory is that some individuals have a reduced responsiveness to arousing events and thus need more (amphetamines or gambling) to achieve the same arousal (Lefevre 1990). However, there appears to be little evidence supporting these contentions (Walker 1990). In fact, the evidence available suggests that heavy gamblers, compared to occasional gamblers, have a greater arousability to the gambling events themselves (Leary and Dickerson 1985) and higher arousability in general (Adams 1988).

Another means by which a pathology of gambling might be established is through the demonstration of physical dependence. If physiological withdrawal effects associated with cessation of gambling could be found, then the way is opened for genetically based differences in the physiological mechanisms associated with that dependence. In the case of drug addictions, the physiological effects of some drugs are known in some detail and the basis for physical dependence established (Sunderwirth 1985). All addictive drugs act directly on the neurotransmission system and produce negative feedback loops whereby chemicals are manufactured by the body which act to minimise the disturbance induced by the drug. The withdrawal syndrome is simply the continuation of the action of these balancing chemicals when consumption of the drug ends.

In order to qualify as a behaviour which might be explained by a pathology of the processes involved in drug effects, problem gambling must first be demonstrated to have a withdrawal syndrome on cessation of involvement. The withdrawal symptoms following cessation of ingestion of opiates include trembling and shaking, heart rate and blood pressure changes, sweating and temperature changes and difficulty in sleeping. Wray and Dickerson (1981) examined the recollections of compulsive gamblers, belonging to Gamblers Anonymous in Britain, concerning how they felt in the first few weeks after stopping gambling. The majority gave answers suggesting relief and happiness at giving up.

However, 30% of the sample recalled some disturbance involving irritability, restlessness, depressed mood, poor concentration and obsessional thoughts. Symptoms such as these are mild and psychological compared to drug withdrawal symptoms which are frequently physiological and typically more severe. Such psychological symptoms might well be expected when a person gives up any exciting pastime that has consumed most of the waking hours over an extended period of time. Furthermore, even if irritability, restlessness, depressed mood, poor concentration and obsessive thoughts are present following the cessation of gambling, for these responses to qualify as withdrawal symptoms it must be shown that they were not present prior to the onset of gambling. It is entirely possible that some gamblers are depressed prior to gambling and that the gambling itself relieves the symptoms which later return when the gambling is terminated. Such symptoms would be falsely assumed to be part of the withdrawal syndrome if appropriate control groups are not used (Hand 1990). At this time, there appears to be no convincing demonstration of withdrawal effects following cessation of heavy gambling.

Gambling Addiction

There is no doubt that heavy gambling can cause financial, personal and social problems. Why people gamble to the extent of causing these problems continues to be a problem for theory, research and therapy. One of the explanations for excessive gambling is that the gambler becomes addicted to the activity. This is an interesting explanation which we will explore further. It is interesting because the term "addiction" is typically used in connection with repeated ingestion of drugs but in the case of gambling there is no drug. Thus, the use of the term "gambling addiction" is a radical departure from the traditional meaning of addiction: it implies that addiction is not a pharmacological property of drugs but a psychological or physiological characteristic of the individual in his or her relationship to an activity or substance. In fact, since there is no pharmacology of gambling, excessive gambling has been referred to as a pure addiction (Custer and Milt 1985; Jacobs 1986).

Can a person become addicted to gambling? In order to answer this question we must first be clear about what is meant by the term "addiction". After all, if it is the drug that is central to the meaning of addiction, then there is no case and all the talk about gambling addictions is misguided and of no value in understanding the origins of gambling problems. However, defining addiction in terms of repeated ingestion of a drug (Davison and Neale 1974; Ullmann and Krasner 1975) avoids the real issue and ignores the possibility that repeated involvement in activities such as gambling may have much in common with repeated use of drugs such as alcohol. Thus, we must first decide whether or not the drug is a necessary part of the concept of addiction.

The Nature of Addiction

The first thing to realise about the concept of "addiction" is that it has no clearly agreed meaning and that describing the phenomenon is not the same thing as explaining it. If we concentrate on describing the phenomenon, then we are looking for a set of characteristics that tell us that an activity is an addiction. Perhaps, at this time, the most widely accepted description of the characteristics of drug dependence are those listed in DSM IIIR (see Table 6.11 for details). Briefly stated, the characteristics of substance dependence are, craving for more of the drug, loss of control over its use, needing more and more to get the same effects (tolerance), withdrawal symptoms, taking the drug to avoid withdrawal symptoms, trying to cut back use, frequent intoxification, giving up other activities and persistent problems caused by use. Alternatives to this list are easily found (see, for example, Jacobs 1986 or Norwood 1988). However, the DSM IIIR list is a synthesis of the ideas and research findings available and thus may be taken to represent other views.

When we examine the DSM IIIR list, it is clear that the items are not independent. In fact, there are probably only three distinct groupings of symptoms: craving and its consequences, tolerance and withdrawal and its consequences. "Craving" is not a well-defined term but is intended to describe the intense and preoccupying desire which the addict has for more of the drug. As we shall see, recent research has clarified the biological basis of craving if not the subjective component associated. Nevertheless, craving the drug is powerfully felt by the addict. Now, many of the other symptoms of dependence listed in DSM IIIR follow from the craving for the drug. Craving more of the drug explains loss of control, explains frequent intoxification, explains why the addict increasingly gives up other activities and explains why the addict continues to take the drug despite the problems it is causing. Tolerance implies that more and more of the drug is being taken and would explain attempts by the addict to cut back. Finally, the onset of painful withdrawal symptoms may cause the addict to continue taking the drug. Of these three components, it is the craving for the drug which appears to be central to the occurrence of addiction.

One early idea that has now been rejected by most people working with drug addictions is that addiction is a response to the pain of the withdrawal syndrome when the addicted person ceases taking his or her drug. Repeated ingestion of heroin, for example, leads to a withdrawal syndrome on cessation which includes vomiting, diarrhoea, stomach cramps, insatiable thirst and other things. Another dose of heroin relieves the sufferer from these symptoms. The idea was that the addict continued to take heroin in order to avoid having to go through this painful state. That is, it was believed that drug addictions were maintained by negative reinforcement. However, a number of observations led to the abandonment of this idea. First of all, if negative reinforcement was the main mechanism supporting the drug habit, why do so many addicts relapse after becoming free of the effects of the drug? Secondly, cocaine is a highly addictive drug which has either no withdrawal effects or, at worst, relatively mild withdrawal effects. Finally, recent research shows that there are opioids (related to heroin) which, although more powerful than heroin in the physical dependence they cause (including a strong withdrawal syndrome), are not addictive in the sense of inducing craving for more and more (Freye 1987).

Similarly, tolerance must be rejected as a central explanatory component of addiction. It does not make sense to say that the addiction occurred because more and more of the drug was required to produce the same effect in the addict. To make sense of addiction, tolerance must be coupled with some motivation to take the drug and even then tolerance effects are a consequence of repeated ingestion of the drug rather than a cause. Thus, the component of addiction as manifest, which is central to the occurrence of addiction, is the craving which develops for the drug.

Craving and Addiction

Craving is experienced by the individual as an intense desire. The desire is not actually for the specific drug but for the positive feelings induced by the drug. Thus, heroin addicts, for example, will exchange taking heroin for taking methadone since the methadone induces the same feelings of pleasure. In terms of behaviour, the craving for the drug results in strenuous activity to obtain it and repeated ingestion when the drug is available.

Recent research with laboratory rats has uncovered the biological basis of craving (Wise 1988). The starting point for this research was an early study of the effects of electrical stimulation of the medial forebrain (the "pleasure centre") of the rat (Olds and Milner 1954). Olds and Milner found that rats could be trained to press a bar in response to brain stimulation. The reinforcing effects of the stimulation were so powerful that natural reinforcers such as food, drink and copulation were ineffective. Indeed, Routtenberg (1964) was able to produce situations in which a rat would starve to death rather than forego the opportunity of further brain stimulation. It was originally thought that the electrical stimulation of the neural pathways was directly responsible for the reward value of the stimulation. However, it now appears that the electrical stimulation brings the brain fibres in contact with dopamine-containing cells and this pharmacological stimulation of the dopaminergic system is responsible for the rewarding properties of the electrical brain stimulation (Wise 1988). This is an important breakthrough in understanding the biological basis of addiction because it is known, again from studies with rats, that addictive drugs, such as cocaine and amphetamines (Yokel and Wise 1975) and the opiates (Mathews and German 1984), achieve their reinforcing effects by increasing synaptic dopamine levels. Thus, the same pharmacological basis for addiction exists for both direct brain stimulation and the effects of cocaine. Interestingly, the negative reinforcement effects of both brain stimulation and drugs act through a different part of the brain (Wise 1988) and thus it appears that craving and avoidance of withdrawal symptoms may be separate processes in humans. The subjective experience of craving is not the same thing as the reward value of the drug but rather the memory of the reward value of the last several occasions on which the drug was used. In the rat as in the human, that memory can be very long-lasting.

The really important aspect to note from the study of the pharmacology of craving for drugs is that drugs act centrally on the reward system in the brain whereas all other pleasurable activities, including gambling, work through the sensory organs and, in the case of activities such as gambling, through significant areas of the neocortex. The actions of drugs such as cocaine and heroin are reinforcing because they stimulate the production of dopamine directly. By contrast, the rewards from eating, drinking (water) and sex which act through well-established pathways but produce their rewarding effects less directly will be less able to produce the control over behaviour that drugs have. And other activities such as gambling, computer games, gardening, and model aeroplanes that produce their effects neither directly nor through well-established pathways but through the neocortex are extremely unlikely to be able to control behaviour using the same mechanisms as addictive drugs. Wise makes this point when he writes,

> If drugs of abuse activate positive reinforcement mechanisms directly and centrally, they may do so with much greater intensity than can ever be summoned by environmental stimuli like food, water, or the reinforcing beauty of nature, art, or music. Whereas the signals from natural reinforcers depend on sensory transducers and the propagation of nerve impulses across axons and synaptic junctions, drugs can activate reinforcement mechanisms centrally, saturating receptor mechanisms that may never be saturated as a consequence of natural reinforcement.
>
> (Wise 1988, p.127)

One last point is established by work showing the way in which drugs of addiction are reinforcing. Since all of the addictive drugs appear to produce their effects by action on the same system (the dopaminergic system), it follows that one drug might substitute for another in the same way that methadone substitutes for heroin. Thus, taking cocaine may re-establish a heroin addiction by reminding the individual of previous pleasure. Moreover, dual addictions and polyaddictions should be relatively common. There is substantial evidence supporting such an expectation (Lacey and Evans 1986).

Is Gambling Addictive?

To answer this question affirmatively, we need to establish that heavy gambling can be similar to drug addiction at three levels: descriptively similar, involving the same processes and achieving the same functions. Thus, we need to establish first of all that heavy gambling has the same characteristics as the drug addictions. This is a necessary condition but not sufficient to conclude that gambling is addictive. Salt and sugar are superficially similar, but only one is a sweetener. Secondly, we need to establish that gambling involves the same processes of reward as the drug addictions. This too is a necessary but not sufficient condition because although gambling may activate the same processes of reward, these may be peripheral and irrelevant to persistence of the activity. In order to validly draw the conclusion that gambling is addictive in the way that drugs are addictive, we must establish that it is the pleasure of gambling (the same feelings of pleasure induced by drugs) that the heavy gambler craves. One side effect of this last requirement is that gambling addiction and drug addiction can be substituted for one another and we should expect relatively high levels of dual addictions and polyaddictions which include gambling.

The Similarity in Terms of Addiction of Gambling and Drug Taking

If we accept the criteria for psychoactive substance dependence listed in DSM IIIR as the descriptive criteria for addiction, then we can ask the extent to which these criteria also fit excessive gambling. In DSM IIIR the criteria for pathological gambling are remarkably similar to those for psychoactive substance dependence (see Table 6.11).

Although the overlap between criteria for substance abuse and patho-logical gambling in DSM IIIR is considerable, it is also intentional. The criteria for pathological gambling were modelled on those for substance abuse and were based on the assumption that pathological gambling was the same kind of problem as drug addiction (Lesieur 1988, 1990).

Those criteria (for DSM IIIR) were created to mimic the criteria for psycho-active substance dependence. They were quite literally modelled after that and all we

TABLE 6.11
Comparison of the DSM IIIR criteria for substance dependence and pathological gambling

Psychoactive substance dependence	Pathological gambling
At least three of the following	At least four of the following
(1) when not actually using the substance, a lot of time spent looking forward to use of or arranging to get the substance	(1) frequent preoccupation with gambling or with obtaining money to gamble
(2) substance often taken in larger amounts or over a longer period than the individual intended	(2) often gambling larger amounts of money or over a longer period than intended
(3) tolerance: need for increased amounts of the substance in order to achieve intoxication or desired effect, or diminished effect with continued use of the same amount	(3) need to increase the size and frequency of bets to achieve the desired excitement
(4) characteristic withdrawal symptoms	(4) restlessness or irritability if unable to gamble
(5) persistent desire or repeated efforts to cut down or control substance use	(5) repeated efforts to cut down or stop gambling
(6) frequent intoxication or impairment by substance use when expected to fulfil social or occupational obligations, or when substance use is hazardous	(6) often gambling when expected to fulfil social or occupational obligations
(7) important social, occupational or recreational activity given up or reduced because it was incompatible with the use of the substance	(7) some important social, occupational or recreational activity given up in order to gamble
(8) continued substance use despite a persistent social, occupational, psychological, or a physical problem that is caused or exacerbated by the use of the substance	(8) continuation of gambling despite inability to pay mounting debts, or despite other significant social, occupational, or legal problems that the individual knows to be exacerbated by gambling
(9) substance often taken to relieve or avoid withdrawal symptoms	(9) repeated loss of money gambling and returning another day to win back his losses ("chasing")

Modified table from Blume (1987, p.242).

did was exchange the word drugs or alcohol or psychoactive substance . . . for gambling. . . . We decided to use the addiction model.

(Lesieur 1990)

Clearly, the question of whether heavy gambling ever has the characteristics of a drug addiction cannot be answered by comparing the criteria for psychoactive substance dependence and those for pathological gambling in DSM IIIR. For this reason, in DSM IV the criteria for pathological gambling have been derived empirically. The people primarily responsible for this research have been Henry Lesieur and Richard Rosenthal in the United States. Lesieur and Rosenthal (1990) developed a questionnaire based on the criteria listed in DSM III (which stress the impulsive nature of problem gambling), the criteria listed in DSM IIIR (which stress the addictive nature of problem gambling), and on the published research indicating characteristics of pathological gambling. The questionnaires were distributed to 222 pathological gamblers and to 130 substance abusing controls. The items which best discriminated the gamblers from the control group are listed in Table 6.10.

Although there are problems with Lesieur and Rosenthal's study in terms of the formation of the experimental group (how do you collect a group of pathological gamblers without using the criteria for pathological gambling?) and the control group (drug users may be a biased sample of social gamblers), the interesting thing is that the best criteria for discriminating are items 1 and 5. Now, although preoccupation is part of what is involved in craving, the preoccupation of the gambler is with things other than the pleasure afforded by the activity. The gambler relives past gambling experiences and we can assume this means thinking about successes and failures ("bad beats", Rosecrance 1987). And the gambler studies a system—a much more constructive and cognitive activity than is engaged in by the drug addict. Similarly, chasing losses is eminently reasonable if one hopes and expects to win. In any case this item has no direct equivalent in the list for substance dependence.

If any weight can be put on the DSM IV criteria, we should conclude that the description of pathological gambling has only a moderate degree of overlap with the description of psychoactive drug dependence. Nevertheless, it is also true in that there are some similarities between drug dependence and pathological gambling. Only a small proportion of those who gamble or take drugs have problems in controlling their behaviour. In both cases, the group with problems make frequent attempts to cut back but usually fail. These failures can be a source of shame in both groups and the continued involvement is often covered up by members of both groups. These similarities are real, but we should not conclude that therefore pathological gambling is the same kind of thing as drug addiction. Behaviours which we would not normally label as excessive can produce the same list of characteristics. For example, some children are enuretic: they are incontinent while sleeping. Only a small proportion of children have problems controlling their urination. These children try assiduously to control their behaviour but fail and these failures are a source of shame and are covered up whenever possible. We cannot conclude that any behaviour is addictive simply by looking at the consequences of the behaviour. If pathological gambling is an addiction, then we must show that it operates through the same physiological processes as drug addictions and fulfils the same functions for the addicted individual.

The Physiological Basis of Pathological Gambling

Addictive drugs are extremely rewarding because of the direct effect that such drugs have on the dopaminergic system in the brain. Clearly, neither gambling nor any other activity engaged in by a person will replicate the effect of an addictive drug. Nevertheless, in so far as an activity causes pleasure we may assume that it does so by activating the same neural system as addictive drugs. Thus it is conceivable that continued involvement in a pleasurable activity may release sufficient amounts of dopamine for the activity to be a powerful reinforcer. Such a case might be made for natural reinforcers such as food, drink, sex and touch. Gambling, however, does not have such an obvious pleasure component. If we consider slot machines as the closest approximation to a repetitive behaviour that can become excessive, we can ask about the degree of pleasure afforded by the activity. The activity does not provide pleasure by ingestion! And there appears to be no serious claims that it is the action of the machine on the body of the player that causes the pleasure. In fact we can be fairly certain that the pleasure comes either from the anticipation that the machine will soon pay out or from the fact that the machine has just paid out. However, if either of these alternatives are the source of pleasure, then slot machines provide liberal doses of pain. Furthermore, if the felt pleasure is excitement (which may have little to do with the pleasure afforded by addictive drugs) and autonomic arousal is a major component of that excitement (Brown 1990), then recent physiological research does not provide evidence of a significant role for pleasure (Dickerson 1990).

Despite the failure to support the claim gambling gives pleasure in the way that addictive drugs give pleasure, there has been a number of attempts to show that the brain activity of pathological gamblers is different from that of social gamblers or non-gamblers. Specifically, various fluids from the bodies of individuals in these two groups are examined to see whether there are different concentrations of the metabolites of various neurotransmitter chemicals. A significant difference is taken to imply that the relevant neurotransmitter is involved in the gambling behaviour of the pathological gambling group. Thus, Blaszczynski, Winter and McConaghy (1986) compared slot machine players and horse-race punters with a control group of non-gamblers and found that the horse-race punters (but not the slot machine players) had significantly lower base-line levels of β-endorphin than the control group. However, pre- and post-race there was no change in the

β-endorphin level. Roy et al. (1988) compared a group of pathological gamblers with a non-gambling control group. A variety of chemicals from the cerebrospinal fluid, blood plasma and urinary output were examined and it was found that there were significant differences in certain chemicals implicating the noradrenergic system within the brain.

The problem in interpreting such data is that it is not possible to tell from such studies whether altered levels of biochemical agents are a cause or a consequence of the excessive activity. In the case of pathological gambling, large amounts of money are lost and this fact alone would be sufficient to account for the depression that pathological gamblers report. Feelings of depression over extended periods of time may bring about changes at the level of neurochemistry that are then detected as differences in comparison to a non-gambling, non-depressed control group. Clearly, for studies investigating the biochemistry of pathological gambling to reach conclusions about physiological causation, before and after studies must be conducted. Ideally, such studies would monitor the dopaminergic system and show a direct relationship between dopamine activity and persistence at gambling. No such evidence exists.

Do Pathological Gamblers Continue to Gamble for the Pleasure it Gives?

There are references in the literature on gambling to the fact that pathological gamblers behave as if they were "high" on a drug when gambling (for example, Shubin 1977; Custer and Milt 1985):

When these people are gambling they're on as much of a high as if they were on a narcotic. Now, in the late stage those highs aren't anywhere as high as they used to be: but nevertheless, there's still that excitement of gambling.

(Shubin 1977, p.2)

Such references imply that the pathological gambler is motivated by the same intense pleasure that comes from a drug like cocaine, for example. However, claims of this kind must be given little weight in the debate about whether gambling is addictive. The concept of "high" with reference to drugs is quite unclear. Such words can be used for a whole range of behaviours that gamblers may exhibit and so it may be simply the perspective of the observer that shows rather than any meaningful statement about the gambler.

In Chapter 2 we examined the behaviour of gamblers in different gambling activities. It was clear then that there is much more to gambling than the pursuit of pleasure. Undoubtedly, winning at gambling gives pleasure. However, the behaviour of gamblers is more goal-oriented, more skilful, and involves strategic thinking in a way that is quite different from the ingestion of drugs. Dickerson (1984) has pointed out that there are few differences between heavy gamblers who are still pursuing their goals and compulsive gamblers in treatment. This suggests that there is a continuum of involvement in gambling from occasional minor betting through to frequent heavy betting (see also Orford 1985). If there is no difference between heavy gambling and pathological gambling, why is it that some gamblers are categorised as pathological gamblers and treated for their disease?

Various authors have pointed to an alternative perspective to addiction (Oldman 1978; Lesieur 1984; Walker 1985; Rosecrance 1986; Hand 1990). Specifically, inferior gambling strategies may bring about unsupportable financial losses. The gambler is coerced, by the reality of these losses and the debts incurred, into treatment. Treatment may appear to be successful if the gambler gives up his or her hopes of winning or is unsuccessful when the gambler subsequently tries again. This perspective, which is stated in more detail in Chapter 4, makes possible a treatment approach which has no parallel in the treatment of drug addictions. If it is the inferior betting strategies of the gambler which are causing the financial losses and thus the categorisation as addicted or pathological, treatment could focus on teaching the gambler how to gamble more effectively. Once the gambler is using better gambling methods and money management techniques (Allcock and Dickerson 1986), the risk of losing large sums of money is reduced and the gambler might be able to continue for longer periods of time (Sartin 1988). It is this option in the treatment of gambling problems, more than any other aspect, which highlights the differences between "pathological" gambling and drug addictions.

Gambling and General Theories of Addiction

We have seen that specific explanations for heavy gambling are readily available. However, numerous writers have pointed out the similarities between a whole range of excessive behaviours and drug addictions: Excessive eating (Orford 1985) and especially fatty foods, spicy foods and chocolate (Fuller et al. 1988), excessive sexual behaviour (Carnes 1985), loving too much (Norwood 1988), jogging and exercise (Solomon 1980) and computer games (Brown 1990). The belief that addiction covers a range of activities and not simply the ingestion of drugs has led to several attempts to explain gambling within a more general framework of psychological addiction. There are empirical grounds for thinking that this approach may be successful. Numerous writers have remarked on the similarities between different addictions (Peele 1977; Solomon and Corbit 1974) and there is growing evidence supporting this point of view (Gossop and Eysenck 1980; Blaszczynski, Buhrich and McConaghy 1985; Lacey and Evans 1986). For example, Blaszczynski et al. found that heroin addicts and pathological gamblers scored higher on the E.P.Q. addiction scale than did a control group of ordinary medical patients. Such results are weakened by the possibility that the difference between the experimental and control groups could be attributed to the labels received in treatment or to the recognition of why they were in their current predicament rather than to the addiction as such (Oldman 1978; Walker 1985).

In support of the generalist position, Lacey and Evans have developed a clinical category which they label "multi-impulsive personality disorder". The specific impulse disorders include those listed in DSM III (pathological gambling, kleptomania, pyromania, intermittent explosive disorder and isolated explosive disorder) together with the better known substance dependencies such as narcotic addiction, alcohol abuse and bulimia. A review of several thousand cases for multiple impulsive disorders revealed some interesting commonalities. For example, Lacey and Evans were able to formulate diagnostic criteria for the multi-impulsive form of bulimia: gross alcohol abuse, "street drug" abuse, multiple overdoses, repeated self-damage, sexual disinhibition and shoplifting. However, interestingly, the pathological gambling group ($N = 50$) exhibited the lowest involvement rate for drugs and alcohol of all the groups studied. One possible explanation for this discrepancy is that if you are a pathological gambler then it is unlikely that you can afford the money for heavy involvement in drugs and alcohol as well. It may well be the centrality of money to the activity of gambling which sets gambling apart from other psychological addictions. Nevertheless, there is growing evidence for a unitary structure underlying a range of psychological addictions and such evidence calls for a general theory of addictions to be advanced. Whether such a theory will apply to heavy gambling remains to be seen.

A Psychoanalytic Theory of Addiction

A number of psychoanalytically oriented theories have been proposed to explain excessive gambling (Bergler 1957; Halliday and Fuller 1974; Maze 1987), but these theories do not attempt to explain other excessive behaviours, although they might well be extended to do so. Freud wrote briefly concerning a common origin to addictions:

In a letter to Fliess of 22 December 1897, Freud suggested that masturbation is the "primal addiction", for which all later addictions are substitutes.

(Halliday and Fuller 1974, p.174)

Furthermore, Freud stated specifically that excessive gambling is a substitute for masturbation:

The "vice" of masturbation is replaced by the addiction to gambling; . . . The irresistible nature of the temptation, the solemn resolutions, which are nevertheless invariably broken, never to do it again, the stupefying pleasure and the bad conscience which tells the subject that he is ruining himself (committing suicide)—all these elements remain unaltered in the process of substitution.

(Halliday and Fuller 1974, p.172)

Thus, excessive gambling is assumed to be a substitute for masturbation. Such a theory is difficult to test. Nevertheless, three observations are relevant to its validity. First, it is not clear that the structural analogy between masturbation and gambling is as close as Freud believed. In the case of masturbation it is successful completion of the activity which is followed by guilt, whereas in the case of excessive gambling, it is failure which is followed by guilt. Second, Freud was clear about the origin of the guilt that follows masturbation: fear of castration by the father. However, the particular dynamics that would apply to male gambling do not appear equally applicable to female gambling, yet about 50% of high frequency slot machine players are women (Walker 1988). Finally, if masturbation is the primary addiction for which all other addictions are substitutes, then cultural differences in rates of addiction in general and pathological gambling in particular would be expected. Japan has a history of liberal attitudes to masturbation which contrasts with typical Western attitudes (Fuller 1974); thus, since masturbation is not followed by guilt in Japanese society, the addictive cycle is broken and addiction would not be expected to be the problem in Japanese society that it is in Western society. However, Fuller reports that gambling in Japan constitutes up to 18% of recreational spending compared with 2–3% in the United States. Whether or not Fuller's figure for Japan is correct, it would seem difficult to make an argument that excessive gambling is not a problem in Japan today.

In summary, Freud's idea that masturbation is the primary addiction which later addictions replace appears to face difficulties at both the conceptual and empirical levels. However, the arguments are speculative rather than conclusive and the possibility that masturbation fulfils this crucial role cannot be rejected until evidence relative to the central hypothesis is collected.

The Opponent-Process Theory of Motivation

Solomon (Solomon and Corbit 1974; Solomon 1980) has pointed out that the affective phenomena of addictions (affective contrast, affective tolerance and withdrawal symptoms) can be understood as the product of two opposed factors. When the individual first takes heroin, for example, the immediate affect is likely to be intensely pleasurable. However, after the direct effects of the drug have disappeared, the individual is left with negative feelings which may be painful and frightening. These physical symptoms disappear after further time has elapsed and it is not until this point is reached that normalcy is restored. During this negative feeling state the individual might strongly desire a return to the positive affective state induced by the drug. If the drug is taken again, at the same dosage, the high is not quite as powerful as the first time, but the subsequent withdrawal phase is more unpleasant. Thus, the cycle is likely to be repeated again and again. Throughout this cyclic use of the drug, the initial positive state grows weaker and the withdrawal state stronger. For this reason, the individual now takes more of the drug in order to restore the full positive state. Very quickly, the withdrawal state becomes so powerful that the individual begins to take the drug in order to avoid that condition. Solomon hypothesised that these affective phenomena result from two processes: a primary process **a** which is a direct response to the drug and is manifested as a positive affective state **A**; and an opponent process **b** which is stimulated by the presence of state **A** and is manifested by a negative affective state **B**. The actual affective tone of the individual at any point in time is the sum of the **A** and **B** states. This manifest affective response will be positive initially but then negative after removal of the drug. The **a** process is typically rapid at onset and quickly decays after the drug leaves the system. By contrast, the **b** process is slow in onset and slow to extinguish. Thus, after many doses of the drug, the manifest affective response is initially positive under the influence of the **a** process but is quickly converted to a negative state which is powerful and enduring under the influence of the **b** process.

The opponent-process theory is associated with the view that the onset of drug addiction occurs at the point at which the behaviour changes from being oriented to achieving the **A** state to being oriented to avoiding the **B** state. This view also suggests why addictions are so difficult to break. It would appear that the only effective procedure for terminating the **b** process is abstinence from the drug. However, if this painful course of action is undertaken, the consequence according to the opponent-process theory is that the drug once more becomes capable of stimulating the **A** state free from the influence of the opponent **b** process.

While the opponent-process theory can be used to explain many different persistent behaviour patterns such as the heavy use of saunas and daily jogging, its use to explain heavy gambling runs into problems. Straightforward predictions can be made about the expectations for comparisons between the effects of low frequency and high frequency gambling (Walker 1986). One of the strongest pieces of evidence supporting predictions drawn from the opponent-process theory comes from a study of arousal in dogs after receiving electric shocks (Church et al. 1966). Initially, electric shocks to the hind paws produce a large increase in heart rate. After the shock, the heart rate decreases slowly to a point below the baseline reading and does not return to the baseline figure until nearly a minute has elapsed. With a veteran laboratory animal the shock produces a much smaller increase in heart rate initially followed by a much larger and prolonged decrease in heart rate below the baseline level. After two minutes, the heart rate has not returned to the baseline figure. Walker points out that, if gambling is arousing and it is this arousal which causes the heavy gambler to continue with the activity, then opponent-process effects should be observed when the heart rates of occasional and heavy gamblers are compared. Specifically, the occasional gambler should exhibit a large increase in heart rate when beginning to gamble (**a** process) which should decay to the baseline or slightly below (**b** process) when the gambling stops. By contrast, the heavy gambler should exhibit a smaller increase in heart rate when beginning gambling (**a** process competing with **b** process), but should show a marked decrease, prolonged in time, below the baseline (strong **b** process) before the normal heart rate is restored.

The evidence available suggests that the opponent-process predictions are erroneous. Dickerson (1985) and Blaszczynski et al. (1986) have both measured heart rate pre- and post-gambling with the same result: the heart rate remains above the baseline after gambling and slowly decays to the baseline figure. Furthermore, Dickerson measured heart rate during the first three minutes of play on a slot machine by low frequency and high frequency players. From the same baseline figure, high frequency players' heart rates rose higher and stayed higher than low frequency players' heart rates. After gambling ceased, the heart rates of high frequency players took longer to return to normal. At no stage did the heart rates of high frequency players dip below the baseline reading, although for low frequency players a dip after cessation of gambling was exhibited. In every respect this data is diametrically opposed to the predictions drawn from the opponent-process theory.

In summary, although the opponent-process theory makes a parsimonious explanation for the phenomena of drug addiction and possibly for others of the psychological addictions, it does not describe accurately the physiological evidence available concerning heavy gambling.

Gambling Addiction as Escape from Pain

The idea that people gamble in order to escape from stress in their lives has been suggested many times (for example, Custer and Milt 1985; Brown 1987; Hand 1990). The source of the pain is usually assumed to be one of two alternatives. Either the pain is physiologically based (Jacobs 1986; Lefevre 1990) or it is psychologically based (Brown 1990; Gray 1990). Recently, Jacobs (1986) has joined these two sources of pain together in a general theory of addictions. The first factor is the resting state of physiological arousal. According to Jacobs, the addiction-prone individual is either chronically over-aroused or chronically under-aroused throughout life. Furthermore, it is not simply any deviation from the normal range of arousal across individuals that is intended but a chronic and excessive hyper- or hypo-arousal. Thus, the addiction-prone individual is under continual stress to correct this condition. The particular addiction that ensnares the individual is one which suddenly and dramatically gives relief from this stress.

Not all such hyper- or hypo-aroused individuals are addiction prone. A second necessary condition involves the childhood and adolescent life of the individual. According to Jacobs (1986, p.21), the addiction-prone individual has "a childhood and adolescence marked by deep feelings of inadequacy, inferiority, and a sense of rejection by parents and significant others". Similarly, Gray (1990) does not believe that the pain is biologically based but rather that it comes from living in dysfunctional families. In a dysfunctional family, for whatever reason (alcohol abuse, workaholism), the child develops feelings of worthlessness which Gray calls "toxic shame". As the child grows up he or she learns ways of coping with the pain of toxic shame. Such children are at risk for developing addictions.

As a child or adolescent, the individual is likely to engage in wish-fulfilling fantasies which give a measure of relief from the reality of the everyday world. At the same time the disabilities of such individuals prevent them from acquiring the coping skills necessary to deal with the situation. Thus these people have a more difficult situation and a lessened ability to deal with that situation than others in society. When such an individual comes in contact with the addictive substance or activity, the result is a powerful relief from tension and one which such an individual is likely to pursue. The addiction is one way that the stressed individual can cope with his or her situation on a continuing basis. Jacobs points out that the initial contact with the addictive behaviour or substance is a chance event, since the individual has no idea that any real relief can be found in the environment.

Jacobs's theory can be tested directly with respect to the necessary conditions for addiction. In particular, heavy gamblers would be expected to show baseline arousal states which deviate markedly from the normal distribution. Since gambling is an activity which creates excitement, it is reasonable that the addiction-prone individuals who choose gambling as their means of relief will be hypo-aroused as a group. However, there appears to be little evidence to support this important hypothesis (Blaszczynski et al. 1986; Leary and Dickerson 1986). Similarly, heavy gamblers would be expected to report rejection in childhood. Although this view has been expressed as a hypothesis elsewhere (Burns 1987), there appears to be no evidence with which to test the hypothesis. Data obtained retrospectively from pathological gamblers must be treated with caution for reasons indicated earlier.

In summary, Jacobs has presented a general theory of psychological addiction which has the advantage that it generates hypotheses which can be tested. Until the relevant evidence is collected, conclusions about the validity of the theory cannot be reached. However, with the limited evidence available, the assumption that addicted gamblers are hypo-aroused appears unfounded.

7

Treatment Strategies for Problem Gambling

Problem gambling, whether it is called compulsive, pathological or excessive, is one of the social problems in Western societies which is most disruptive to individual well-being and family harmony. Furthermore, whether or not the number of problem gamblers is 1.0%, 0.1%, or 0.01% of the adult population, as various writers have argued, there is a continuing need to find effective techniques for treating the numbers of people who suffer from this problem.

The most widespread resource for problem gamblers is the Gamblers Anonymous organisation. Until the 1980s there were very few alternatives to Gamblers Anonymous for gamblers seeking help. However, the period since 1980 has seen the development of a number of hospital-based programmes involving various therapeutic techniques. Although the hospital-based approaches have relied heavily on group therapy, a number of programmes have also incorporated behaviour modification techniques. Treatments within a psychodynamic perspective have become less frequently reported possibly because of the length of treatment required. Similarly, the favoured treatment of the 1960s, aversion therapy, appears to be less popular now. By contrast, the more unusual methods being used with problem gamblers which have recently been reported may point to new directions in the future for this area of therapy.

Gamblers Anonymous

Gamblers Anonymous is a voluntary organisation limited to compulsive gamblers and modelled on the ideas and methods of Alcoholics Anonymous. The organisation held its first meeting in 1957 in the United States and since that time has spread throughout the world. In 1964, the first meeting in the United Kingdom was held in London. This meeting came about largely through the efforts of the Reverend Gordon Moody. In many places Gamblers Anonymous is the only agency to which gamblers in trouble can turn. There are perhaps about 400 groups (called *chapters*) in the United States and over 1,000 such groups worldwide.

Gamblers Anonymous accepts the disease model of compulsive gambling described in Chapter 6. In particular, they regard the disease as essentially incurable. According to Gamblers Anonymous, no member can afford to relax their guard against the urges to gamble. Relapse into compulsive gambling remains just one bet away for the rest of the individual's life. Thus, the therapy recommended by Gamblers Anonymous is an ongoing process.

The Therapy

Gamblers Anonymous uses the strategies of mutual support, encouragement and holding the gambler to an honest, realistic accounting of his attitudes and behavior.

(Custer and Milt 1985, p.272)

According to Gamblers Anonymous, in order for the therapy to be successful, the compulsive gambler must really want to stop gambling. He or she must come to Gamblers Anonymous voluntarily and sincerely want to help themselves. Cromer (1978) has described the early stages of the passage through Gamblers Anonymous as *degradation*. Degradation is complete when the compulsive gambler confesses the full extent of his or her gambling and the manipulations, deceits and crimes that have been involved. The first step involves the gambler filling out a questionnaire containing twenty questions (Table 6.9) about the impact gambling is having on his or her life. If the gambler answers *yes* to seven or more questions, then the gambling is considered a matter of concern and the gambler is admitted to the group. The *yes* answers to the twenty questions give a basis for the main step towards accepting the true state of affairs concerning the gambling. This step involves standing up at the first meeting and beginning with the words, "I am a compulsive gambler." The gambler is then encouraged to "come clean" about all that has been involved.

The strength of Gamblers Anonymous is the conviction of the whole group that compulsive gambling can be beaten. Once the gambler has publicly acknowledged the problem, the group provides support for the public commitment to abstain from gambling. This support does not end at the end of the meeting but continues through time. This point is made by "Taxi" Tom, a member of Gamblers Anonymous in Britain for more than twenty-one years:

After the meeting, I spoke to Gordon Moody and many others. It was heart-warming. The whole room was electric with resolve to arrest our addiction. I received a booklet, our "bible" it was called, it had twenty questions on the last page. Answer "yes" to seven and you were a "Compulsive Gambler". I actually answered the whole twenty—even the last one: "Have you ever contemplated suicide?" I also received a Telephone List, to ring any members should I get the "Urge" to gamble.

(Taxi Tom 1986, p.3)

TABLE 7.1
The twelve steps of Gamblers Anonymous

1.	We admitted we were powerless over gambling—that our lives had become unmanageable.
2.	Came to believe that a Power greater than ourselves could restore us to a normal way of thinking and living.
3.	Made a decision to turn our will and our lives over to the care of this Power of our own understanding.
4.	Made a searching and fearless moral and financial inventory of ourselves.
5.	Admitted to ourselves and another human being the exact nature of our wrongs.
6.	Were entirely ready to have these defects of character removed.
7.	Humbly asked God (of our understanding) to remove our shortcomings.
8.	Made a list of all persons we had harmed, and became willing to make amends to them all.
9.	Made direct amends to such people wherever possible, except when to do so would injure them or others.
10.	Continued to take personal inventory and when we were wrong promptly admitted it.
11.	Sought through prayer and meditation to improve our conscious contact with God as we understood him, praying only for knowledge of His will for us and the power to carry that out.
12.	Having made an effort to practice these principles in all our affairs, we tried to carry this message to other compulsive gamblers.

Thus the new member of Gamblers Anonymous has someone to contact when the urge to gamble comes. This may make the difference between an immediate relapse and abstention until the next meeting. Long-term members of Gamblers Anonymous report that the urge to gamble again is always present and, even twenty years on, the need to take each day one at a time remains (Harry P. 1983).

The personal testimonies of the members of Gamblers Anonymous are called *therapies*. A member tells and retells his therapy on numerous occasions. In this way members strengthen their resolve not to give in to the urge to gamble. Any attempt to diminish responsibility or minimise the harm caused by gambling or to understate the extent of gambling is likely to attract a chorus of disbelief from the other members.

Beyond therapy, meetings focus on the twelve steps to recovery which are based on those used by Alcoholics Anonymous. The twelve steps of Gamblers Anonymous are shown in Table 7.1.

Steps 8 and 9 are of particular importance. Most compulsive gamblers are heavily in debt when they join Gamblers Anonymous. A repayment plan is demanded by steps 8 and 9 and this is made one of the immediate goals. Furthermore, members who have repaid their own debts refuse to help pay any of the outstanding debts of new members. The importance of refusal to bail out the compulsive gambler is now widely recognised across different treatment programmes.

One of the problems faced by the recovering gambler is the void in life created by not gambling. During the desperation phase of gambling, virtually every waking minute will have been focused on the anticipation of gambling and the requirement for gambling money. Now that gambling is being avoided, the recovering gambler will have a lot of spare time. Gamblers Anonymous provides part of the answer by focusing attention on the demands of the next meeting and the rewards to be obtained in the form of praise if gambling is avoided. The other answer is found in directing energies toward work and leisure activities and individual therapies are often concerned with developments in these two areas. Work and leisure involvement help the recovering gambler in two ways: less time and energy for gambling or thoughts associated with gambling and alternative sources of stimulation and excitement.

After one year of abstention from gambling, the member becomes eligible for the one-year pin which is considered an important milestone on the way to recovery. Achieving this goal perhaps more than anything else is the sign of success for Gamblers Anonymous in the contest with each member's urge to gamble.

Treatment Effectiveness

Gamblers Anonymous is concerned with preventing members from returning to gambling. From their perspective, the best chance for life lies in regular attendance at meetings. From this point of view, the success rate for Gamblers Anonymous approaches 100% for those members who continue to attend meetings for the rest of their lives. Those who discontinue attending meetings and return to gambling have not completed their treatment. This approach to measuring the effectiveness of the treatment is clearly unsatisfactory since no living member of Gamblers Anonymous has completed therapy. A more realistic appraisal of effectiveness will include both members and drop-outs over a set period of time.

Unfortunately, there are a number of barriers preventing a full evaluation of the effectiveness of Gamblers Anonymous and the number of attempts to evaluate the treatment provided is remarkably small. Among the barriers to proper evaluation are:

1. Anonymity. No case records are kept, no attempt is made at objective evaluation, and the only evidence is the subjectively based self-report of the member. These self-reports are themselves not available to an outsider on the regular basis necessary for evaluation.
2. Sample bias. Gamblers Anonymous accepts only those who come voluntarily and who meet the twenty questions criterion. Membership is continually changing and some members attend multiple meetings. These factors rule out the possibility of comparison with a control group.

TABLE 7.2
Number and % attending Gamblers Anonymous for varying lengths of time

Category of attendance	Number	%
Only one meeting	52	22
2–9 meetings	109	47
10–< one year pin	29	13
One—two year pin	4	2
Still attending	38	16
Total	232	100

From Brown 1985, p.265.

3. The criterion for success in Gamblers Anonymous is complete abstention. Among those who drop out and among those who "fall" there is no measure of the success that Gamblers Anonymous has achieved. It is quite possible that many of those who attended Gamblers Anonymous for a small number of meetings gained the strength to resist the urge to gamble compulsively without needing to attend further meetings.

The only major attempt to evaluate the effectiveness of Gamblers Anonymous appears to be the study of drop-outs and continuers in Britain by Brown (1985, 1986, 1987). Brown made use of the fact that Gamblers Anonymous, unlike Alcoholics Anonymous, keeps minutes of each meeting showing who attended. In a retrospective study of three Gamblers Anonymous groups, Brown analysed the minutes of all meetings held within a five-year period. In all there were 232 new members in that period. Table 7.2 shows the lengths of time over which new members attended.

The majority of new attenders (69%) dropped out after attending less than ten meetings. We do not know how many of these returned to gambling or how many began gambling again at a problem level. Brown counts these drop-outs as treatment failures for evaluation purposes, although he acknowledges the unknown status of this group.

Table 7.3 shows the drop-outs over the first ten meetings and demonstrates that the most likely result for a new member is that he or she will not attend again after the first or second meeting. The more meetings attended, the smaller the number of drop-outs. However, this should not be interpreted as meaning that those who stay longer are more likely to continue. Column 3 in Table 7.3 shows that the likelihood of dropping out following the current meeting and this probability is remarkably consistent and independent of how many meetings (up to seven) have been attended previously. A new member has a one in three chance of dropping out before the next meeting, at least over the first seven

TABLE 7.3
Drop-outs over the first ten Gamblers Anonymous meetings

Meeting number	No. drop out	% of attenders
1	52	31
2	36	33
3	23	31
4	13	26
5	12	32
6	9	25
7	4	25
8	8	—
9	1	—
10	3	—
Total	161	

Based on Brown 1985, p.267.

meetings. From the point of view of Gamblers Anonymous, this figure must be disappointing.

When claims are made for the effectiveness of a therapy or treatment, some kind of follow-up and statistic for long-term improvement is mandatory. While there is no established period of time for long-term follow-up, a minimum of two years would seem desirable for the treatment of compulsive gamblers. For periods of up to one year and longer, the gambler may not gamble because of debts and loss of funds for gambling. Although the gambling debts may persist beyond two years, those debts will be less pressing. Furthermore, control of money in the family is likely to have been placed with the spouse initially. During the first year of abstention, gambling may not have occurred because of lack of opportunity. After two years, the gambler may have regained some control over money and therefore may be in a position to start gambling again.

For reasons such as these, Brown set the criterion for maintained improvement as two years of abstinence. With this rather strict criterion, we can ask how effective was the programme. What percentage of new members attain their two-year pin? Brown's figures for those members who potentially could have abstained for two years show that only seventeen (15%) of 114 new members were actually awarded their two-year pin.

A 15% success rate is not high. Part of the reason for this low figure is the strict criterion of absence from gambling for two years. Perhaps some of those who leave before reaching the two-year pin do not return to gambling. Perhaps also, some return to gambling but not at the level which had caused them to seek help in the first place. However, this latter possibility is rejected by Gamblers Anonymous which regards compulsive gambling as an ever present threat for the kind of person whom they accept in the first place.

One last point needs to be made concerning Gamblers Anonymous. The organisation is voluntary and makes no financial demands on members or the community. It is therefore a low cost treatment for a major social problem. Although Brown's data suggests that the long-term success rate of Gamblers Anonymous is low, those who are helped receive that help at no cost to the general community. It is therefore a cost-effective treatment for large numbers of compulsive gamblers. While alternative programmes may hope to achieve a greater success rate it is unlikely that any will be equally cost-effective.

Group Psychotherapy

Group psychotherapy refers to a heterogeneous collection of approaches that have in common the use of group processes to bring about change in behaviour and possibly change in the personality of the group members. Individual psychotherapy is likely to take much the same direction but with the role of the group replaced by the psychotherapist. Group psychotherapy is often joined with other aspects of therapy so that the gambler may also be seen alone in individual therapy, be seen together with the spouse in conjoint marital therapy, receive peer counselling and take part in Gamblers Anonymous meetings. However, programmes using group psychotherapy usually regard this component as the primary means of change. The use of group psychotherapy for the treatment of compulsive gambling was initiated by Bob Custer in 1971 at the Veterans Administration Hospital in Brecksville, Ohio. Since then similar programmes have spread to a number of Veterans Administration hospitals throughout the United States. These programmes are frequently identified by their location such as the Brecksville programme. Other programmes have been started in major public and private hospitals and are typically referred to by the name of the hospital such as the Taylor Manor programme conducted at the Taylor Manor hospital in Ellicott City, Maryland (Franklin and Richardson 1988).

Background Theory

Certainly, we were going to continue to deal with the gambling, per se, trying to motivate the patient to give up the gambling, to get his gambling under control. But right along with that we had to deal with the personality and behavior problems—the dishonesty, impatience, intolerance and manipulation, inability to plan and make decisions, avoidance of responsibility, insensitivity to the feelings and needs of others, poor problem-solving ability.

(Custer and Milt 1985, p.301)

Custer and Milt regard compulsive gambling as a psychological illness with psychological causes. The essence of compulsive gambling is the inability of the gambler to resist the urge to gamble: the gambling is out of control. Thus compulsive gambling is like compulsive eating, compulsive alcohol consumption and compulsive drug-taking. They believe that compulsive gambling is a psychological addiction.

According to Custer and Milt, compulsive gambling is caused at least in part by maladaptive personality traits. These traits are seen as preceding the onset of gambling. Unless some change to these traits is brought about by therapy, the success of the programme in preventing is likely to be minimal. Thus, the Brecksville programme is oriented to changing personality attributes such as, impatience, poor problem-solving ability, poor planning, poor decision-making and irresponsibility. Characteristics such as these make it difficult for a person to cope with the everyday stresses of living. Gambling becomes an escape. Thus treatment must aim not only at supporting the patient's resolve not to gamble again but at equipping him or her with coping strategies that are currently missing.

Franklin and Richardson carry the logic of broad-based intervention a step further. Given that the gambler is in difficulties financially, at home, in his or her employment, in interpersonal relations and is psychologically unstable, it follows that therapy must be tailored to help the gambler deal with the problems in each of these areas. Thus, the evaluation of therapy must include measures of change which go beyond simple abstinence. One of the strengths of the Taylor Manor programme is that they have developed a broad-based assessment instrument, the modified Addiction Severity Index (Franklin and Richardson 1988).

The Therapy

Therapy must provide opportunities to practise and to learn the rewards of responsibility: acceptance, patience, self-discipline and sensitivity. These are the qualities which the process of group therapy is designed to bring out and foster—as it were, a training ground for tolerance.

(Spanier 1987, p.112)

Group therapy involves a small number of patients meeting with a psychotherapist in repeated sessions over a period of time. Traditionally, the psychotherapist is expected to be non-directive. Certainly, group therapy is not intended to discover deep psychological processes underlying neurosis but rather to allow group processes to bring pressure to bear on individuals and thus bring about behaviour and character changes. Typically, a group member will tell his or her story and the others will comment on aspects of the story as they see fit. This spoken autobiography is claimed to be one of the potent components of the overall therapy (Adkins, Taber and Russo 1987). Since the gamblers themselves have a range of character defects such as being manipulative, stubborn, insensitive and deceitful, conflict is bound to occur. Group therapy allows patients to confront one another about undesirable behaviour. Change comes about because the gambler is too insecure to resist group pressure and stand up to group censure. As Spanier states, group therapy becomes a training ground in which more useful and adaptive qualities can be learned.

Group therapy is often complemented by other techniques which can be used with small groups. Films may be shown depicting the downward path of the compulsive gambler and the advantages that can be gained by resisting the urge to gamble. Relaxation training allows the gamblers to learn the skills for coping with anxiety and social skills training is used to provide techniques for dealing with commonly arising situations: the "friend" who suggests having a bet, the spouse who is angry and unforgiving and the creditors and their demands.

In the Brecksville programme, Custer added to the group work individual counselling on a range of issues summarised in the acronym GAMBLING (Gambling Alienation Marital problems Behavior problems Legal problems Indebtedness Needs Goalessness). Individual counselling was aimed at working out plans for coping with these aspects of the problem. Another important focus of individual counselling was the construction of a plan to make restitution to all those who had lent money or been harmed by the gambler's actions. Finally, each patient was also encouraged to attend Gamblers Anonymous.

Treatment Effectiveness

One of the problems in assessing the effectiveness of group psychotherapy and other hospital-based approaches is that there is little agreement on what are the specific goals of therapy and what should be the criteria by which change is measured. There does appear to be agreement that abstinence from gambling should not be the sole goal of therapy or the only measure of success; the improvement in the lifestyle of the gambler should also be included (Franklin and Richardson 1988).

Russo, Taber, McCormick and Ramirez (1984) conducted an outcome study of the Brecksville in-patient treatment programme for pathological gamblers. They describe a six-bed in-patient programme. The goals are abstinence, decreased desire to gamble and restoration of social functioning. The thirty-day intensive programme consists of group psychotherapy, education on addiction and health and regular participation in GA. One hundred and twenty-four patients were followed up one year after discharge. Sixty of these completed the follow-up survey. Thirty-three out of the sixty had been completely abstinent for the year. Five reported continuation of gambling at the same or an accelerated rate. Thirty-four reported improved financial status. Forty-one reported less depression and thirty-eight said their personal relationships had improved. The main problem with this study is the status of the 50% of the sample who did not respond.

Taber et al. (1987) have subsequently reported a follow-up of pathological gamblers after treatment. The same treatment programme at Brecksville was the focus of concern. Sixty-six patients aged 24–74 who were male veterans participated in the twenty-eight-day in-patient programme. Of these sixty-six, fifty-seven were involved in a follow-up six months later in a before and after study with no control group. The amount of gambling was 15.7 days/month before treatment which was reduced to 4.74 days/month gambling six months after treatment. The group now spent less, attended GA more, was less distressed, showed more impulse control, had more employment, showed lower alcohol abuse and were less inclined to suicide and self-mutilation.

In terms of the treatment goal of abstinence from gambling, thirty-two gamblers had not gambled in the previous six months. This constitutes a 48% success rate. While this success rate appears to compare favourably with the success rate achieved by Gamblers Anonymous, there are two major reasons to be cautious in drawing such a conclusion. First of all, part of the treatment programme involves attendance at Gamblers Anonymous meetings and this attendance is expected to continue after the completion of treatment. Thus, we do not know which is the effective component of treatment: the twenty-eight-day Brecksville in-patient programme or the attendance at Gamblers Anonymous. It is possible that the psychotherapy and education parts of the Brecksville programme are ineffective and that the high abstention rate at the six-month follow-up is due entirely to the attendance at Gamblers Anonymous meetings.

One way in which we can gain an idea of the relative effectiveness of the in-patient programme and the attendance at Gamblers Anonymous meetings is by examining the abstinence rates of those who continued to attend Gamblers Anonymous and those who dropped out. This kind of *post facto* analysis is dangerous because we have no way of knowing whether those who subsequently attended Gamblers Anonymous meetings differ in any important way from those who do not (for example, severity of gambling problem). Nevertheless, this comparison is all we have to work on in trying to disentangle the confounded factors. Taber et al. report that at the six-month follow-up, the abstinent group had attended significantly more Gamblers Anonymous meetings (mean = 5.9) than had the non-abstinent group (mean = 1.6). They conclude,

Clearly, participation in Gamblers Anonymous, which was the primary aftercare resource for these patients, was an important factor in their continued abstinence.

(Taber et al. 1987, p.760)

TABLE 7.4
Items from the modified Addiction Severity Index

Finances	Scale score	Judgement criteria
	0—1	Not applicable, secure
	2—3	Solvent (some savings, good credit)
	4—5	Marginal (no savings, some credit)
	6—7	Bankrupt
	8—9	Destitute (no means of support)
Abstinence	Scale score	Judgement criteria
	0—1	Not gambling
	2—3	Infrequent gambling
	4—5	Occasional gambling
	6—7	Binge gambling
	8—9	Actively gambling

From Franklin and Richardson 1988, pp.402–403.

Thus, the data suggests that attendance at Gamblers Anonymous meetings is an important factor in maintaining abstinence and, thus, it is difficult for us to assess the contribution of the in-patient programme.

The second reason for caution is that a six-month follow-up may be too early to determine whether the pathological gambler has quit gambling for good. The analysis of the effectiveness of Gamblers Anonymous was based on the two-year pin for abstinence for gambling. The two-year criterion is a good choice, since the period of time involved allows the gambler to have regained financial control. At six months many gamblers may not be gambling not because they have given up gambling but because they have not yet gained sufficient financial stability or control over their own finances to make the return to gambling worthwhile. What will be the success rate of the Brecksville programme at the two-year follow-up? According to Taber et al., the longer term follow-ups are proceeding. However, at this time they have not yet become available.

A one-year follow-up for gamblers passing through the Taylor Manor programme has been published (Franklin and Richardson 1988). Franklin and Richardson modified the Addiction Severity Index developed for the assessment of recovery from substance abuse. The index has nine component subscales measuring stability and disruption in a variety of spheres of life. The gambler receives a rating between 0 and 9 on each subscale where 0 reflects no problem and 9 the highest level of disruption. The nine subscales measure: (1) personal depression and distress; (2) family relationship and interpersonal concerns; (3) vocational concerns; (4) financial concerns; (5) legal issues; (6) G.A. attendance; (7) treatment participation; (8) a measure of abstinence; and (9) a measure of substance abuse. The nine-point subscales are relatively coarse and have attached judgement criteria in many cases. Table 7.4 shows the scale divisions and criteria for scale 4 (financial) and scale 8 (abstinence).

The modified ASI was used to assess eighty pathological gamblers at admission and again twelve months after discharge. Only three of the original eighty could not be included in the follow-up. Significant improvement was found on five of the nine scales. Table 7.5 shows the change towards controlled gambling and abstinence. After one year 46% of the gamblers had abstained from gambling. Since the Taylor Manor programme also encourages attendance at Gamblers Anonymous after completion of the treatment, the same question arises here as was addressed for the Brecksville programme: can the effectiveness of the treatment be attributed to attendance at Gamblers Anonymous or is it a result of the psychotherapy? Table 7.5 shows that attendance at Gamblers Anonymous meetings did not increase significantly following completion of the Taylor Manor programme. This suggests that the treatment has been effective for nearly 50% of the gamblers: the best published results reported for psychotherapy. Nevertheless, caution is again recommended in the interpretation of these results.

There are three reasons for caution. First of all, as Franklin and Richardson acknowledge, the evaluation of the programme involves only before and after measures and not a controlled trial with some gamblers, chosen randomly, receiving the treatment programme when others do not. The impact of this failure is that we know neither the spontaneous recovery rate nor the recovery rate for a placebo treatment programme (which would include attendance at Gamblers Anonymous meetings). It is possible, though unlikely, that with gamblers such as those treated at the Taylor Manor hospital, spontaneous recovery may be an important factor. The second reason for caution concerns a related issue: type of gambler treated. It appears that at least 22 gamblers scored between 0 and 3 on the finance subscale on admission to the programme. These gamblers were thus solvent and sometimes secure financially. This level of financial security is inconsistent with the image of the pathological gambler as someone concerned with getting money from wherever

TABLE 7.5
Evaluation of the Taylor Manor treatment programme (Franklin and Richardson 1988; sample size n = 77)

Scale score	Level of gambling at admission	Level of gambling one year follow-up	Attend GA at admission	Attend GA one year follow-up
8–9	67	15	51	48
6–7	9	8	12	9
4–5	0	15	11	11
2–3	0	2	2	4
0–1	1	37	1	5
	significant $p < 0.01$		not significant	

Based on Franklin and Richardson 1988, tables 1 and 2.

possible in order to have another gamble. Gamblers entering treatment generally have massive debts. For example, the mean debt of 81 patients entering the out-patients programme at St Vincent's North Richmond Community Center on Staten Island, New York, was $54,661 (Blackman, Simone and Thoms 1986). Thus a sizeable proportion of the gamblers accepted for treatment at Taylor Manor may not have had severe gambling problems at the level generally reported by Gamblers Anonymous members. The final reservation about the Taylor Manor programme is the period of abstinence. A one-year follow-up should not be regarded as conclusive where pathological gambling is concerned. The committed gambler may have to wait considerably longer before he or she is again in a position to resume gambling.

Conjoint Marital Therapy

Conjoint marital therapy is a form of group psychotherapy sometimes used instead of conventional group psychotherapy (Boyd and Bolen 1970) and sometimes as a supplement (Tepperman 1985). Couples are seen together rather than the individual gambler attending without his or her spouse. Couples may be seen alone or in a group with several other couples. Since the close interpersonal relationships of the pathological gambler are nearly always in crisis, it would seem appropriate to include the spouse where possible. However, the reasons for involving the spouse in therapy go deeper than the observation that the quality of the husband-wife relationship is often extremely poor.

Background Theory

According to Boyd and Bolen, the pathological gambling of the husband may be a defence against the stresses threatening the marriage. The husband and wife may have worked out mutually dependent roles in a complex game which stabilises the marriage. At the core of this game is the role of "martyr" for the wife and the "sick, compulsive gambler" for the husband.

Symptoms of pathological gambling must be understood in the larger context of an even more complicated marital symptom and interaction complex. Analogous to the individual intrapsychic dynamics, gambling in the marital relationship also serves the defensive function of stabilizing a pathological marriage at a level of minimal disequilibrium that is mutually tolerable by the marital partners.

(Boyd and Bolen 1970, p.89)

It is clear that if both husband and wife are taking part in a game which holds their marriage together, then therapy for the gambler without his partner is likely to be ineffective. If change is to come about, then therapy must allow both partners to become less defensive and to face the problems in the relationship together and at the same time.

The Therapy

The group psychotherapy offered by Boyd and Bolen (1970) and by Tepperman (1985) differ considerably in structure and content. Boyd and Bolen's approach was exploratory and relatively unstructured, whereas Tepperman structured his programme around the twelve steps of Gamblers Anonymous. Boyd and Bolen's sessions took place once per week for a year, whereas Tepperman held twelve sessions, each session investigating the meaning of a different step. Tepperman ran two groups with ten couples in each group, whereas Boyd and Bolen ran two groups with four or five couples in each group. However, despite these differences, the general aim was similar: to allow couples to begin working through their problems in a situation where each partner could be less defensive.

The progress of Boyd and Bolen's groups can be broken down into phases. The early phase consisted of discussions about gambling, with the therapists being non-directive. Husbands swapped gambling stories while the wives commiserated with each other about their plight. In the second phase, the therapists began striving to have the partners talk to each other rather than make assumptions about what the other person's thoughts or reactions might be. The aim was to replace the accusations, complaints and arguments by more constructive dialogue in which each partner is inquiring about and trying to understand the other. In the third phase the therapists became more involved by making explicit the games that the husband-wife pairs were playing. As these more authentic communications became more common, the gambler would become more resistant to the attractions of gambling but, interestingly, the wife began to show psychopathology.

As therapy progressed, there was noticeable improvement in the husband as manifested by increased assertiveness, decreased gambling, and decreased depression. With improvement in their husbands and the initial investigation of their own personal difficulties, the wives universally experienced depressive reactions. At this point the wives became increasingly aware that their husbands' gambling was a mutual problem symptomatic of marital discord.

(Boyd and Bolen, p.80)

By the end of the year, change and improvement in the couples' relationship was marked by more cohesiveness, frankness, mutuality and authenticity.

Treatment Effectiveness

Boyd and Bolen's groups continued for one year. During this time one couple left therapy. Of the remaining eight gamblers, three were fully abstinent at the end of the year and had been for several months prior to that time. The other five gamblers were near cessation.

In the Tepperman study, twenty Gamblers Anonymous/Gam Anon couples were accepted into two experimental groups, and twenty similar couples were accepted into the control groups. Each experimental group ran for twelve sessions, focusing on the individual meaning associated with each of the twelve steps. The members of the experimental groups were led by a Father John who used Rogerian techniques. The control group treatment is not specified but may be assumed to be attendance at Gamblers Anonymous. Ten experimental and ten control couples dropped out of the programme. Dropping out involved not only quitting the marital therapy but also failure to attend Gamblers Anonymous and a return to gambling. The drop-outs were mainly newer Gamblers Anonymous members.

Since the same number of subjects dropped out of both the experimental and control groups, it can be assumed that the experimental treatment was not a clear advantage over Gamblers Anonymous alone in preventing a return to gambling. Both the Tepperman and Boyd and Bolen studies highlight a clear need for standardised measures of improvement. Being near cessation is difficult to interpret in the Boyd and Bolen study and in the Tepperman study no statistics are given concerning persistence in attending Gamblers Anonymous and no details are given concerning the time and rate of improvement.

Psychoanalysis

Gambling is but *one* of the long series of unconsciously self-provoked, self-created, and self-perpetuated, self-damaging tragedies in their lives.

(Bergler 1957, p.128)

Although several writers have offered insights into the nature of gambling from a psychoanalytic perspective (see Chapter 4), where psychoanalytic therapy is concerned, only one person appears to have provided an assessment of the effectiveness of the therapy. Bergler (1957) has provided a detailed account of several cases treated analytically and has indicated the factors that are associated with success and failure in treating compulsive gamblers.

Background Theory

According to Bergler, compulsive gambling must be understood as a neurosis. No matter what the gambler might say about his or her reasons for gambling, those explanations will always cover the true reasons for gambling. The important aspect of gambling for the compulsive gambler is the losing and the consequences that follow from losing. It does not matter whether the gambler believes that he or she has a winning system or whether they can prove that their system works; it does not matter whether the gambler claims that he or she gambles for excitement; and it does not matter whether the reason given for gambling is some kind of escapism. The truth is that every compulsive gambler gambles for masochistic reasons. All of the overt reasons given by the gambler can be shown to be false: if gambling to win, then why continue when losing; and if for the excitement or escapism, then why at such a cost.

If it is true that the gambling is motivated by masochistic needs, then the explanation for the gambling will be found in the history of the gambler and especially in the childhood relations with parents. And if it is true that the gambling fulfils an unconscious wish for punishment, then it is likely that the gambler will show other forms of maladaptive behaviour which achieve the same goal. Thus we should not be surprised if the gambler has a problem with alcohol or other drugs.

The gambler's problems go back primarily to the early relationship with the mother. This relationship is misperceived. When the mother refuses to offer the breast, she is perceived as being malicious. Essentially, the gambler grows up believing that the world is unjust. Time and again in therapy Bergler exposes his patients as collectors of injustices. Psychologically, these injustices are proof that the gambler's mother was a bad mother. Gambling is an effective means of collecting injustice. Failed gambling is bad luck but brings a great deal of antagonism from the gambler's family, especially the gambler's spouse.

The Therapy

The two main techniques in psychoanalytic therapy are the use of *transference* and *resistance* as means to attack and break down the neurotic structures on which the patient relies. *Transference* is the name given to the situation in which the patient comes to treat the analyst as an important figure and uses the same neurotic displays and emotional pressures against him or her as are typical of the relationship with spouse or parent. The patient gains emotional insight into the neurotic behaviour through the confrontations with the analyst. *Resistance* refers to the negative feelings brought about in the patient during interactions with the analyst. The analyst tries to upset the neurotic ritualised patterns of the patient. Since these rituals are the basis of the patient's stability, the analyst's words are dangerous and his arguments and assertions are therefore resisted.

Thus, psychoanalytic therapy aims to uncover the real reasons for the gambling behaviour and to show that the gambler's conscious thoughts about gambling are a cover for more important beliefs and goals. Since these beliefs and goals are unconscious, the gambler will not in general agree with the interpretations of the analyst. However, by showing how the patient uses the same limited range of stratagems repeatedly despite their failure and by linking these stratagems back to their use in childhood, the analyst hopes to give the patient insight into his or her own unconscious motivations. Once this insight has been obtained, the consciously organised rationalisations of the neurotic behaviour become unnecessary. The gambling loses its meaning and its thrill and the former gambler begins the task of learning new and more adaptive ways of interacting with the world.

Treatment Effectiveness

There are certainly no grounds for recommending that a gambler who wants to cease betting should enter psychoanalysis.

(Dickerson 1984, p.101)

The assessment of Bergler's effectiveness in treating compulsive gambling by psychoanalysis is made difficult by the fact that Bergler regards statistics of this kind as unreliable and because Bergler himself does not provide exact numbers. Thus, the percentages stated in this section must be regarded as only roughly describing the effectiveness of psychoanalysis.

First of all, we must determine how many gamblers came to Bergler with their problems. Bergler states that he treated, by psychoanalysis, sixty patients over thirty years of practice as a psychiatrist. Analysis typically took one to one and a half years to complete. However, some gamblers were seen for less time than this and either did not start or did not complete analysis. Bergler gave each patient a trial period of four to six weeks. At the end of that time the patient was either accepted into analysis or treatment was terminated. According to Bergler, approximately 25% of the compulsive gamblers seen were terminated before being admitted into full analysis. Thus, approximately fifteen of the sixty gamblers were not cured or improved. Of the remaining forty-five gamblers, about a quarter are considered to be spurious successes because, although their gambling stopped, analysis had not dealt with the underlying neuroses. Such patients were likely to maintain their masochistic way of life by replacing gambling with some other means whereby they could be further punished. If we place the number of spurious successes at eleven, there remains approximately thirty-four gamblers who were fully cured by analysis. This figure is consistent with Bergler's assertion that,

TABLE 7.6
The effectiveness of psychoanalysis in the treatment of compulsive gambling

	Number		% of total
Gamblers seeking treatment	160	*	100
Gamblers who enter therapy	60		38
Gamblers discontinuing after 4 weeks	15	*	10
Gamblers continuing after trial period	45	*	28
Gamblers whose gambling only is cured	11	*	7
Gamblers completely cured	34	*	21

Note: * indicates that these figures are estimates based on Bergler's statements (Bergler 1957, pp.128–134) and may be slightly inaccurate.
Estimates based on the reports of Bergler (1957).

Hence, with good conscience, the claim of the therapeutic accessibility of gamblers to psychoanalytic procedure is put forward on the basis of thirty-odd cured patients.
(Bergler 1957, p.134)

Bergler also reports seeing approximately one hundred patients once or twice in consultation. None of these entered analysis. In most cases they did not return either because they did not want the treatment, because they lived in another state and were referred to Bergler's colleagues, or because they could not afford the treatment. In evaluating Bergler's psychoanalytic methods, it is important what status is given to these non-starters in therapy. In a worst case scenario all of these non-starters would be counted as failures. However, they are clearly in a different category from those who terminated treatment at the end of the four to six week test period. In this worst case, approximately forty-five patients out of approximately one hundred and sixty ceased gambling, thus yielding a 28% success rate. This is, undoubtedly, a conservative estimate of the number of gamblers treated analytically who stopped gambling as a result. Bergler calculates his success rate a little differently. Since sixty entered analysis and approximately thirty-four were completely cured of their neurosis, the success rate is approximately 57%. These estimates are shown in Table 7.6.

Since Bergler does not give precise figures, it is easy to see that errors of interpretation might occur when assessments are made of his work. It appears that such errors have been made by Brown (1985) and by Blaszczynski (1988) who estimate that approximately 200 gamblers sought help and of these 80 entered therapy. These figures appear to misunderstand the intent of Bergler's assertion that 25% of patients were terminated after the four to six week trial period. In order for Bergler's statements to be consistent, these 25% must refer to a proportion of the sixty gamblers entering analysis and not to another group not included in the sixty. Dickerson provides estimates similar to those in Table 7.6 although he assumes that three gamblers receiving full analysis were not cured. There appears to be no basis on which to make this assumption.

In evaluating the effectiveness of psychoanalysis for the treatment of compulsive gambling, two problems occur in relation to Bergler's work. First of all, Bergler chose which gamblers were suitable for analysis. Thus, up to 25% of patients were not accepted past the four to six week trial period. By comparison, Gamblers Anonymous and the various hospital programmes accept all compulsive gamblers who wish to stop gambling. Nevertheless, over 50% of all gamblers entering psychoanalysis with Bergler were cured of their neurosis. Secondly, Bergler provides no follow-up data. From the theory it is clear that a patient who is *cured* has no psychological need to gamble. However, we do not know if such gamblers abstained from gambling after the completion of therapy and we have no data concerning possible relapses. The five case studies provided by Bergler all suggest that gambling ceased for good, that the treated gamblers did abstain and that this abstinence from gambling was maintained over a period of years. It seems likely then that the "thirty-odd" gamblers whom Bergler reports as cured were indeed free of gambling for the rest of their lives but, unfortunately, we have no hard evidence on which to base this speculation. Nevertheless, the strength of the evidence presented by Bergler is sufficiently compelling for us to disagree with Dickerson's conclusion presented at the beginning of this section.

Behaviour Modification

Whereas the psychoanalytic perspective views problem gambling as a manifestation of a neurotic personality, behaviour theories regard gambling as simply behaviour which has been acquired by typical learning processes. It follows that gambling behaviour can be extinguished by appropriate manipulation of the environment. From a psychoanalytic perspective, even if behaviour modification procedures do stop the gambling in the short term, since the underlying neurosis remains, the gambling will either return or be replaced by some other maladaptive behaviour. From a pragmatic point of view, it would perhaps be better if psychoanalytic theory was wrong about the origins and treatment of gambling problems. Whereas psychoanalysis takes a year or more of weekly consultations with a psychiatrist (Bergler 1957), behavioural therapies typically require much shorter treatment times such as one week as an in-patient or six weeks as an out-patient. Thus, if behaviour therapies can be shown to be effective in reducing or stopping gambling, they are likely therefore also to be cost effective.

A range of behavioural techniques have been applied to the treatment of gambling problems. In order to extinguish the gambling, both imagined and real reinforcements have been used. Since imaginal procedures are conducted in the hospital or clinical rooms by a therapist talking to the gambler, they are not greatly different from psychotherapy in form. However, whereas psychotherapy focuses on the broader consequences of the gambling, behaviour therapies focus on the details of the gambling behaviour itself. Within behavioural approaches there are two main categories of methods: those based on classical conditioning and those based on instrumental conditioning. Classical conditioning aims to modify the conditioned response of excitement by pairing the stimulus cues for gambling with a competing response such as boredom. Instrumental conditioning aims to modify the reinforcement schedule by punishing the gambling response directly.

Since the major research on behavioural methods (Blaszczynski 1988) compares different techniques, it will be useful to briefly describe what is involved in the different methods. The techniques based on the classical conditioning paradigm include in vivo desensitisation, imaginal desensitisation, systematic desensitisation, relaxation therapy, covert sensitisation and satiation therapy. The techniques based on the instrumental conditioning paradigm include aversion therapy and behavioural counselling.

In vivo desensitisation	involves pairing cues for gambling with no gambling behaviour and feelings of boredom. Typically, the gambler is taken to the gambling location and stands by without gambling for extended periods of time. The therapist suggests that the whole situation is uninteresting.
Imaginal desensitisation	differs from in vivo desensitisation by having the gambler imagine the cues for gambling and then pairing these imagined cues with a competing response such as feelings of boredom.
Systematic desensitisation	refers to a gradient of increasingly powerful cues for gambling. At each step any arousal that the gambler is experiencing is extinguished by imagined scenes of tranquillity or direct muscular relaxation.
Relaxation therapy	consists of training in relaxation techniques which can be used when the urge to gamble arises.
Satiation therapy	involves presenting the gambler with no other stimuli and no other activities but those associated with gambling.

Aversion therapy	electric shocks typically administered to the finger, hand or arm form the punishment for gambling. The punishment may be paired with a specific gambling response or may be randomly interspersed throughout the gambling session.
Behavioural counselling	involves the use of a contract not to gamble or not to gamble more than a preset amount. The gambler is rewarded if the contract is honoured and punished if it is broken. The negative consequences of gambling are made salient to the gambler through face-to-face counselling.

Aversion Therapy

Aversion therapy refers to interventions which produce a negative response when the undesired behaviour is exhibited. Typically, the gambling behaviour is paired with an electric shock. Repeated pairings diminish the pleasure associated with gambling and induce anxiety when the gambling behaviour is initiated. Although electric shock is the aversive stimulus most frequently chosen in the treatment of compulsive gambling (Barker and Miller 1988; Goorney 1988; Seager 1970; Cotler 1971; Koller 1972; and McConaghy et al. 1983), an intravenous injection of apomorphine, which induces nausea and vomiting, has also been tried with some success (Salzmann 1982).

Background Theory

According to Barker and Miller, the timing of the unpleasant stimulation is very important. The electric shock or other aversive stimulus should immediately precede or be contiguous with the gambling behaviour for maximum effectiveness. The aversive stimulus should be terminated when the gambling behaviour ceases. In this way, repeated pairings of the aversive stimulus with the gambling behaviour induces conditioned aversion to the gambling behaviour and associated stimuli. Barker and Miller caution against allowing the aversive stimulus to occur after the gambling and related gratification have taken place. Such timing transforms the aversive stimulus into a punishment. Punishment may suppress the behaviour in the short term but is likely to be ineffective in the long term.

Given that the timing of the aversive stimulus is important, when should the stimulus be applied to maximise the effectiveness of the therapy? Clearly, the cues which elicit the pleasurable sensations and excitement should be located and used to define the times at which to apply the aversive stimulus. Goorney (1968), for example, identified the following events as ones which provided the patient with pleasurable emotions: buying the morning newspaper and making the selections for the day's races; fantasies concerning horses, prices and profits; anticipating and listening to the results of races which were given over the radio in the late afternoon; and, where possible, watching the races on television. Shocks were given every fifteen seconds or so in ten-minute sessions throughout the day. Six sessions were arranged to precede and coincide with: selecting from the newspaper; three sessions throughout the morning while the patient fantasised about the races; during radio results; and during televised replay in the evening. Similarly, Cotler (1971) required his patient (a poker player) to self-administer an electric shock each time the patient won a pot and just prior to gathering in the chips.

Goorney's use of fantasy in three sessions raises another aspect of aversion therapy. Whereas most reports state that the aversive stimulus was paired with actual gambling behaviour, at least in part (Barker and Miller 1968; Goorney 1968; Seager 1970; Cotler 1971; Koller 1972; and, Salzmann 1982), more recently some studies have paired the aversive stimulus with imagined gambling (McConaghy et al. 1983; Blaszczynski 1988). Since these latter two studies report weak levels of improvement for aversion therapy, it may well be the case that aversion conditioned to real gambling cues is important.

The Therapy

Aversion therapy requires relatively few sessions before the treatment is complete. The time in therapy for reported cases varies from as little as five hours (Koller 1972) to as much as twelve hours (Barker and Miller 1966). During this time as many as 700 electric shocks are delivered (Barker and Miller 1968, Case 2). Large variations are found from study to study on whether many shocks are given in one sustained session of gambling or whether smaller numbers of shocks are given in a large number of brief gambling sessions. For example, Barker and Miller (1966) used four 3-hour sessions whereas Goorney (1968) used forty-five 10-minute sessions. Theoretically, variations of this kind are relatively unimportant. By contrast, the timing of the delivery of the aversive stimulation is fundamentally important, but interestingly, large variations in practices exist here also.

Ideally, the points at which the gambler makes gambling-related responses which are associated with pleasurable arousal must be determined and the aversive stimulus arranged to precede or coincide with these points. In practice, such precision may be a goal which cannot be attained. Nevertheless, by careful recording of the details of the gambler's behaviour and feelings in relation to gambling, many of the appropriate points may be located. Goorney appears to have come closest to achieving this goal in locating three times in the day which the gambler anticipates with excitement. Similarly, by having shocks delivered after poker wins and just before the extreme pleasure of raking in the pot, Cotler ensured that the timing for this aspect of the pleasure in playing poker was correct. Again, Seager had his patients thumb through newspapers and delivered the electric shocks on each occasion that the racing column was reached. It is probably correct to assume that this is a behaviour which is generally anticipated with pleasure by betting shop enthusiasts. However, not all reports show the same level of care in designing the schedule of aversive stimulation. Frequently, the electric shocks are simply delivered randomly throughout the gambling session. This is typically the case for aversion therapy delivered to patients whose gambling problem is slot machines (Koller 1972; Salzmann 1982; Barker and Miller 1966; Barker and Miller 1968). In fact, Barker and Miller (1966) state with confidence that 672 shocks were delivered at random to all stages of the gambling behaviour. Unfortunately, in so doing, many of the shocks will miss their mark and perhaps the whole sequence may be regarded as punishing slot machine play rather than specifically producing aversive conditioning. If this is the case, we should not expect the treatment to be effective in the longer term.

Other aspects of the therapy also vary from study to study. Many applications of aversion therapy fail to ensure that the conditioning takes place in the usual gambling environment. Since the gambling environment contains an array of cues for gambling and associated excitement, it would seem mandatory that aversion therapy be conducted in that place. However, in most studies, conditioning took place in hospital rooms (Barker and Miller 1966; Barker and Miller 1968; Seager 1970; Koller 1972; McConaghy et al. 1983). Only Cotler (1971) and Salzmann (1982) were careful to conduct the therapy in the appropriate gambling environment.

In several studies, slides, overheads or films were made of the gambling behaviour and electric shocks were delivered on a random and/ or intermittent basis while the scene was replayed. For example, in Case 3, Barker and Miller (1968) made a three-minute film of the patient in one of his betting shops. Similarly, Seager (1970) showed betting shop gamblers slides of the betting shop, lists of horses and betting tickets. Even further removed from realistic gambling and the associated excitement is the technique used by McConaghy et al. (1983). These investigators had their subjects supply phrases which described aspects of their gambling behaviour which they found exciting. The phrases were written on cards which were subsequently turned over and read aloud at ten-second intervals. The problem with techniques such as these is that there is no guarantee that the gambler actually feels excited by the images used. Gambling is exciting but not necessarily looking at oneself gambling or describing the gambling scene.

Given the variation in technique from study to study, it should not be surprising to find that the success reported by different investigators ranges widely. We shall also see that the assessment of the effectiveness of aversion therapy is complicated by other factors as well.

Treatment Effectiveness

Despite the variation in technique from study to study, it is likely that the best assessment of the effectiveness of aversion therapy will come from a summation of the results. However, since no single study appears to have used the therapy under ideal arrangements, it is perhaps fair to say that aversion therapy is at least as effective as the available figures show and may be more effective if used under ideal conditions. Table 7.7 summarises the data currently available about the effectiveness of aversion therapy.

Table 7.7 reveals that the overall success rate for aversion therapy in producing abstention from gambling is about 23%. However, the reliability of this estimate can be expected to be low. There are several reasons for expecting unreliability. First of all, there is the wide variation in actual techniques used. Secondly, the results obtained by McConaghy et al. (1983) and Blaszczynski (1988) may be inappropriately low because of the major differences between their techniques and the other studies with which they are being summed. Finally, in at least one study (Seager 1970), the follow-up data is confounded by the availability of psychotherapy as an adjunct and the recommendation that the patients also attend Gamblers Anonymous meetings.

TABLE 7.7
Outcomes for aversion therapy in the treatment of gambling problems

Authors	Sample	Follow-up	Abstaining	Improved
Barker and Miller (1968)	3	2 years	1	2
Goorney (1968)	1	1 year	1	—
Seager (1970)*	16	1 to 3 years	5	3
Cotler (1971)	1	1 year	—	1
Koller (1972)*	12	½ to 2 years	5	1
McConaghy et al. (1983)*	10	1 year	0	1
Blaszczynski (1988)*	10	2 years	0	1
Total	53		12	9

Note: * indicates studies in which some gamblers could not be followed up. All such cases are treated as failures in the data given.

Aversion therapy appears to have fallen in popularity over the last twenty years. This may be partly accounted for by the relatively poor results achieved. However, a more major factor may be the belief that it is unethical to deliver noxious stimuli to patients when there is no clear evidence that the approach is effective (Dickerson 1984, p.101).

In Vivo Desensitisation

In vivo desensitisation has not been a popular therapy, at least as reported in studies of the treatment of problem gambling, although occasional references to its use can be found (Greenberg and Rankin 1982; Blaszczynski 1988).

Background Theory

In vivo desensitisation involves the gambler being placed in the gambling context so that the conditioned stimuli for gambling are present. However, the gambling behaviour is prevented so that the therapeutic intervention becomes an extinction trial from the perspective of classical conditioning. The gambler learns to make other responses, in the presence of the gambling-related stimuli, such as walking out of the betting shop or placing the coins back in the purse or pocket. Strictly speaking, a single session of an hour in a betting shop or slot machine club contains a series of trials (betting shop rituals or the sounds and sights of slot machines). Thus, therapeutic sessions function as massed extinction trials provided that the gambler does not gamble. The behaviours conditioned to the gambling-related stimuli, the actions of gambling and the feelings of excitement are less likely to occur in future in response to those stimuli after each trial than formerly was the case.

The Therapy

The therapy is remarkably simple. The therapist accompanies the gambler to the betting shop, casino or slot machine parlour and enables the patient to experience all of the usual cues but this time without gambling. This is probably not as difficult as might be expected, because the gambler-patient is likely to have few or no funds with which to make a bet or to insert into a machine. Greenberg and Rankin added covert sensitisation in order to strengthen the gambler's ability to resist the urge to gamble: on feeling the urge to have a bet, the gambler would snap an elastic band on the wrist and imagine the disastrous consequences of starting to gamble again. The procedure might be conducted over a number of sessions and an extended period of time (Greenberg and Rankin 1982) or repeated once a day for seven consecutive days (Blaszczynski 1988).

Treatment Effectiveness

The only controlled trials reported for in vivo desensitisation are those by Greenberg and Rankin working at the Maudsley Hospital in London and Blaszczynski working at the Prince of Wales Hospital in Sydney, Australia. Greenberg and Rankin treated twenty-six gamblers, although only about half of these received in vivo desensitisation (the other half received behavioural counselling concerning ways in which to avoid being tempted to gamble). In Blaszczynski's study, one group of ten gamblers received brief in vivo desensitisation (four fifteen-minute sessions each day) whereas a second group of ten gamblers received prolonged in vivo desensitisation (a one-hour session each day). The follow-up period in these two studies are quite variable (0 to $2\frac{1}{2}$ years for Greenberg and Rankin and 2 to 5 years for Blaszczynski). The results of these studies at the follow-up are shown in Table 7.8.

Clearly, in vivo desensitisation is not highly effective as carried out either by Blaszczynski or by Greenberg and Rankin. An abstention rate of 10% with a further 20% improved is reported by Blaszczynski if failure to contact at the time of the follow-up is counted as no improvement in gambling. Similarly, only 20% of the Greenberg and Rankin sample were exhibiting controlled gambling at the time of follow-up (nine months or more). Perhaps the main reason for the relatively poor showing of in vivo desensitisation is that, even if the theoretical basis for treatment is valid, full extinction of the gambling behaviour and associated excitement is unlikely to occur with such a short period of time in which extinction trials are held. An over-learned behaviour such as gambling may take months or years of trials before it is extinguished.

Imaginal Desensitisation

The use of imaginal desensitisation as a treatment approach for pathological gambling has been pioneered by McConaghy and Blaszczynski

TABLE 7.8
The effectiveness of in vivo desensitisation

	(Blaszczynski) Length of session		(Greenberg and Rankin) in vivo desensitisation and behavioural counselling
	15 mins	One hour	
Stopped	1	1	0
Controlled	3	1	5
Variable control	—	—	7
Uncontrolled	2	2	14
Not known	4	6	—
Total	10	10	26

Data from Blaszczynski 1988, p.153 and Greenberg and Rankin 1982, p.365.

(McConaghy et al. 1983; Blaszczynski 1985). Recently, Blaszczynski (1988) has completed a controlled test of imaginal desensitisation. This is an important study because it is the first controlled comparison of different therapies.

Background theory

Pathological gambling is based on the action of behavioural completion mechanisms. According to McConaghy (1980), we build up neuronal models for repeated behaviours. Repetitive behavioural sequences are run off with little associated arousal. However, if an event occurs which blocks the behavioural sequence, arousal results. Such arousal is typically a negative experience which is felt as annoyance in most cases but in more extreme cases may be felt as anger or panic. A common example is the annoyance we feel while driving a car when held up in traffic. The arousal is dissipated by the completion of the behavioural sequence that was initiated.

According to McConaghy, gambling is a repetitive behaviour which is maintained by the behavioural completion mechanism. The gambling behavioural sequence is elicited by the environmental cues associated with that gambling. The betting shop and environs is a stimulus set which triggers gambling for many horse-race punters. However, whereas the majority of punters are able to walk past the betting shop without a bet when engaged in some other activity, the pathological gambler is unable to do so. The arousal generated by the blocked behavioural completion mechanism is too intense and is sufficiently aversive to cause the gambler "to complete the behaviours even though initially they did not wish to do so" (Blaszczynski 1988, p.67). McConaghy et al. (1983) suggest that imaginal desensitisation may be effective in reducing the general level of arousal generated by the behavioural completion mechanism. With decreased arousal, the negative feeling associated with that arousal will be less intense and the gambler is therefore in a better position to resist the gambling behaviour.

The Treatment

Each gambler is asked to describe scenes associated with gambling. These scenes are then reduced to their core components and re-phrased so that they can be suggested to the gambler during therapy. Finally, the ending is changed so that although the gambler has visualised a range of stimuli associated with gambling, he or she does not in fact complete the behaviour. A typical scene is described by McConaghy et al.:

TABLE 7.9
Aversion therapy and imaginal desensitisation after one year

Degree of response to the therapy at the one-year follow-up	Number of subjects	
	Aversion ($n = 10$)	Desensitisation ($n = 10$)
Gambling urge		
Absent	0	5
Markedly reduced	1	2
Slightly reduced	2	1
Unchanged	7	2
Gambling behaviour		
Absent	0	2
Controlled	2	5
Markedly reduced	1	0
Slightly reduced	0	2
Unchanged	7	1

From McConaghy et al. 1983, p.369.

You are going home from work and know your wife is away. You decide to go to the club and put a few dollars through the poker machines. You enter the club and find a free machine. You are about to put a coin in but feel bored. You leave without gambling.

(McConaghy et al. 1983, p.368)

Clearly, these instructions will increase the gambler's level of arousal substantially if the theory is correct. Thus the imagined scene must be followed immediately by a relaxation procedure. The gambler is taught a relaxation technique based on tensing and relaxing muscles in the arms, legs and face. Following each scene, the gambler employs the relaxation technique and signals to the therapist when relaxation has been achieved. Therapy then proceeds to another scene and the process is repeated. Altogether four scenes are dealt with in a fifteen-minute session. The gambler may have three sessions a day over a short period of time such as a week. It is important to note that the gambling is imaginary and that the scenes are not placed in a hierarchical sequence of increasing arousal levels as would occur in systematic desensitisation.

Treatment Effectiveness

Controlled studies of treatment effectiveness for pathological gambling are rare. Thus, the study published by McConaghy et al. (1983), although reporting results for small samples, is particularly interesting. Ten gamblers received imaginal desensitisation and ten received aversion therapy also based on imagined gambling stimuli. The results are shown in Table 7.9.

Table 7.9 shows that this first controlled trial provided strong support for imaginal desensitisation as a more effective treatment than aversion

TABLE 7.10
Imaginal desensitisation versus alternative therapies

	Original N	Follow-up N	Abstinent	Controlled	No change
Imaginal desensitisation	60	33	10	16	7
Aversion therapy	20	6	0	2	4
Relaxation therapy	20	14	6	2	6
In vivo exposure	20	10	2	4	4

From Blaszczynski 1988, p.153.

therapy. Seven out of ten gamblers in the imaginal desensitisation group have improved compared to three out of ten in the aversion therapy group. However, note that five of the gamblers undergoing the imaginal desensitisation therapy are now reported as controlled gamblers. If abstinence is taken as the criterion, then the success rate drops to 20%.

In 1988, as a part of his doctoral dissertation, Blaszczynski reported a much larger controlled comparison between imaginal desensitisation and a variety of other behaviour therapies. Twenty gamblers were randomly allocated to imaginal desensitisation or to the alternative treatment in each of six studies:

Study 1   Imaginal desensitisation versus aversion therapy (1983 data)
Study 2   Imaginal desensitisation versus aversion therapy
Study 3   Imaginal desensitisation versus relaxation therapy
Study 4   Imaginal desensitisation versus relaxation therapy
Study 5   Imaginal desensitisation versus brief in vivo exposure
Study 6   Imaginal desensitisation versus prolonged in vivo exposure.

Relaxation therapy is the same as imaginal desensitisation except that the gambling scenes are replaced by pleasant relaxing scenes.

Unfortunately, only 63 out of the original 120 gamblers could be followed up two years later. Of the remainder, 33 could not be traced and 13 refused to participate. The results for the 63 gamblers followed up two years later are shown in Table 7.10.

It can be seen that this kind of research is hindered substantially by inability to follow up over extended periods of time. However, for those gamblers who could be followed up, imaginal desensitisation performs better than the alternative therapies. 43% of gamblers receiving imaginal desensitisation are known to have improved at follow-up compared with 30% for relaxation therapy, 30% for in vivo exposure and 10% for aversion therapy.

An interesting aspect of these results is the implications they have for McConaghy's theory of behavioural completion mechanisms. McConaghy predicted that both aversion therapy and imaginal desensitisation would be effective in reducing general arousal and thereby enabling the gambler to experience the gambling cues without succumbing to the urge to gamble. Table 7.10 shows that aversion therapy was clearly less effective than imaginal desensitisation. Such a result does not invalidate the notion of a behavioural completion mechanism, but McConaghy is left with the problem of explaining the large difference in effectiveness for the two therapies.

Satiation Therapy

Satiation therapy fits the stereotype of "reverse psychology". When the author was still at school, he obtained vacation employment filling bags with chocolates and assorted sweets behind the scenes in a large department store. It was the store's policy to allow staff employed in this way to eat as much as they wanted. The store managers had found by direct experience that satiation therapy was effective!

Background Theory

Satiation therapy has been used in a variety of situations. For example, in one case a hospital patient was hoarding towels. By giving the patient as many towels as she wanted, the hoarding behaviour was extinguished (Ayllon 1963). With respect to gambling, satiation therapy implies allowing the gambler to engage in the activity as much as is desired and preventing involvement in other alternative activities. The idea is that if the gambling behaviour is the result of some learned drive to gamble, then the drive can be extinguished through satiation (this would not occur, of course, for primary drives). It is the urge to gamble which must be extinguished not the association of specific cues with gambling. Thus, although quite different in the approach taken to treatment, satiation therapy has a similar goal to imaginal desensitisation and aversion therapy.

The Treatment

Peck and Ashcroft (1972) appear to be the only people to report the use of satiation therapy with gamblers. Their report refers to five horse-betting gamblers treated by this means. The gambler is admitted as an in-patient and conditions are arranged so that there is little else to do but think about, talk about and bet on the races. The only magazines are racing magazines. Staff will talk of nothing else and the racing commentaries are played over the radio.

Treatment Effectiveness

Unfortunately, the Peck and Ashcroft report does not provide measures, descriptions or detailed evaluations. However, according to the authors, "For four out of the five patients gambling ceased to be a major problem."

Behavioural Counselling

Dickerson (1984) refers to an unpublished paper by H. R. Montgomery and S. Kreitzer presented at the California State Psychological Association Convention at Santa Barbara, California, in 1968. In that paper, Montgomery and Kreitzer specified the foci for behavioural therapies which aim to enable the gambler to exercise self-control over his or her gambling behaviour. Therapies should aim at achieving change in the following three aspects of the gambler's behaviour:

1. The gambler choosing not to gamble when opportunity occurs.
2. Choosing to stop when losing.
3. Involvement in non-gambling activities.

(Dickerson 1984, p.112)

While behavioural counselling involving change of this kind is likely to be very common, there are very few reports on methods or effectiveness and no controlled trials with even moderate sample sizes.

Background Theory

The basis of change lies in the ability of the therapist, in conjunction with the gambler and other significant people in the gambler's life, to arrange environmental contingencies in such a way that the gambler is less likely to come in contact with gambling venues, less likely to remain gambling when in such environs and less likely to form relationships among other gamblers. It is assumed that gambling is a rewarding activity in which the gambler engages for those rewards. However, the attractions of gambling have placed the activity outside the self-control of the gambler. If the opportunity to gamble is severely limited and if other enjoyable activities are arranged to replace gambling, then the rewards from the new activities and the relationships formed with other non-gamblers may be sufficient for the gambler to regain control over his or her life.

These positive reinforcements for not gambling can be supported by negative reinforcement made salient in a behavioural contract between the gambler and a significant other (usually the gambler's spouse). Typically, the gambler agrees to a limited access to gambling in return for meeting certain obligations. Failure to meet obligations results in withdrawal of the gambling privilege. By meeting obligations, this unfavourable outcome can be avoided.

The Treatment

There is no standard treatment regime and, in fact, very few studies report the details of the behavioural contingencies arranged through counselling. Thus, in describing the treatment, it is perhaps best to briefly indicate what has been done in specific cases. Two single case studies (Dickerson and Weeks 1979; Rankin 1982) will be used to exemplify the approach. One interesting detail about these studies is that in each case the aim of treatment was control over, rather than abstinence from, gambling. Whenever limited access to gambling is made part of the contract, controlled gambling is the obvious goal for treatment. Nevertheless, there is no necessary reason why the goal should be control rather than abstinence. First of all, the behavioural contract may specify no gambling rather than limited gambling. And, secondly, even if limited gambling is made part of the contract, as time progresses and other activities replace gambling, the gambling behaviour may fall away altogether.

Dickerson and Weeks specify three components in their behavioural counselling programme: (1) control over the cash money flow; (2) alternative activities to gambling; and (3) long-term support and follow-up. Since the gambler whom they were treating was a betting shop gambler, the counselling was oriented to ways in which the attractions of the betting shop could be avoided. As part of the contract it was agreed that the gambler should not enter betting shops. Since the gambler could place 50p on one horse each Saturday, it was arranged that the bet would be laid by an intermediary. The wife was to handle all cash transactions and to facilitate this collected his pay packet from work each week. Another part of the contract dealt with alternative activities to gambling. These activities were to include the wife and were to be decided on jointly. They included going to theatres and clubs, family get-togethers, shopping expeditions and the like. The programme adopted by Rankin followed a similar pattern. Again the wife handled all money. Limited gambling was permitted up to a limit of £5 a week with no reinvestment of winnings and no carryover of funds from one week to the next.

Treatment Effectiveness

Both treatment programmes were successful. At a follow-up fifteen months from the time of referral, Dickerson and Weeks found that all of the controls were still in place. The gambler now placed his own bets but only if time permitted. Marital argument had decreased but the wife still maintained control over the family income. Even after the elapsed time, the couple still considered such a move too risky. In the case of the gambler treated by Rankin, follow-up was maintained for two years. The controls placed on this gambler were not as great as those reported by Dickerson and Weeks. Perhaps for this reason, there were more relapses by Rankin's gambler. However, the amount bet and aspects of the betting on the three occasions of relapse were quite different in character from the betting prior to treatment. The first relapse at four weeks involved reinvesting some of the winnings (but not all). The second relapse involved betting £20 on a major race. Finally, the third relapse occurred after a £25 bonus at work. £15 was invested in an accumulated bet which won £5,000. Of this £100 was bet the next day. However, the remainder of the winnings was spent on home improvements or given to his wife.

Neither case involved abstinence from gambling, but in both cases controlled gambling was restored. The possibility of controlled gambling as a treatment goal is an important issue and one which we will consider in more detail later. However, the cases presented by Dickerson and Weeks and by Rankin invite immediate comment on this issue. The central question concerns whether it is likely that these individuals will retain control over their gambling. The gambler seen by Dickerson and Weeks had been betting up to £1,000 on horses and had been listening to the races every day in extended lunch hours. After treatment, he was allowed a bet of 50p per week and no listening to the races. What are we to make of such a change? If the man had given up gambling or lost interest in gambling, why would he bet at all? On the other hand, if he was still interested in picking horses, then how could that interest be maintained with a 50p bet each week, no discussion with gambling friends and highly limited access to the results of races? Perhaps, the 50p bet had become a ritual with meaning in the relationship but not in terms of gambling. However, the effective follow-up was only about one year. If this gambler is maintaining his interest in horses despite his meagre involvement, then one must question the durability of the change that has been brought about.

The gambler treated by Rankin has much greater access to gambling. He too appears to have maintained his interest in the sport despite heavily reduced betting. However, the £5,000 win should be a source of concern for the therapist, since it is known that big wins early in a career (when the bets are small and infrequent) are often a precursor to problem gambling. This event hits at the core of the problem with controlled gambling: whatever the cause of the heavy gambling in the first case, a large win may stimulate the factors which caused the heavy gambling to occur. Viewed another way, since controlled gambling often becomes uncontrolled gambling after a big win, and, since the gambler has returned to controlled gambling, the cycle is complete. Will another large win cause the cycle to be repeated? £5,000 must be strong inducement to return to gambling for more of the action and more of the returns.

Cognitively Based Treatment Strategies

Cognitive therapies attempt to modify the thought patterns of an individual so that the undesired behaviour is no long triggered. Although a number of case studies can be found which use a variety of cognitive treatments, there appear to be no large-scale studies of the kind reported for psychotherapy or behaviour therapy. This state of affairs is particularly surprising given the arguments presented in Chapter 5 which attempt to show how gambling is maintained by irrational thinking. Thus, one of the important goals to be achieved in this chapter will be the specification of a cognitively based treatment programme which might be used in the treatment of pathological gambling. However, first we will complete our survey of what has been achieved in the treatment of pathological gambling by cognitive methods.

Thought Stopping

Thought-stopping techniques have been used previously in the control of obsessive-compulsive behaviours such as hand-washing (Maurer 1985). Typically, the patient monitors his or her impulses to gamble and when thoughts concerning the possibility of gambling are detected, one or more of a variety of thought-stopping or thought-replacement techniques is instigated. For example, a common thought-stopping routine involves the use of a rubber band on the wrist. When the impulse to gamble is detected, the gambler snaps the rubber band and says aloud, *stop*. The thought about gambling is then replaced by a previously rehearsed alternative. Thus, the gambler might replace "I'll go down to the club and make some money on the slots" by "I'll go down to the library and borrow a really good thriller." Similarly, the thought "I am so angry at my wife that I am going to gamble for a few hours" might be replaced by "I certainly am angry at my wife and after I have cooled down I will talk with her about my concerns."

According to Maurer (1985), it is important to include with thought-stopping procedures a range of other techniques to support the intention to cease gambling. First of all, it is important to develop a plan for repaying loans. Secondly, the gambler should learn mood management procedures such as stress management techniques, relaxation training and self-hypnosis. Maurer has found that spouse involvement is a positive factor in maintaining the involvement of the gambler in the treatment programme. Gamblers seen alone typically attend for three or four visits whereas couples average ten visits. Finally, Maurer recommends attendance at Gamblers Anonymous meetings and marital therapy following the completion of treatment (Maurer 1985, p.215).

Cognitive Restructuring

Much of what passes for pathology in gambling is relatively straightforward, mistaken belief that it is possible to win consistently even in games of pure chance.

(Baucum 1985, p.201)

In Chapter 5, a sociocognitive theory of gambling involvement was described. It is the central argument of this book that gambling is maintained by irrational thinking and thus that treatment of gambling problems should focus on changing the relevant irrational beliefs to beliefs which are consistent with the reality of gambling. Although this view has been expressed elsewhere (Baucum 1985; Walker 1985), surprisingly there does not appear to be a single case reported in the literature where cognitive restructuring has been used in the treatment of pathological gambling. Thus, in this section a potentially valuable treatment strategy based on cognitive restructuring will be described.

The major steps in the successful treatment of gambling problems can be stated:

(1) The gambler must stop gambling (gambling may be resumed at a later date);
(2) Alternative activities to gambling are initiated or resumed;
(3) A plan for repayment of debts must be initiated;
(4) The motivation to gamble must be moderated or eliminated.

Most programmes for the treatment of compulsive or pathological gambling would endorse most or all of these steps. The main difference between a treatment strategy based on cognitive restructuring and other therapies is in the implementation of step 4. Whereas other treatment approaches may attempt to decondition the excitement attached to gambling, improve the relationship between the gambler and his or her spouse, eliminate character or personality defects, or simply bolster the gambler's resolve to stop gambling, cognitive restructuring attempts to change mistaken beliefs held by the gambler about his or her involvement in gambling. It is assumed that the gambler is motivated to gamble by the belief that he or she will win in the long run. The problem gambler does not stop when behind because he or she believes that the losses will be recouped: persistence, larger bets and a bit of luck will set the accounts straight. Similarly, the problem gambler does not stop when ahead because this is precisely the time when a fortune can be made.

Unfortunately, perseverance with a losing strategy is bound to be a failure in the long run. It is precisely this belief which the gambler must come to accept if his dangerous gambling behaviour is to stop.

In order to complete step 4, a detailed account of the gambling must be obtained. *Detailed* does not mean the details of frequency, duration, money lost, precipitating factors and so on that might be part of a detailed case history but, rather, the steps, procedures, strategies, rituals and so on that the gambler employs when gambling. If the gambler is unable to remember or to recount this aspect of the gambling, it may be necessary to accompany him or her on a gambling session. Each form of gambling has its own structure (see Chapters 2 and 3) and the therapist will need to be aware of this structure in order to accurately understand the significant features of the gambler's play.

It is possible to foresee some of the strategies the gambler will employ in order to win. Some likely strategies for slot machine players are listed below. Similar lists can be drawn up for other forms of gambling, especially where false beliefs are generally held (for sources of such material, see Wagenaar 1988 and Solonsch 1989). However, it is important to realise that each gambler may have his or her own special knowledge and that this material must be located anew for each new gambler.

Slot Machines

- a favourite place related to potential to win
- a favourite machine or type of machine
- rituals associated with playing the machine
- prevent others from playing this machine until the gambler has finished with it
- special methods of play (for example, always maintain a minimum number of credits in the machine, press quickly for a fast spin, etc.)
- ability to predict when a big pay-out will occur.

Unusual Treatment Methods for Gambling Problems

Possibly because the mainstream treatment approaches have been far from fully effective in dealing with cases of problem gambling, a whole range of methods has arisen based on unusual conceptions of the nature of gambling problems. Some of these methods, such as hypnosis and logotherapy, appear to be similar in technique to methods which have been described earlier. Hypnosis can be seen as an extreme form of imaginal desensitisation whereas logotherapy requires a treatment with many of the behavioural features of satiation therapy. Similarly, the Adlerian approach seeks to uncover the hidden agenda of the gambler in much the same way as classical Freudian psychoanalysis. More unusual are methods such as win therapy, which seeks to transform "bad" gamblers into "good" gamblers, and brief therapy, which uses a form of "reverse psychology" to undermine the gambling behaviour.

Hypnotherapy

There appears to be only one reference to the treatment of compulsive gambling by hypnosis (Griffiths 1982). However, since this was a case where the gambling problems had become severe and where the therapy was spectacularly successful, it is important that the approach be considered. The theory behind the use of hypnosis is similar to that explained for imaginal desensitisation. It is assumed that the gambling is maintained by the excitement associated with the action of gambling. This excitement can be lessened or removed by hypnotic suggestion. Griffiths employed hypnosis based on eye-fixation with progressive relaxation and deepening procedures. He reports that the patient was a good subject for hypnosis, a statement which immediately raises the question of how widely applicable hypnotherapy would be in general.

The patient was a thirty-six-year-old man who had had a lifelong problem with gambling. At the time of treatment he was threatened by divorce, heavily in debt, pursued by creditors and threatened by criminal charges. He received one session of therapy which aimed at deconditioning the excitement associated with gambling, and rekindling the excitement associated with other activities. A second "reinforcement" session was the last received. At this final session the patient had lost all interest in gambling. No follow-up details are given, but for the statement that "Since this final session, no recurrence of the symptom has been seen to date."

Logotherapy

The neurotic who learns to laugh at himself may be on the way to self-management, perhaps to cure.

(Allport 1956)

Frankl (1967) has described a therapy based on his philosophical perspective of humans searching for meaning in life. Among the problems encountered by people is one which he calls anticipatory anxiety. Nearly everyone has experienced anticipatory anxiety before important events such as examinations, speeches and performances. This anxiety can be so intense as to threaten the ability of the person to complete the activity. Anticipatory anxiety becomes maladaptive when it brings about the failure which the person most fears. For a person prone to blushing, anticipatory anxiety induces a particularly intense blush when it is most important to remain composed. Similarly, stuttering, palpitations, clammy hands and the like are maintained by anticipatory anxiety. Frankl invented a technique, which he called paradoxical intentions, which would dissipate anticipatory anxiety. The technique involves instructing the client to exhibit the symptoms at their strongest level rather than trying to inhibit them. Thus, the person who blushes, at the next opportunity is to blush for as long and as deeply as he can. In attempting to exhibit the symptoms, the person fails because the anticipatory anxiety is no longer present.

Victor and Krug (1967) reported a case in which paradoxical intentions were used to treat compulsive gambling. The gambler had been gambling for many years but recently the amount of time spent gambling had become so great that it interfered with every other aspect of his life. He was so busy gambling that he did not have time to buy his wife a Christmas present. Victor and Krug do not specify precisely the kind of gambling which was causing trouble, but references to "gambling joints" and to "horses and cards" suggest that the game which was absorbing time was some kind of card game. Whatever the game, the gambler nearly always lost. When winning, the stakes would be increased until, eventually, he lost all that he had won.

The patient had received seven months of group psychotherapy before attending for individual counselling. Treatment by paradoxical intentions began during counselling and continued for several weeks (length unspecified). The treatment consisted of the instruction to gamble for three hours and then to record the details in a diary. The patient was required to gamble each day. At the end of three weeks the patient had lost all of his ready money. The therapist suggested he sell his watch or a picture so that he could continue and instructed that as soon as he had the cash he was to let the therapist know and to resume gambling.

Being instructed to gamble may be assumed to diminish the anticipatory excitement. At another level, being ordered to gamble may have a reverse effect. If the gambling is conducted as an act of defiance or as a means of being punished, as psychoanalytic theories assume, then being ordered to gamble (to be "bad") undermines its psychological significance to the individual. The impact on the patient can be seen from comments he recorded in his diary:

I determined to follow these instructions exactly as they were laid out. . . . The idea seized me and frightened me. I was now under instructions to do the thing that was wasting my life, causing me continuous heartache and making all my efforts useless.

(Victor and Krug 1967, p.812)

At the time at which the paper was written, the gambler had abstained from gambling for "several months" (details not supplied). There was one notable exception to his loss of interest in gambling: he took a large bet of $700 with a gambling friend that he would not be seen again in the gambling joints!

Minimal Interventions

Minimal intervention refers to any treatment of a problem which requires considerably less time from a therapist than is typically needed by psychotherapy. One of the main forms of minimal intervention is the self-help manual. With the aid of the manual the client becomes his or her own therapist. Self-help manuals for behaviour problems have an extensive history (Glasgow and Rosen 1978). In the area of alcohol problems, self-help manuals have been developed by Miller and Munoz (1982) and by Robertson and Heather (1983). Evaluations of the effectiveness of minimal intervention for drinking problems suggests that they are at least as effective as therapist interventions (Miller, Gribskov and Mortell 1981; Orford and Edwards 1977).

A self-help manual for people with gambling problems has been developed by Dickerson in Australia (Allcock and Dickerson 1986; Dickerson 1987). The manual is modelled on the one for drinking problems used by Robertson and Heather and contains the following sections:

1. Definition of the potential user or problem gambler;
2. An examination of why people gamble;
3. How to self-monitor;
4. Functional analysis of gambling behaviour;
5. Goal/limit setting;
6. Self-reinforcement;
7. Alternative incompatible behaviours;
8. How to maintain gains in the longer term.

(From Dickerson 1990, p.89)

The manual allows the gambler to choose whether abstinence or controlled gambling is the goal. If the goal is control, then the advice focuses on ways to limit the time and money spent on gambling, the need to maintain an accurate record of the gambling, thinking accurately about gambling expectations and rewarding oneself for maintaining control over the gambling. Advice is also given about actual gambling behaviour which is more controlled and therefore less dangerous financially.

Slightly different advice is offered if the goal is to stop gambling altogether. Most importantly, access to cash must be controlled. Wages must be collected by someone else or be paid straight into a bank account. Withdrawal of money should depend on two signatures. Keep limited sums of cash in the house, and so on. Particularly in relation to

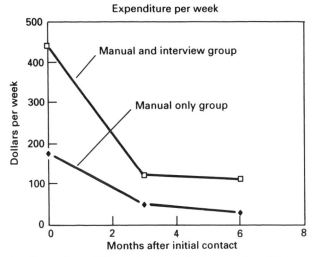

FIG. 7.1 Change in gambling behaviour following use of a self-help manual.

access to money, it is important to have someone else involved. Another important area is involvement in other activities. Since problem gambling typically absorbs most of one's free time each week, it is important to become involved in other activities that will enable attention and energy to be directed away from gambling. The use of relaxation techniques is advised as a way of keeping the gambling urge under control and the gambler should avoid things and places that might trigger the urge to gamble.

How effective is a self-help manual in dealing with problem gambling? Dickerson (1990) has reported a six-month follow-up of twenty-nine problem gamblers who have received the self-help manual. Of the twenty-nine gamblers, sixteen received the manual and a set of questionnaires by post and thirteen completed a structured interview and were given the manual. The average losses for the whole group amounted to $5,464 per year. Gambling sessions typically lasted two hours or more and occurred on average three to five times per week. All but one of the sample would be categorised pathological gamblers according to the DSM IIIR criteria. The effects of the self-help manual on gambling behaviour are shown in Figure 7.1.

It is clear that whether or not the gambler was given a structured interview, gambling decreased following use of the manual. Dickerson also found that the number of sessions of gambling per week also decreased. Unfortunately, there was no control group so it is impossible to determine whether the lessened gambling would have occurred whether or not the manual was used. Perhaps many of the gamblers in this study were ready to cut back and would have done so even if they had not participated in the study. Again, as with many other treatments, the follow-up is too recent to be convincing. It is possible that most of the gains in this study will be eroded as time elapses. Nevertheless, we should avoid having unrealistically high expectations for this approach. Its strength lies in the low costs involved. However, pathological gamblers may need more support in their endeavours to control their gambling than can be given in a self-help manual. Furthermore, although advice is given to think rationally about gambling, habitual gamblers may need persuasion that the expectations for gambling given in the manual apply in their particular case.

Win Therapy

At the Seventh International Conference on Gambling and Risk Taking held in Reno in 1987, one paper attracted considerable criticism. Among papers reporting the nature of pathological gambling and the effectiveness of therapeutic measures designed to have the gambler stop gambling for good, the paper presented by Howard Sartin challenged many of the assumptions implicit in the preceding papers (Sartin 1988). According to Sartin, the real pathology in pathological gambling is the loss of money; not an obsessive-compulsive personality, not a defective relationship with the spouse, and not a disease from which the gambler will never fully recover. Sartin's view of pathological gambling leads to a radically different approach to treatment. Win therapy has the straightforward aim of converting losing gamblers into winning gamblers. For those who believe that pathological gambling is a disease, or who believe that the pathological gambler has an unconscious wish to lose, or who believe that the pathological gambler cannot exercise self-control over gambling, win therapy is nonsense. Such people would argue that any successes Sartin might achieve will be with gamblers whose problems are less intense and not with pathological gamblers.

Win therapy applies to horse racing and not to other forms of gambling. The gambler contracts to avoid gambling again until he or she has received sufficient training in handicapping (the art of assessing the true expectations for each horse: see Chapter 2) to have a positive expectancy for betting on horses. Expert handicappers are employed to teach the gamblers who are referred to as investors. The details of the handicapping methods are not supplied by Sartin although he has indicated that furlong times (the speed with which a horse completes each furlong in a race) play a central role (Sartin 1984). When a losing gambler (Sartin insists that negative labels be abandoned) has mastered the methods of handicapping, he or she can now proceed to gamble with less risk.

Sartin reports having treated 1,387 gamblers by win therapy. Only 1.8% of the gamblers appear to have a pathology that goes beyond the fact of losing and the consequences that follow. Seventy-two per cent of the sample have been able to resume gambling in a healthy, profitable way. A further 6% resumed gambling but relapsed into heavy, losing gambling and are counted as failures. The remainder of the sample were still in training at the time of the Reno conference. Sartin offers no follow-up data other than to state that, in relation to the the successful group, "Under regular monitoring they continue to manifest a healthy psychological protocol" (Sartin 1988, p.367).

What are the implications of Sartin's unorthodox approach? There appear to be a number of limitations to win therapy which must be taken into account. (1) Severity of gambling problems: At the Reno gambling conference, it was asserted that the gamblers treated by Sartin were not pathological gamblers but controlled gamblers. The argument continues that if Sartin had been working with pathological gamblers then they would not have been able to control their gambling in the way suggested. However, Sartin refers to the gamblers as meeting the DSM III diagnostic criteria for pathological gambling. Even if many of the gamblers had sufficient incomes to support their failures at gambling, nevertheless they cannot be said to differ from those gamblers being treated in the regular hospital programmes. Without further evidence to the contrary, we must accept Sartin's claim that these are in fact pathological gamblers of the type being treated elsewhere. (2) Biased sample of gamblers: Sartin points out that win therapy appears to be more effective with horse-racing gamblers than with casino gamblers or sports betters. His explanation is in terms of the different personality structures of these groups of gamblers. However, more likely, casino gamblers do not wish to give up their preferred method of gambling just because more favourable outcomes might be obtained from betting on the horses. Although Sartin did accept some non-horse-racing gamblers into treatment, it appears that the majority were horse punters rather than other kinds of gamblers. Nevertheless, gamblers with preferred games other than horse betting could be treated within Sartin's framework. For example, it would be possible to extend win therapy to casino gambling since, in the case of blackjack at least, card counting allows a small but positive expected outcome (see Chapter 3). (3) Failure to deal with the problem of absence from home: One of the important factors promoting antagonism and bitterness in the gambler's close relationships is the amount of time spent gambling and away from those significant others. Although this problem may be lessened by win therapy since the amounts lost in gambling sessions would be much less, it is likely that most spouses would not be satisfied with continued gambling as a goal for therapy. Furthermore, if escape from the family is one of the motives for

TABLE 7.11

Comparison of the effectiveness as measured by abstinence of four treatment approaches to pathological gambling

Broad therapeutic strategy	Study reported by	Gamblers treated N	Percentage abstaining from gambling at follow-up		
			6 months	1 year	2 years
Gamblers Anonymous	Brown	114	—	—	15
Psychotherapy	Taber	66	48	—	—
	Franklin et al. and Russo et al.	204	—	31	—
Psychoanalysis	Bergler	60	75	—	—
Behaviour therapy	Mixed	53	—	23	—
	Blaszczynski and Barker and Miller	93	—	—	14

continued gambling, then win therapy may exacerbate the problem by ensuring that the gambler can continue to gamble for much longer periods of time without losing. (4) Finally, if the criterion for effective treatment of pathological gambling is long-term abstinence, then win therapy is quite ineffective. However, with regard to this last point, Sartin's view is clear:

Like most psychiatrists, I have done a lot of work with patients/clients with behavioral manifestations that are rooted in sexual problems characterized by "Disorders of impulse control". Were I, or any other practitioner, to prescribe ABSTINENCE in lieu of cure for such problems, I would be laughed out of practice by patients and peers alike.

(Sartin 1988, p.383)

Abstinence or Control as the Goal of Treatment

According to the doctrine of Gamblers Anonymous, control as a treatment goal for compulsive gambling is an absurdity. Since the compulsive gambler cannot control his or her urges to gamble, controlled gambling is a contradiction of terms. The unacceptability of controlled gambling as a treatment goal is endorsed by most groups working within the medical model of pathological gambling. However, we have seen that for many programmes control and abstinence are equally valid alternatives (see, for example, behaviour therapy or minimal intervention) and that for some approaches controlled gambling is the only acceptable goal (as is the case for win therapy). Furthermore, the abstinence rate at follow-up declines rapidly as the period of time to follow-up increases from six months to two years. Table 7.11 shows figures derived from the reports of major programmes treating pathological gambling with abstention as the major criterion for success. The major omissions from Table 7.11 are the results of the studies published by: Greenberg and Rankin (1982), where the aim appears to have been control rather than abstention; Sartin (1988), where the aim was re-education rather than abstention; and a number of studies where the follow-up data has not yet been published in full (this includes the work of Blackman, Simone and Thoms 1986 and Dickerson 1987).

High rates of abstention are reported six months after the completion of treatment although the 75% cited for psychoanalysis may be inflated by an undisclosed number of gamblers who were seen but not accepted into analysis and by the fact that systematic follow-ups were not reported by Bergler. Thus, a best guess of effectiveness of treatment generally after six months have elapsed is 50%. One year after completion of treatment the abstinence rate has fallen to approximately 25% and by the two-year follow-up abstinence has dropped further to about 15%. While a decline in abstinence rates would be expected as the period since treatment increases, the rapid decline shown by these figures suggests that the long-term effectiveness of treatments for pathological gambling is low, independent of the type of treatment offered. There are three possible explanations for the rapid decline in abstention from gambling following treatment:

1. Pathological gambling is an illness from which most people so afflicted do not recover. Gambling may cease for a time, but unless vigilance is maintained, possibly for the rest of one's life, a relapse is very likely to occur and to recur. This explanation is essentially the view of Gamblers Anonymous.
2. The treatments reviewed do not deal with the central cause of gambling problems. Most pathological gamblers cannot continue gambling after treatment because they have no money with which to do so. However, many of the gamblers treated are simply serving time until they can again try their luck. The decline in abstention occurs because eventually most gamblers will reach a financial position where they can again begin to gamble. It is the contention of this book that the neglected factor in the treatment of pathological gamblers is the irrational thinking which gamblers use in the gambling activity.
3. Abstention from gambling is an unrealistic goal. In areas such as America and Western Europe, most people gamble at some time each year and gambling is widely promoted as a recreational activity. Gambling itself is not pathological. Therefore, the problem which everyone faces when gambling is self-control. Thus, the objective of treatment should be controlled gambling and not abstaining from gambling altogether. With control as the criterion, many of the treatments reviewed will be seen to be highly effective.

In this section we will compare treatment strategies again, but this time with controlled gambling as the criterion rather than absence of gambling. In the final section we will speculate about a possible treatment programme built around the goal of restructuring the irrational thinking of pathological gamblers.

Table 7.12 shows the reported rates of controlled gambling for the treatment programmes reviewed. Controlled gambling will include all levels of gambling that are no longer a problem to the person involved and will therefore include abstention from gambling. There are several observations to be made about the data entered in Table 7.12. First of all, some gamblers have been followed up after a greater period than two years; this applies in particular to the studies conducted by Blaszczynski (1988). Secondly, what counts as controlled gambling is not well defined. For example, it is not immediately clear what is meant, in relation to gambling, by terms such as: "markedly reduced" (McConaghy et al. 1983); "variable control" (Greenberg and Rankin 1982); and "binge gambling" (Franklin and Richardson 1988). Thirdly, where follow-ups occurred over different periods of time, for example six months to two years for Koller (1972), all the results are placed at the shorter end of the range. Finally, the overall figures are heavily biased by two results: Brown (1987) for Gamblers Anonymous and Sartin (1988) for win therapy. The data for Gamblers Anonymous does not include the unknown number of former G.A. members who returned to controlled gambling but did not continue attending meetings. Thus the 15% figure for Gamblers Anonymous is undoubtedly an underestimate with respect to a criterion of controlled gambling. Sartin's large sample dominates the data for the six-month follow-up. However, the figure for the early follow-up fortunately remains constant at 72% whether or not Sartin's data is included.

When we examine Table 7.12 we see that the same rapid decline in controlled gambling is evident that was observed for the abstinence criterion in Table 7.11. The high level of controlled gambling after six months (72%) drops to 50% after one year and to 27% after two years. However, if the Gamblers Anonymous data is omitted, on the grounds that it may be a serious underestimate of reality, then the level of controlled gambling after two years is 37%. Thus, although the picture remains unclear, there is weak evidence that controlled gambling may be maintained in as many as one in three pathological gamblers receiving treatment. Again, this level of success is no basis for satisfaction.

Concluding Comment on Treatment

From a broader perspective the central question for treatment concerns the overall health of those who return to gambling in a controlled way

TABLE 7.12

Comparison of the effectiveness as measured by controlled gambling of different treatment approaches to pathological gambling

Broad therapeutic strategy	Study reported by	Date	Gamblers treated N	Number controlling their gambling after		
				6 months	1 year	2 years
Gamblers Anonymous	Brown	1987	114	—	—	17
		Total	114	—	—	15%
Psychotherapy	Russo et al.	1984	124	—	46	—
	Franklin and Richardson	1988	80	—	54	—
	Taber	1987	66	38	—	—
	Bolen and Boyd	1968	10	8	—	—
		Total	280	60%	49%	—
Psychoanalysis	Bergler	1958	60	45	—	—
		Total	60	75%	—	—
Behaviour therapy	Blaszczynski	1988	120	—	—	42
	Barker and Miller	1968	3	—	—	3
	Rankin	1982	1	—	—	1
	Seager	1970	16	—	8	—
	Aversion case studies		2	—	2	—
	Dickerson and Weeks	1979	1	—	1	—
	Greenberg and Rankin	1982	26	12	—	—
	Koller	1972	12	6	—	—
	Peck and Ashcroft	1972	5	4	—	—
		Total	186	51%	58%	37%
Cognitive therapy	Bannister	1977	1	—	1	—
Brief therapy	Walker	1985	1	—	1	—
Win therapy	Sartin	1988	1,387	999	—	—
Hypnotherapy	Griffiths	1982	1	1	—	—
Logotherapy	Victor and Krug	1967	1	1	—	—
	Grand total control	6 months	1,568	72	—	—
		1 year	225	50	—	—
		2 years	237	27	—	—

compared with those who abstain. It is possible, for example, that avoiding gambling focuses attention on the forbidden activity and leaves the former gambler continually frustrated. Freud has suggested that it is the people with the strongest conscience who experience the strongest temptation to sin. Is it the case that the former gambler, who now abstains, pays a price in psychological well-being?

Blaszczynski (1988), in his treatment study of 120 pathological gamblers, was able to follow up 63 treated gamblers after an interval of between two and nine years. These former pathological gamblers were asked to categorise themselves as totally abstinent from gambling or as continuing to gamble at the time of contact. Those who were gambling were asked further whether they considered their gambling to be controlled or uncontrolled. For 56 of the gamblers, confirmation of the self-assessment was obtained from the spouse of the gambler or some other significant person. Of the 63 contacted, 18 were abstinent, 24 were gambling in a controlled way and 21 were gambling in an uncontrolled way. The comparison of these three groups of formerly pathological gamblers on measures of psychological well-being can indicate whether or not total abstinence is associated with psychological health.

In the area of close relationships, one-third of both the abstainers and the controlled gamblers reported that their relationship with their spouses had improved and approximately half of each group reported that their relationships with other family members had improved. In measures of psychological health there were no differences between the abstainers and the controlled gamblers. In particular, the abstainers were not more anxious or depressed nor did they replace the gambling behaviour with excessive consumption of alcohol or cigarettes.

The results of Blaszczynski's study are particularly important for two reasons. First, the data gives no reason for discriminating between control and abstinence as a preferred goal for treatment. There are no significant differences between treated gamblers who resume their gambling but in a controlled manner and those who stop gambling and have not gambled at all for long periods. That result in itself is of major importance in the quest for the best treatment strategy for pathological gamblers. However, the second reason concerns the aetiology of gambling. Whether personality problems cause the gambling problem or the gambling problem causes psychological ill-health is a hotly debated issue. Some like to have a bet each way by suggesting that both factors are operating. However, Blaszczynski's data suggests that the gambling problem causes the psychological ill health. All of the gamblers were treated for pathological gambling as defined in DSM III. On a whole range of measures of psychological health, these gamblers uniformly differed from the norms in the direction of ill health prior to treatment. These differences included measures of neuroticism, psychoticism, anxiety, hostility, paranoia and obsessive-compulsive personality. If the gambling problem was a symptom of an underlying personality defect, then one would expect some measure of personality to persist in the bias following treatment but independently of category (abstainer, controlled, uncontrolled). In fact, the scores of the abstainers and controlled gamblers at follow-up do not differ from the normative sample. By contrast, the uncontrolled gamblers maintain their deviation from the norms. Put simply, effective treatment eliminates or strongly diminishes evidence of a personality disorder, but the same treatment when ineffective leaves the personality disorder in place. Such a result must strengthen the claims of treatment strategies which focus on the symptom at the expense of those that focus on the underlying problem.

Concluding Comments

Legal gambling is very popular. Racecourses and betting shops, casinos, lotteries and other forms of gambling are attractive to large numbers of people. Given that gambling is an important leisure activity throughout Europe, the United States and most other principalities, it is surprising that so little is known about the activity. Since gambling contributes to the social problems in these different communities, it is a matter of importance not only to understand the reasons for involvement in general but also the factors that promote excessive involvement in gambling. There is a relatively large number of theories explaining ordinary and problem levels of involvement but relatively little data which are helpful in discriminating between these theories. This imbalance between theory and research is one in need of immediate action.

Detailed Descriptions of Gambling in Natural Settings

Theories of gambling cannot develop much further without a richer set of descriptions of real gambling behaviour in natural settings. Not enough is known about the social basis of regular gambling despite the work of Rosecrance and Hayano. It is likely that careful observation will reveal the extent to which problem gambling arises either because of the involvement or because of the absence of involvement with a community of other like-minded gamblers. Is it that life in the gambling community becomes sufficiently important to keep the gambler gambling despite major losses or is it that the problem gambler loses a sense of proportion precisely because he or she has not been integrated into a community of gamblers who would help him or her restrain overambitious gambling? This issue cannot be resolved by one or two careful studies of different forms of gambling. Descriptions must be provided for the whole range of gambling games and in different cultural contexts. Without a sufficient range of games and a sufficient diversity of contexts, the ability to make generalised statements will be reduced and the ability to reject false theories will be limited.

It is not just detailed accounts of the social settings in which gambling takes place that are too few in number and range. Surprisingly, there are very few accounts of the move-by-move gambling behaviour itself. What is it that keeps the gambler at the task over relatively long periods of time. Different theories suggest arousal, reinforcement, expectation of reward and false beliefs are central. However, the evidence lies in the move-by-move gambling behaviours or strategies of the individual. The recent work of Dickerson provides the best example of the kind of detailed studies that are required to sort out the basis of persistence at different forms of gambling. However, even in Dickerson's studies, more information is needed. For example, if expectation of reward or false beliefs are important, then the descriptions and explanations of the gambler must be monitored in real time. Ladouceur and Griffiths have analysed the talk of gamblers but have not related what is said to the details of the game or variations in the behaviour of the gambler. Without this level of detail, it may prove impossible to reject any of the contending theories.

The use of natural settings may be essential, although even this has not been established beyond doubt. Anderson and Brown have demonstrated that unless a real game in its natural setting is played, the arousal of regular blackjack players remains low. Is this the case for all gambling games? Again, the behaviours and strategies of gamblers may depend upon their level of arousal, but this has not been demonstrated. It may be that the important aspects of persistence at gambling can be studied in artificial settings with all the advantages that such settings entail. While much research on gambling behaviour is based on scepticism about the usefulness of involving non-gambling university students in laboratory games for monopoly money, moderate deviations from the natural setting may not have the impact that has been assumed by some workers. For example, real poker games involving real excitement can be played in laboratory rooms rather than private homes. The advantages gained in detailed monitoring of such games may outweigh any loss in the realism of the setting.

The Role of Cognitions in Persistence at Gambling

There has been insufficient attention paid to the belief structure of gamblers about their chosen gambling activity. By contrast, excitement and its physiological correlates have been made the core construct of most explanations of why gamblers persist. It is to be hoped that the foregoing chapters have taken a step towards righting this imbalance. It is not the claim here that excitement has no role in gambling but rather that it has been overemphasised in theorising about the nature of gambling. Gambling, like all contests, produces variations in excitement. There are identifiable situations that produce peaks in excitement and rather more circumstances where the game is less than exciting. Unfortunately, despite the numerous writers who support excitement as the key to explaining regular and heavy gambling involvement, there is relatively little research published which measures excitement or arousal throughout a session of gambling. What little research there is supports generalised statements about excitement, such as excitement is highest at the start of a slot machine session or that excitement increases during the racing commentary.

In Chapter 5 we identified a range of cognitions which have been linked to persistence at gambling. The illusion of control over the game, biased evaluation of outcomes, belief in luck as a personal characteristic or manipulable entity, entrapment and a range of other false beliefs have been collectively called "irrational thinking". While there is little doubt that irrational thinking is present among most or all regular and heavy gamblers, there appears to have been no serious attempt to explore the interaction of beliefs with the move-by-move strategies employed by gamblers. Until such research is available, it will not be possible to disentangle cause and effect involving cognitions about gambling and the gambling activity. It is possible that irrational thinking occurs after the event as a means of explaining or "rationalising" the sequence of events and outcomes that have occurred. According to such a view, the gambling behaviour is caused by other variables and the observed irrational thinking is only a consequence. In this book we have suggested that the role for cognition, in general, and irrational thinking, in particular, is causal in both the decision to gamble and subsequent persistence with gambling.

The central construct in explaining gambling is strategic thinking. Gambling is an example of problem solving and the guiding analogy for a cognitive account of gambling is the game of chess rather than the pleasures of cocaine or heroin. All gambling is conducted in the context of games where the goal of the game also determines the outcome of the gamble. The game may be one that is observed by the gambler, as in the case of the horse race, or one in which the gambler participates as a player, as in blackjack. However, in either case the gambler is involved in attempting to predict the outcome and to bet accordingly. Thus, the gambling is a meta-game in which the goal is winning. Unfortunately, for the gambler, the gambling game is not a fair contest and the overall expectation for all regular and heavy gamblers is loss. It is this asymmetry which is assumed by cognitive theory to impact on the thinking of the gambler, to promote irrational thinking and to produce the range of gambling phenomena. Recent research on cognitions during gambling, especially that of Ladouceur in Canada and Griffiths in England, suggests that the regular and heavy gambler makes greater use of irrational thinking than the occasional or "social" gambler. However, until more detailed research is conducted, the triggers to irrational thinking will remain unknown.

The Nature of Gambling Problems

The dominant view of problem gambling is that the gambler has become addicted to gambling. Gambling is a dependence without a drug. At the Seventh International Conference on Gambling and Risk Taking, held in Reno in 1987, there was very nearly complete agreement among the views expressed by clinicians that excessive gambling is best understood as an addiction. The addiction model, however, appears to have lost ground since then. At the Eighth International Conference on Gambling and Risk Taking, held in London in 1990, some clinicians openly rejected the addiction model and the new criteria for diagnosing patho-logical gambling showed a modest shift away from conformity with the criteria for diagnosing psychoactive substance abuse. Part of the reason for this change may be the increasing recognition that gambling is a complex activity involving a range of different processes and thus not easily categorised with other "self destructive" behaviours. Neverthe-less, the prevailing view is that money is not the central issue but is incidental to gambling problems.

In the account given in this book, money is the core of gambling problems. The problem gambler seeks to win money and believes that he or she will do so with persistence. However, persistence produces increasing debts. Gambling becomes, increasingly, the only means by which those debts can be paid. The fluctuations in fortunes experienced by the gambler maintain the illusion that the debts can be paid in this way. The big win proves that the gambler is right and the big loss simply increases the desperate need of the gambler for a big win. Thus problem gambling is best viewed as an interaction between mistaken beliefs about the possibilities of winning and the real circumstances of gambling which cause debts. The hope of making money keeps the gambler involved, but the reality of the debts incurred cause the break-down of the gambler's personal and social life. According to this view, gambling does not directly cause personal problems such as depression, nor does it cause social problems such as the breakdown of relationships with significant others. Gambling directly causes debt which in turn causes the range of other observable problems.

The reason for persistence in the face of mounting debts and increas-ing problems in other sectors of life is not simply false beliefs about the nature of gambling. Beliefs do not constitute a motivation in themselves. They must be coupled with a source of motivation in order to produce behaviour. Although the motivation for gambling may appear to be the acquisition of money, there may be deeper underlying reasons. At the very least, gambling may be seen as a challenge or contest in which the individual attempts to show his or her true self or in which the individual attempts to create a sense of self. Psychoanalytic theory offers alternative motivations for gambling which trace the origin of problem gambling back to childhood development. What the gambling means to the individual may only be discovered in the context of understanding their life story. Unfortunately, the motives of gamblers are not readily apparent and questionnaire research asking for the reasons why a person gambles is likely to give nothing more than a superficial explanation.

The failure to understand and agree on the nature of problem gambling has had several major consequences both at the level of measurement and at the level of treatment. When we wish to know the prevalence rate of problem gambling, the answer must not only specify the rate but also which problem is being addressed. Prevalence rates for problem gambling vary with the criteria that are used. It makes a difference whether the prevalence rate is that for compulsive gambling, pathological gambling, excessive gambling or heavy gambling. Even if we ask about the prevalence rate for pathological gambling, the criteria for this one category have changed three times in little more than a decade. Perhaps the best method of approaching the question of prevalence is by specifying the nature of the "problem" as precisely as we can in terms of measurable characteristics of the gambler or the gambling. For example, the theory proposed in Chapter 5 suggests that the central "problem" is loss of money. Although measuring loss of money introduces a different set of problems, these may be technical problems which are soluble rather than conceptual problems which are not. The question of what problems actually confront the gambler is difficult to answer. Perhaps the most useful data will be provided by the spouse. At the other extreme, the practice of asking "cured" gamblers or gamblers in treatment about the problems faced by the gambler is fraught with the danger of obtaining unreliable and biased information. Unfortunately, many of the studies of compulsive or pathological gambling have used this approach.

Finding an Effective Treatment for Gambling Problems

A wide range of treatments have been tried for problem gambling, but the success rate of these therapies has not been high. Evaluation of treatment methods is complicated by the fact that some gamblers may well have "given up" gambling for good by the time they receive treatment. A prior question for treatment is whether the goal of therapy should be abstinence or control. According to some perspectives, controlled gambling is not a realistic option. Since the controlled gambler is still gambling, the possibility that circumstances will induce loss of control remains present. Given that the gambler has invested so much of life in the one activity and has built a network of friends through the activity, the goal of abstinence itself may be less than ideal.

The sociocognitive theory put forward in this book leads to the straightforward expectation that cognitive therapies will be the most effective in coping with gambling problems. Both rational emotive therapy and cognitive restructuring should prove effective in reducing the inclination to gamble. Moreover, techniques which directly address the irrational thinking of the gambler should be investigated. For example, Ladouceur et al. (1989) have recorded and subsequently corrected the irrational beliefs of video poker players, thus reducing the urge to continue playing that game. Perhaps the most radical approach to therapy is simply to correct the mistaken beliefs and defective strategies of gamblers by training the gambler in good money management and optimal gambling strategies. The gambler can then continue with the gambling but without the risk of heavy losses. According to the theories expressed in this book, such an approach may be effective in reducing the flow of problems from the gambling losses sustained.

References

Abramson, Seligman, and Teasdale. Learned helplessness in humans: Critique and reformulation. *Journal of Abnormal Psychology,* 1978, 87, 49–74.

Abt, V., Smith, J.F., and Christiansen, E.M. An explanation of gambling behavior. In Eadington, W.R. (ed.), *The Gambling Studies: Proceedings of the Sixth National Conference on Gambling and Risk Taking,* 1985, 3, 159–171.

Adams, H.B. Studies in REST: REST, arousability, and the nature of alcohol and substance abuse. *Journal of Substance Abuse Treatment,* 1988, 5, 77–81.

Adkins, B.J., Taber, J.I., and Russo, A.M. The spoken autobiography: a powerful tool in group psychotherapy. *Social Work,* 1985, 435–439.

Allcock, C. Professional gambling: profit or piffle. In Caldwell, G.T., Dickerson, M.G., Haig, B., and Sylvan, L. (eds.), *Gambling in Australia.* Sydney : Croom Helm, 1985.

Allcock, C. Pathological gambling. *Australian and New Zealand Journal of Psychiatry,* 1986, 20, 259–265.

Allcock, C., and Dickerson, M.G. *The Guide to Good Gambling.* New South Wales : Social Science Press, 1986.

Allport, G. *The Individual and His Religion.* New York : Macmillan, 1956.

Alvarez, A. Introduction. In Yardley, H.O., *The Education of a Poker Player.* Glasgow : Fontana/Collins, 1980.

American Psychiatric Association. *Diagnostic and Statistical Manual of Mental Disorders,* (3rd edition) DSM III. Washington : American Psychiatric Association, 1980.

American Psychiatric Association. *Diagnostic and Statistical Manual of Mental Disorders,* (3rd edition) DSM III (Revised). Washington : American Psychiatric Association, 1987.

Anderson, G., and Brown, R.I.F. Real and laboratory gambling, sensation-seeking and arousal. *British Journal of Psychology,* 1984, 75, 401–410.

Anderson, G., and Brown, R.I.F. Some applications of reversal theory to the explanations of gambling and gambling addictions. *Journal of Gambling Behavior,* 1987, 3, 179–189.

Arrow, K.J. *Essays in the Theory of Risk-Bearing.* Amsterdam : North Holland, 1970.

Ayllon, T. Intensive treatment of psychotic behavior by stimulus satiation and food reinforcement. *Behavior Research and Therapy,* 1963, 1, 53.

Baldwin, R., Cantey, W., Maisel, H., and McDermott, J. The optimum strategy in blackjack. *Journal of the American Statistical Association,* 1956, 51, 429–439.

Bannister, G. Cognitive behavior therapy in a case of compulsive gambler. *Cognitive Therapy and Research,* 1977, 13, 223–227.

Barker, J.C., and Miller, M. Aversive therapy for compulsive gambling. *Lancet,* 1966, 1, February 26, 491–492.

Barker, J.C., and Miller, M. Aversion therapy for compulsive gambling. *The Journal of Nervous and Mental Disease,* 1968, 146, 285–302.

Baucum, D. Arguments for self-controlled gambling as an alternative to abstention. In Eadington, W.R. (ed.), *The Gambling Studies: Proceedings of the Sixth National Conference on Gambling and Risk Taking,* University of Nevada, Reno, 1985.

Baudot, J.-C. *Slot Machines of Europe and America.* Kent, England : Costello, 1988.

Bergler, E. *The Psychology of Gambling*. London : International Universities Press, 1970. (First published in New York : Hill and Wang, 1957.)

Beyer, A. *My $50,000 Year at the Races*. New York : Harcourt Brace Jovanovich, 1975.

Bird, R., and McCrae, M. Gambling markets: A survey of empirical evidence. In Caldwell, G.T., Dickerson, M.G., Haig, B., and Sylvan, L. (eds.), *Gambling in Australia*. Sydney : Croom Helm, 1985.

Blackman, S., Simone, R.V., and Thoms, D.R. Treatment of gamblers. *Hospital and Community Psychiatry*, 1986, 37, 404.

Blaszczynski, A.P. Clinical studies in pathological gambling: Is controlled gambling an acceptable treatment outcome? Thesis submitted for the Degree of Doctor of Philosophy, University of New South Wales, Australia, 1988.

Blaszczynski, A.P., Buhrich, N., and McConaghy, N. Pathological gamblers, heroin addicts and controls compared on the E.P.Q. "Addiction Scale". *British Journal of Addiction*, 1986, 80, 315–319.

Blaszczynski, A.P., Wilson, A.C., and McConaghy, N. Sensation seeking and pathological gambling. *British Journal of Addiction*, 1986, 81, 113–117.

Blaszczynski, A.P., Winter, S.W., and McConaghy, N. Plasma endorphin levels in pathological gambling. *Journal of Gambling Behavior*, 1986, 2, 3–14.

Blume, S.B. Compulsive gambling and the medical model. *Journal of Gambling Behavior*, 1987, 3, 237–247.

Bond, N.A. Basic strategy and expectation in casino blackjack. *Organizational Behaviour and Human Performance*, 1974, 12, 413–428.

Boyd, W.H., and Bolen, D.W. The compulsive gambler and spouse in group psychotherapy. *International Journal of Group Psychotherapy*, 1970, 20, 77–90.

Brenner, G.A., and Brenner, R. *A Profile of Gamblers*. Montreal (Québec) : Centre de Recherche et Développement en Économique, 1987.

Brockner, J., and Rubin, J.Z. *Entrapment in Escalating Conflicts: A Social Psychological Analysis*. New York : Springer-Verlag, 1985.

Brockner, J., Shaw, M.C., and Rubin, J.Z. Factors affecting withdrawal from an escalating conflict: Quitting before it's too late. *Journal of Experimental Social Psychology*, 1979, 15, 492–503.

Brown, R.I.F. The effectiveness of Gamblers Anonymous. In Eadington, W.R. (ed.), *The Gambling Studies: Proceedings of the Sixth National Conference on Gambling and Risk Taking*, 1985, 5, 258–284.

Brown, R.I.F. Arousal and sensation-seeking components in the general explanation of gambling and gambling addictions. *The International Journal of the Addictions*, 1986, 21, 1001–1016.

Brown, R.I.F. Dropouts and continuers in Gamblers Anonymous: Life-context and other factors. *Journal of Gambling Behavior*, 1986, 2, 130–140.

Brown, R.I.F. Dropouts and continuers in Gamblers Anonymous: Part 2. Analysis of free-style accounts of experiences with GA. *Journal of Gambling Behavior*, 1987, 3, 68–79.

Brown, R.I.F. Dropouts and continuers in Gamblers Anonymous: Part 3: Some possible specific reasons for dropout. *Journal of Gambling Behavior*, 1987, 3, 137–151.

Brown, R.I.F. Dropouts and continuers in Gamblers Anonymous: Part 4: Evaluation and summary. *Journal of Gambling Behavior*, 1987, 3, 202–210.

Brown, R.I.F., and Robertson, S. Home computer and video-game addictions in relation to adolescent gambling: Conceptual and developmental aspects. Paper presented at the *Eighth International Conference on Risk and Gambling*, London, August 1990. (To be published in Eadington, W.R., *Proceedings*, 1991.)

Browne, B.R. Going on tilt: frequent poker players and control. In Eadington, W.R. (ed.), *Gambling Research: Proceedings of the Seventh International Conference on Gambling and Risk Taking*, Reno, University of Nevada-Reno, 1988.

Brunk, G.G. A test of the Friedman-Savage gambling model. *Quarterly Journal of Economics*, 1981, 96, 341–348.

Burns, F.S. The compulsive gambling debate in Australia: Myth or fact. Paper presented at the *Seventh International Conference on Gambling and Risk Taking*, Reno, August 1987.

Caillois, R. *Man, Play and Games.* Great Britain : Thames and Hudson, 1961.

Caldwell, G.T. The gambling Australian. In Edgar, D.E. (ed.), *Social Change in Australia.* Melbourne : Cheshire, 1974.

Caldwell, G.T., Young, S., Dickerson, M.G., and McMillen, J. *Casino Development for Canberra: Social Impact Report.* Canberra : Commonwealth of Australia, 1988.

Caltabiano, N. Community reactions to gender and ethnic origin: the case of the compulsive gambler. Thesis submitted for the Degree of Doctor of Philosophy, James Cook University of North Queensland, 1989.

Carlson, N.R. *Physiology of Behavior.* Boston : Allwyn & Bacon, 1991.

Carlton, P.L., and Manowitz, P. Physiological factors as determinants of pathological gambling. *Journal of Gambling Behavior,* 1987, 3, 274–285.

Carnes, P. *The Sexual Addiction.* Minneapolis : CompCare, 1983.

Cayuela, R. Characteristics and situation of gambling addiction in Spain: Epidemiological and clinical aspects. Paper presented at the *Eighth International Conference on Risk and Gambling,* London, August 1990. (To be published in Eadington, W.R., *Proceedings,* 1991.)

Ceci, S.J., and Liker, J.K. A day at the races: a study of IQ, expertise, and cognitive complexity. *Journal of Experimental Psychology: General,* 1986, 115, 255–266.

Chapman, L.J., and Chapman, J.P. Genesis of popular but erroneous diagnostic observations. *Journal of Abnormal Psychology,* 1967, 14, 271–280.

Chew, S. A generalisation of the quasilinear mean with applications to the measurement of income inequality and decision theory resolving the Allais paradox. *Econometrica,* 1983, 51, 1065–1092.

Clotfelter, C. T. On the regressivity of state-operated "number" games. *National Tax Journal,* 1979, 32, 543–547.

Cohen, J. *Psychological Probability.* London : George Allen and Unwin, 1972.

Cornish, D.B. *Gambling: A Review of the Literature and its Implications for Policy and Research.* London : Home Office Research Study, No.42, 1978.

Cotler, S.B. The use of different behavioral techniques in treating a case of compulsive gambling. *Behavior Therapy,* 1971, 2, 579–584.

Cromer, G. Gamblers Anonymous in Israel: a participant observation study of a self-help group. *The International Journal of the Addictions,* 1978, 13, 1069–1077.

Crossman, R. Five card stud: some calculations. In Walker, M.B. (ed.), *Faces of Gambling.* Sydney : National Association for Gambling Studies, 1987.

Cummings, W.T., and Corney, W. A conceptual model of gambling behavior: Fishbein's theory of reasoned action. *Journal of Gambling Behavior,* 1987, 3, 190–201.

Custer, R.L., and Milt, H. *When Luck Runs Out.* New York : Facts on File Publications, 1985.

Daley, K. Encouraging "habitual" gambling on poker machines. In Walker, M.B. (ed.), *Faces of Gambling.* Sydney : National Association for Gambling Studies, 1987.

Davison, G.C., and Neale, J.M. *Abnormal Psychology: An Experimental Clinical Approach.* New York : John Wiley and Sons, 1974.

Devereux, E.C. Gambling and social structure. Ph.D. dissertation, Department of Sociology, Harvard University, 1949. Reprinted New York : Arno Press, 1980.

Devinney, R.B. Gamblers: A personality study. *Dissertation Abstracts International,* 1979, 40(1-B), 429–430.

Dickerson, M.G. Unpublished Ph.D., 1974. Referred to in Cornish, D.B., *Gambling: A Review of the Literature. . . .* London : Home Office Research Study No.42, 1978.

Dickerson, M.G. *Compulsive Gamblers.* London : Longman, 1984.

Dickerson, M.G. The importance of a field study approach to gambling research. In McMillen, J. (ed.), *Gambling in the 80's.* Brisbane : National Association for Gambling Studies, 1986.

Dickerson, M.G. A preliminary exploration of a two-stage methodology in the assessment of the extent and degree of gambling related problems in the Australian population. Paper presented at the *Eighth International Conference on Risk and Gambling,* London, August 1990. (To be published in Eadington, W.R., *Proceedings,* 1991.)

Dickerson, M.G. Internal and external determinants of persistent gambling and impaired control. Paper presented at the *Eighth International Conference on Risk and Gambling*, London, August 1990. (To be published in Eadington, W.R., *Proceedings*, 1991.)

Dickerson, M.G., and Adcock, S. Mood, arousal and cognitions in persistent gambling: Preliminary investigation of a theoretical model. *Journal of Gambling Behavior*, 1987, 3, 3–15.

Dickerson, M.G., and Hinchy, J. Minimal treatment intervention for problem gamblers. In Walker, M.B. (ed.), *Faces of Gambling*. Sydney : National Association for Gambling Studies, 1987.

Dickerson, M.G., and Hinchy, J. The prevalence of excessive and pathological gambling in Australia. *Journal of Gambling Behavior*, 1988, 4, 135–151.

Dickerson, M.G., and Hinchy, J. Minimal treatments and problem gamblers: A preliminary investigation. *Journal of Gambling Behavior*, 1990, 6, 87–102.

Dickerson, M.G., and Weeks, D. Controlled gambling as a therapeutic technique for compulsive gamblers. *Journal of Behaviour Therapy and Experimental Psychiatry*, 1979, 10, 139–141.

Dickerson, M.G., Fabre, J., and Bayliss, D. A comparison of TAB customers and poker machine players. In McMillen, J. (ed.), *Gambling in the 80's*. Brisbane : National Association for Gambling Studies, 1986.

Dickerson, M.G., Hinchy, J., and Legg-England, S. Minimal treatments and problem gamblers: A preliminary investigation. *Journal of Gambling Studies*, 1990, 6, 87–102.

Dickerson, M.G., Hinchy, J., and Fabre, J. Chasing, arousal and sensation seeking in off-course gamblers. *British Journal of Addiction*, 1987, 82, 673–680.

Dickerson, M.G., Hinchy, J., Cunningham, R., and Legg-England, S. On the operant determinants of persistent gambling behaviour II: a comparison of low-, medium-, and high-frequency poker machine players. *Journal of Applied Behaviour Analysis*, 1990.

Dickerson, M.G., Hinchy, J., Schafer, M., Whitworth, N., and Fabre, J. The use of a hand-held microcomputer in the collection of physiological, subjective and behavioral data in ecologically valid gambling settings. *Journal of Gambling Behavior*, 1988, 4, 92–98.

Dickerson, M.G., Walker, M.B., Legg-England, S., and Hinchy, J. Demographic, personality, cognitive and behavioural correlates of off-course betting involvement. *Journal of Gambling Behavior*, 1990, 6.

Don, M. The effects of compulsive gambling on the family. In Walker, M.B. (ed.), *Faces of Gambling*. Sydney : National Association for Gambling Studies, 1987.

Downes, D.M., Davies, B.P., David, M.E., and Stone, P. *Gambling, Work and Leisure: A Study Across Three Areas*. London : Routledge and Kegan Paul, 1976.

Drapkin, T., and Forsyth, R. *The Punter's Revenge*. London : Chapman and Hall, 1987.

Dumont, M., and Ladouceur, R. Evaluation of motivation among video-poker players. *Psychological Reports*, 1990, 66, 95–98.

Eadington, W.R. Approaches to the legalization and commercialization of casino gambling throughout the world: causes and public policy concerns. In Walker, M.B. (ed.), *Faces of Gambling*. Sydney : National Association for Gambling Studies, 1987.

Eadington, W.R. Economic perceptions of gambling behavior. *Journal of Gambling Behavior*, 1987, 3, 264–273.

Eadington, W.R. Ethical and policy considerations in the spread of commercial gambling. Paper presented at the *Eighth International Conference on Risk and Gambling*, London, August 1990. (To be published in Eadington, W.R., *Proceedings*, 1991.)

Edwards, W. Probability-preferences among bets with differing expected values. *American Journal of Psychology*, 1954, 67, 56–67.

Eysenck, H.J. *Dimensions of Personality*. London : Routledge and Kegan Paul, 1947.

Eysenck, H.J. *The Scientific Study of Personality*. London : Routledge and Kegan Paul, 1967.

Eysenck, H.J. *The Structure of Human Personality*. London : Methuen, 1970 (3rd edition).

Eysenck, H.J. *The Inequality of Man*. San Diego : Edits Publishers, 1975.

Fischer, S. The use of fruit machines by children. *The Society for the Study of Gambling Newsletter*, 1989, 16, 13–33.

Fischer, S. The preadult use of amusement machines in the U.K. Paper presented at the *Eighth International Conference on Risk and Gambling*, London, August 1990. (To be published in Eadington, W.R., *Proceedings, 1991.*)

Fishbein, M., and Ajzen, I. *Belief, Attitude, Intention, and Behavior: An Introduction.* Reading, Massachusetts : Addison-Wesley, 1975.

Frankl, V.E. *Psychotherapy and Existentialism.* Middlesex, England : Penguin, 1967.

Franklin, J., and Richardson, R. A treatment outcome study with pathological gamblers: Preliminary findings and strategies. In Eadington, W.R. (ed.), *Gambling Research: Proceedings of the Seventh International Conference on Gambling and Risk Taking,* Reno, University of Nevada-Reno, 1988.

Freud, S. Dostoevsky and parricide. In Halliday, J., and Fuller, P. (eds.), *The Psychology of Gambling.* London : Harper & Row, 1974.

Freye, E. *Opioid Agonists, Antagonists and Mixed Narcotic Analgesics: Theoretical Background and Considerations for Practical Use.* London : Springer Verlag, 1987.

Fuller, N.P., Taber, J.I., and Wittman, G.W. On the irrelevance of substances in defining addictive disorders. In Eadington, W.R. (ed.), *Gambling Research: Proceedings of the Seventh International Conference on Gambling and Risk Taking,* Reno, University of Nevada-Reno, 1988, 5, 95–111.

Fuller, P. Introduction. In Halliday, J., and Fuller, P. (eds.), *The Psychology of Gambling.* London : Harper & Row, 1974.

Gaboury, A., and Ladouceur, R. Irrational thinking and gambling. In Eadington, W.R. (ed.), *Gambling Research: Proceedings of the Seventh International Conference on Gambling and Risk Taking,* Reno, University of Nevada-Reno, 1988.

Gamblers Anonymous. *Gamblers Anonymous Leaflet.* Los Angeles : Gamblers Anonymous Publishing, 1977.

Gardner, H. *Frames of Mind.* New York : Basic Books, 1983.

Gilovich, T. Biased evaluation and persistence in gambling. *Journal of Personality and Social Psychology,* 1983, 44, 1110–1126.

Gilovich, T., and Douglas, C. Biased evaluations of randomly determined gambling outcomes. *Journal of Experimental Social Psychology,* 1986, 22, 228–241.

Glasgow, R.E., and Rosen, G.M. Behavioral bibliography: A review of self-help behavior therapy manuals. *Psychological Bulletin,* 1978, 85, 1–23.

Glass, C.D. Differences in internal-external locus of control and tolerance-intolerance for ambiguity among pathological, social and non-gambling groups. *Dissertation Abstracts,* 1982, 43, 524.

Goffman, E. *Interaction Ritual.* Garden City, N.J. : Doubleday, 1967.

Goorney, A.B. Treatment of a compulsive horse race gambler by aversion therapy. *British Journal of Psychiatry,* 1968, 114, 329–333.

Gossop, M.R., and Eysenck, S.B.G. A further investigation into the personality of drug addicts in treatment. *British Journal of Addiction,* 1980, 75, 305–311.

Graham, J. *Amusement Machines: Dependency and Delinquency.* London : Home Office Research Study No. 101.

Graham, J.R., and Lowenfeld, B.H. Personality dimensions of the pathological gambler. *Journal of Gambling Behavior,* 1986, 2, 58–67.

Gray, J.D. Understanding the dynamics of addictions. Paper presented at the *Eighth International Conference on Risk and Gambling,* London, August 1990. (To be published in Eadington, W.R., *Proceedings, 1991.*)

Greenberg, D., and Rankin, H. Compulsive gamblers in treatment. *British Journal of Psychiatry,* 1982, 140, 364–366.

Greene, J. The gambling trap. *Psychology Today,* 1982, 50–55.

Grichting, W.L. The impact of religion on gambling in Australia. *Australian Journal of Psychology,* 1986, 38, 45–58.

Griffin, P.A. Mathematical expectation for the public's play in casino blackjack. Paper presented at the *Seventh International Conference on Gambling and Risk Taking,* University of Nevada-Reno, Reno, Nevada, 1987.

Griffiths, F.V. A case of compulsive gambling treated by hypnosis. *International Journal of Clinical and Experimental Hypnosis,* 1982, 30, 195.

Griffiths, M.D. An analysis of "Amusement Machines: Dependency and Delinquency". *The Society for the Study of Gambling Newsletter,* 1989, 16, 34–48.

Griffiths, M.D. A study of the cognitive activity of fruit machine players. Paper presented at the *Eighth International Conference on Risk and Gambling,* London, August 1990. (To be published in Eadington, W.R., *Proceedings,* 1991.)

Guilford, J.P. *The Nature of Human Intelligence.* New York : McGraw-Hill, 1967.

Haig, B. Expenditure on legal gambling. In Caldwell, G., Dickerson, M.G., Haig, B., and Sylvan, L. (eds.), *Gambling in Australia.* Sydney : Croom Helm, 1985.

Halliday, J., and Fuller, P. *The Psychology of Gambling.* London : Harper & Row, 1974.

Hand, I. A socio-behavioral model of compulsive gambling: Social gambling—pathological gambling—addictive gambling. Paper presented at the *Eighth International Conference on Risk and Gambling,* London, August 1990. (To be published in Eadington, W.R., *Proceedings,* 1991.)

Hardy, F. *Four-legged Lottery: A Novel.* London : T.W. Laurie, 1958.

Harry, P. Compulsive gambling. Paper presented at a one-day symposium on gambling, Sydney, Rozelle Hospital, 1983.

Hayano, D.M. The professional poker player: career identification and the problem of respectability. *Social Problems,* 1977, 24, 556–564.

Hayano, D.M. Communicative competency among poker players. *Journal of Communication,* 1980, 30, 113–120.

Hayano, D.M. *Poker Faces: The Life and Work of Professional Card Players.* Berkeley : University of California Press, 1982.

Hayano, D.M. The professional gambler: fame, fortune and failure. *Annals, AAPSS,* 1984, 474, 157–167.

Henslin, J.M. Craps and magic. *American Journal of Sociology,* 1967, 73, 316–330.

Hersant, Y. Introduction. In Baudot, J.-C., *Slot Machines of Europe and America.* Kent, England : Costello, 1988.

Hong, Y.-Y., and Chiu, C.-Y. Sex, locus of control, and illusion of control in Hong Kong as correlates of gambling involvement. *The Journal of Social Psychology,* 1988, 128, 667–673.

Huizinga, J. *Homo Ludens.* New York : Roy Publishers, 1950.

Hunter, R. Problem gambling in a gambling town: The experience of Las Vegas. Paper presented at the *Eighth International Conference on Risk and Gambling,* London, August 1990. (To be published in Eadington, W.R., *Proceedings,* 1991.)

Hyndman, R. Calculating the odds. In Walker, M.B. (ed.), *Faces of Gambling.* Sydney : National Association for Gambling Studies, 1987.

Ide-Smith, S.G., and Lea, S.E.G. Gambling in young adolescents. *Journal of Gambling Behavior,* 1988, 4, 110–118.

Inglis, K. Gambling and culture in Australia. In Caldwell, G.T., Dickerson, M.G., Haig, B., and Sylvan, L. (eds.), *Gambling in Australia.* Sydney : Croom Helm, 1985.

Jablonski, B. Locus de controle e o comportamento de jogar. *Arquivos Brasileiros de Psicologia,* 1985, 37, 19–26.

Jacobs, D.F. A general theory of addictions: a new theoretical model. *Journal of Gambling Behavior,* 1986, 2, 15–31.

Jacobs, D.F. Illegal and undocumented: a review of teenage gambling and the plight of children of problem gamblers in America. In Shaffer, H.J., Stein, S.A., Gambino, B., and Cummings, N. (eds.), *Compulsive Gambling: Theory, Research, and Practice.* Massachusetts/Toronto : Lexington Books, 1989.

Johnson, J. Gambling as a source of government revenue in Australia. In Caldwell, G.T. et al. (eds.), *Gambling in Australia.* Sydney : Croom Helm, 1985.

Jung, C.G. *Psychological Types.* New York : Harcourt, 1923.

Kahneman, D., and Tversky, A. The psychology of preferences. *Scientific American,* 1982, Jan., 136–142.

Kallick, M., Suits, D., Dielman, T., and Hybels, J. *A Survey of American Gambling Attitudes and Behaviors.* Ann Arbor : University of Michigan, 1976.

Kallick-Kaufmann, M. The micro and macro dimensions of gambling in the United States. *Journal of Social Issues,* 1979, 35, 7–26.

Kaplan, H.R. Gambling among lottery winners: before and after the big score. *Journal of Gambling Behavior,* 1988, 4, 171–182.

Karlin, S. *Mathematical Methods and Theory in Games, Programming and Economics.* Reading, Massachusetts : Addison-Wesley, 1959.

Kelly, G.A. *The Psychology of Personal Constructs.* New York : Norton, 1955.

King, K.M. Neutralizing marginally deviant behavior: Bingo players and superstition. *Journal of Gambling Behavior,* 1990, 6, 43–62.

Koller, K.M. Treatment of poker-machine addicts by aversion therapy. *The Medical Journal of Australia,* 1972, 1, 742–745.

Kuhlman, D.M. Individual differences in casino gambling? In Eadington, W.R. (ed.), *Gambling and Society.* Springfield, Illinois : Thomas, 1976.

Kuley, N.B., and Jacobs, D.F. The relationship between dissociative-like experiences and sensation seeking among social and problem gamblers. *Journal of Gambling Behavior,* 1988, 4, 197–207.

Kusyszyn, I., and Rutter, R. Personality characteristics of heavy gamblers, light gamblers, non-gamblers, and lottery players. *Journal of Gambling Behavior,* 1985, 1, 59–63.

Lacey, J.H., and Evans, C.D.H. The impulsivist: A multi-impulsive personality disorder. *British Journal of Addiction,* 1986, 81, 641–649.

Ladouceur, R., and Gaboury, A. Effects of limited and unlimited stakes on gambling behavior. *Journal of Gambling Behavior,* 1988, 4, 119–126

Ladouceur, R., and Mayrand, M. Charactéristiques psychologiques de la prise de risque monétaire des joueurs et des non-joueurs à la roulette. *International Journal of Psychology,* 1986, 21, 433–443.

Ladouceur, R., and Mireault, C. Prevalence estimates of pathological gambling in Québec, Canada. Paper presented at the *Eighth International Conference on Risk and Gambling,* London, August 1990. (To be published in Eadington, W.R., *Proceedings,* 1991.)

Ladouceur, R., Mayrand, M., and Tourigny,Y. Risk taking behavior in gamblers and non-gamblers during prolonged exposure. *Journal of Gambling Behavior,* 1987, 3, 115–122.

Ladouceur, R., Sylvain, C., Duval, C., Gaboury, A., et al. Correction des verbalisations irrationelles chez des joueurs de poker-video. *International Journal of Psychology,* 1989, 24, 43–56.

Langer, E.J. The illusion of control. *Journal of Personality and Social Psychology,* 1975, 32, 311–328.

Lau, R.R., and Russell, D. Attribution in the sports pages. *Journal of Personality and Social Psychology,* 1980, 39, 29–38.

Leary, K., and Dickerson, M.G. Levels of arousal in high- and low- frequency gamblers. *Behaviour Research and Therapy,* 1985, 23, 635–640.

Lee, W. *Decision Theory and Human Behavior.* New York : Wiley, 1971.

Lefevre, R. Compulsive gambling and addictions—Implications for treatment. Paper presented at the *Eighth International Conference on Risk and Gambling,* London, August 1990. (To be published in Eadington, W.R., *Proceedings,* 1991.)

Leigh, N. *Thirteen Against the Bank.* New York : Penguin, 1977.

Lesieur, H.R. The compulsive gambler's spiral of options and involvement. *Psychiatry,* 1979, 42, 79–87.

Lesieur, H.R. *The Chase: Career of the Compulsive Gambler.* Cambridge, Mass. : Schenkman, 1984.

Lesieur, H.R. Altering the DSM-III criteria for pathological gambling. *Journal of Gambling Behavior,* 1988, 4, 38–47.

Lesieur, H.R., and Blume, S.B. The South Oaks Gambling Screen (SOGS): A new instrument for the identification of pathological gamblers. *American Journal of Psychiatry,* 1987, 144, 1184–1188.

Lesieur, H.R., and Rosenthal, R.J. Pathological gambling and the new criteria: DSM IV. Paper presented at the *Eighth International Conference on Risk and Gambling*, London, August 1990. (To be published in Eadington, W.R., *Proceedings*, 1991.)

Lesieur, H.R., and Rosenthal, R.J. Pathological gambling: A review for the *DSM-IV source book*, 1991. (To be published.)

Li, W.L., and Smith, M.H. The propensity to gamble: Some structural determinants. In Eadington, W.R. (ed.), *Gambling and Society*. Springfield : Charles C. Thomas, 1976, 189–206.

Lopes, L.L. Model-based decision and inference in stud poker. *Journal of Experimental Psychology: General*, 1976, 105, 217–239.

Lorenz, V.C. Family dynamics of pathological gamblers. In Galski, T. (ed.), *A Handbook on Pathological Gambling*. Springfield, Il. : Charles C. Thomas, 1987.

Lorenz, V.C., and Shuttlesworth, D.E. The impact of pathological gambling on the spouse of the gambler. *Journal of Community Psychology*, 1983, 11, 67–76.

Lorenz, V.C., and Yaffee, R.A. Pathological gambling: psychosomatic, emotional and marital difficulties as reported by the gambler. *Journal of Gambling Behavior*, 1986, 2, 40–49.

Lorenz, V.C., and Yaffee, R.A. Pathological gambling: psychosomatic, emotional and marital difficulties as reported by the spouse. *Journal of Gambling Behavior*, 1988, 4, 13–26.

Lovibond, S.H. The aversiveness of uncertainty: An analysis in terms of activation and information theory. *Australian Journal of Psychology*, 1968, 20, 85–91.

Lowenhar, J.A., and Boykin, S. Casino gaming behavior and the psychology of winning and losing: How gamers overcome persistent failure. In Eadington, W.R. (ed.), *The Gambling Studies: Proceedings of the Sixth National Conference on Gambling and Risk Taking*, 1985, 3, 182–205.

Machina, M. "Expected utility" analysis without the independence axiom. *Econometrica*, 1982, 50, 217–232

MacMillan, G.E. People and gambling. In Caldwell, G.T., Dickerson, M.G., Haig, B., and Sylvan, L. (eds.), *Gambling in Australia*. Sydney : Croom Helm, 1985.

Mahigel, E.S. Nonverbal communication at the poker table: A descriptive analysis of sender-receiver behaviour. Unpublished thesis, University of Minnesota, 1969.

Mathews, R.T., and German, D.C. Electrophysiological evidence for excitation of rat ventral tegmental area dopaminergic neurons by morphine. *Neuroscience*, 1984, 11, 617–626.

Matthews, D. Ratings—why they work or fail. In Walker, M.B. (ed.), *Faces of Gambling*. Sydney : National Association for Gambling Studies, 1987.

Maurer, C.D. An outpatient approach to the treatment of pathological gambling. In Eadington, W.R. (ed.), *The Gambling Studies: Proceedings of the Sixth National Conference on Gambling and Risk Taking*, 1985, 5, 205–217.

Maze, J.R. The concept of attitude. *Inquiry*, 1973, 16, 168–205.

Maze, J.R. *The Meaning of Behaviour*. London : Allen and Unwin, 1983.

Maze, J.R. Lady Luck is gambler's mother. In Walker, M.B. (ed.), *Faces of Gambling*. Sydney : National Association for Gambling Studies, 1987.

McConaghy, N. Behavior completion mechanisms rather than primary drives maintain behavioral patterns. *Activitas Nervosa Supplement (Praha)*, 1980, 22, 138–151.

McConaghy, N., Armstrong, M.S., Blaszczynski, A., and Allcock, C. Controlled comparison of aversive therapy and imaginal desensitization in compulsive gambling. *British Journal of Psychiatry*, 1983, 142, 366–372.

McCormick, R.A. Pathological gambling: A parsimonious need state model. *Journal of Gambling Behavior*, 1987, 3, 257–263.

McCormick, R.A., Russo, A.M., Ramirez, L.F., and Taber, J.I. Affective disorders among pathological gamblers seeking treatment. *American Journal of Psychiatry*, 1984, 141, 215–218.

McGlothlin, W.H. A psychometric study of gambling. *Journal of Consulting Psychology*, 1954, 18, 145–149.

McNair Anderson 1983.

McNair Anderson 1983b.

Miller, W.R., and Munoz, R.F. *How to Control Your Drinking: A Practical Guide to Responsible Drinking*. Albuquerque, Mexico : University of New Mexico Press, 1982.

Miller, W.R., Gribskov, C., and Mortell, R. The effectiveness of a self-control manual for problem drinkers with and without therapist contact. *International Journal of Addictions*, 1981, 16, 829–839.

Mollo, V., and Gardener, N. *Card Play Technique*. London : Faber and Faber, 1977.

Montgomery, H.R., and Kreitzer, S. Compulsive gambling and behaviour therapy. Unpublished paper, 1968. Referred to in Dickerson, M.G., *Compulsive Gamblers*. London : Longman, 1984.

Moody, G.E. Playing with chance. In Eadington, W.R. (ed.), *The Gambling Studies: Proceedings of the Sixth National Conference on Gambling and Risk Taking*, 1985, 3, 317–329.

Moran, E. Gambling as a form of dependence. *British Journal of Addiction*, 1970, 64, 419–428.

Moran, E. Pathological gambling. *British Journal of Psychiatry*, Special publication no.9: *Contemporary Psychiatry*. London : Royal College of Psychiatrists, 1975.

Moran, E. Gambling: What we now know. Plenary paper presented at *the Eighth International Conference on Risk and Gambling*, London, July, 1990.

Moravec, J.D., and Munley, P.H. Psychological test findings on pathological gamblers in treatment. *The International Journal of the Addictions*, 1983, 18, 1003–1009.

Morris, R.P. An exploratory study of some personality characteristics of gamblers. *Journal of Clinical Psychology*, 1957.

Mort-Green, J. Please God, save me from the "good thing"—the certainty. In McMillen, J. (ed.), *Gambling in the 80's*. Brisbane : National Association for Gambling Studies, 1986.

Norwood, R. *Letters From Women Who Love Too Much*. London : Arrow, 1988.

O'Hara, J. The jockey club and the town in colonial society in Australia. Paper presented at the *Eighth International Conference on Risk and Gambling*, London, August 1990. (To be published in Eadington, W.R., *Proceedings*, 1991.)

Oldman, D.J. Chance and skill: a study of roulette. *Sociology*, 1974, 8, 407–426.

Oldman, D.J. Compulsive gamblers. *Sociological Review*, 1978, 26, 349–371.

Olds, and Milner, P.M. Positive reinforcement produced by electrical stimulation of septal area and other regions of rat brain. *Journal of Comparative and Physiological Psychology*, 1954, 47, 419–427.

Orford, J. Hypersexuality: Implications for a theory of dependence. *British Journal of Addiction*, 1978, 73, 299–310.

Orford, J. *Excessive Appetites*. London : John Wiley and Sons, 1985.

Orford, J., and Edwards, *Alcoholism: A Comparison of Treatment and Advice, with a Study of the Influence of Marriage*. Oxford : Oxford University Press, 1977.

Peck, D.F., and Ashcroft, J.B. The use of stimulus satiation in the modification of habitual gambling. *Proceedings of the Second British and European Association Conference on Behaviour Modification*, Kilkenny, Ireland, 1972.

Peele, S. Redefining addiction I: Making addiction a scientifically and socially useful concept. *International Journal of Health Services*, 1977, 7, 103–124.

Peterson, Seligman, and Vaillant. Pessimistic explanatory style is a risk factor for mental illness: A thirty-five year longitudinal study. *Journal of Personality and Social Psychology*, 1988, 55, 23–27.

Pokorny, M.R. Compulsive gambling and the family. *British Journal of Medical Psychology*, 1972, 45, 355–364.

Quiggin, J. A theory of anticipated utility. *Journal of Economic Behaviour and Organisation*, 1982, 3, 323–343.

Quiggin, J. Lotteries: an economic analysis. In Walker, M.B. (ed.), *Faces of Gambling*. Sydney : National Association for Gambling Studies, 1987.

Rankin, H. Control rather than abstinence as the goal in the treatment of excessive gambling. *Behaviour, Research and Therapy*, 1982, 20, 185–187.

Reid, R.L. The psychology of the near miss. In Eadington, W.R. (ed.), *The Gambling Studies: Proceedings of the Sixth National Conference on Gambling and Risk Taking*, 1985, 3, 1–12.

Revere, L. *Playing Blackjack as a Business.* Secaucus, N.J. : Lyle Stuart, 1980.

Robertson, I., and Heather, N. *So You Want to Cut Down Your Drinking? A Self-Help Manual for Controlled Drinking.* Edinburgh : Scottish Health Education Group, 1983.

Rosecrance, J. Compulsive gambling and the medicalization of deviance. *Social Problems,* 1985, 32, 275–284.

Rosecrance, J. You can't tell the players without a scorecard: a typology of horse players. *Deviant Behavior,* 1986, 7, 77–97.

Rosecrance, J. Why regular gamblers don't quit: a sociological perspective. *Sociological Perspectives,* 1986, 29, 357–378.

Rosecrance, J. "The next best thing": A study of problem gambling. *The International Journal of the Addictions,* 1986, 12, 1727–1739.

Rosecrance, J. Attribution and the origins of problem gambling. In Walker, M.B. (ed.), *Faces of Gambling.* Sydney : National Association for Gambling Studies, 1987.

Rosecrance, J. Professional horse race gambling: working without a safety net. In Eadington, W.R. (ed.), *Gambling Research: Proceedings of the Seventh International Conference on Gambling and Risk Taking,* Reno, University of Nevada-Reno, 1988, 3, 11–37.

Rosecrance, J. *Gambling Without Guilt: The Legitimation of an American Pastime.* Pacific Grove, California : Brooks/Cole, 1988.

Ross, M., and Siccoly, F. Egocentric biases in availability and attribution. *Journal of Personality and Social Psychology,* 1979, 37, 322–336.

Roston, R.A. Some personality characteristics of male compulsive gamblers. *American Psychologist,* 1965, 548.

Rotter, J.B. Generalized expectancies for internal versus external control of reinforcement. *Psychological Monographs,* 1966, 80 (Whole number 609).

Routtenberg, A. Self-starvation caused by "feeding center" stimulation. *American Psychologist,* 1964, 19, 502–507.

Roy, A. A search for biological substrates to pathological gambling. In Eadington, W.R. (ed.), *Gambling Research: Gamblers and Gambling Behavior.* Nevada : University of Nevada-Reno, 1988, vol.5.

Roy, A. Biological aspects of pathological gambling. Paper presented at the *Eighth International Conference on Risk and Gambling,* London, August 1990. (To be published in Eadington, W.R., *Proceedings,* 1991.)

Rule, B.G., Nutter, R.W., and Fischer, D.G. The effect of arousal on risk-taking. *Personality,* 1971, 2, 239–247.

Russo, A.M., Taber, J.I., McCormick, R.A., and Ramirez, L.F. An outcome study of an inpatient treatment program for pathological gamblers. *Hospital and Community Psychiatry,* 1984, 35, 823–827.

Salzmann, M.M. Treatment of compulsive gambling. *British Journal of Psychiatry,* 1982, 141, 318–319.

Sartin, H.G. The dynamics of incremental velocity and energy distribution. Paper presented at the *Handicapping Expo '84,* Meadowlands Hilton, October 17–20, 1984.

Sartin, H.G. Win therapy: An alternative diagnostic and treatment procedure for problem gambling. In Eadington, W.R. (ed.), *Gambling Research: Proceedings of the Seventh International Conference on Gambling and Risk Taking,* Vol. 5, pp. 365–391. Reno : University of Nevada-Reno, 1988.

Scarne, J. *Scarne's New Complete Guide to Gambling.* London : Constable, 1975.

Scott, D. *Winning.* Sydney : Puntwin, 1978.

Scott, D. Exotic betting. In Walker, M.B. (ed.), *Faces of Gambling.* Sydney : National Association for Gambling Studies, 1987.

Seager, C.P. Treatment of compulsive gamblers by electrical aversion. *British Journal of Psychiatry,* 1970, 117, 545–553.

Shubin, S. The compulsive gambler. *Today in Psychiatry,* 1977, 3, 1–3.

Skinner, B.F. *Science and Human Behavior.* New York : Free Press, 1953.

Skinner, B.F. *About Behaviorism.* New York : Vintage Books, 1974.

Skolnick, J.H. *House of Cards.* Boston : Little, Brown and Company, 1978.

Solomon, R.L. The opponent-process theory of acquired motivation. *American Psychologist,* 1980, 35, 691–712.

Solomon, R.L., and Corbit, J.D. An opponent-process theory of motivation. *Psychological Review,* 1974, 81, 119–145.

Solonsch, M. The conceptualization and evaluation of the concept of skill in gambling. Unpublished Honours thesis, Department of Psychology, Australian National University, 1989.

Solonsch, M. An analysis of skill in gambling. Paper presented at the *Eighth International Conference on Risk and Gambling,* London, August 1990. (To be published in Eadington, W.R., *Proceedings,* 1991.)

Spanier, D. *Easy Money: Inside the Gambler's Mind.* London : Secker & Warburg, 1987.

Strickland, L.H., and Grote, F.W. Temporal presentation of winning symbols and slot machine playing. *Journal of Experimental Psychology,* 1967, 74, 10–13.

Sullivan, G. *By Chance a Winner—The History of Lotteries.* New York : Dodd, Mead and Co, 1972.

Summers, J.J., Borland, R., and Walker, M.B. *Psychology: An Introduction.* Brisbane : Jacaranda-Wiley, 1989.

Sunderwirth, S.G. Biological mechanisms: Neurotransmission and addiction. In Sunderwirth, S.G. (ed.), *The Addictions.* 1985

Sylvestre, R. Le marché québécois des loteries. Referred to in Brenner, G.A., and Brenner, R. *A Profile of Gamblers.* Montreal (Québec) : Centre de Recherche et Développement en conomique, 1987. Survey originally reported in 1977.

Syme, D. Recent New Zealand gambling industry developments. *NAGS Newsletter,* 1989, No.2, 6–12.

Taber, J.I. Compulsive gambling: An examination of relevant models. *Journal of Gambling Behavior,* 1987, 3, 219–223.

Taber, J.I., McCormick, R.A., and Ramirez, L.F. The prevalence and impact of major life stressors among pathological gamblers. *The International Journal of the Addictions,* 1987, 22, 71–79.

Taber, J.I., McCormick, R.A., Russo, A.M., Adkins, B.J., and Ramirez, L.F. Follow-up of pathological gamblers after treatment. *American Journal of Psychiatry,* 1987, 144, 757–761.

Taxi Tom. *Growing Up the G.A. Way.* England : Gamblers Anonymous, 1986.

Tec, N. *Gambling in Sweden.* Totowa, N.J. : Bedminster Press, 1964.

Tepperman, J.H. The effectiveness of short-term group therapy upon the pathological gambler and wife. In Eadington, W.R. (ed.), *The Gambling Studies. The Phenomenon of Pathological Gambling: Psychological Theories and Treatment Strategies.* Nevada : University of Nevada-Reno, 1985, 5, 185–198.

Thorp, E.O. *Beat the Dealer.* New York : Vintage Books, 1962.

Thorp, E.O. *The Mathematics of Gambling.* Secaucus, N.J. : Gambling Times, 1984.

Trompf, G.W. Gambling and religion: some aspects. In Walker, M.B. (ed.), *Faces of Gambling.* Sydney : National Association for Gambling Studies, 1987.

Tuck, E.O. Blackjack—Is there anything more to be said? In Walker, M.B. (ed.), *Faces of Gambling.* Sydney : National Association for Gambling Studies, 1987.

Ullmann, L.P., and Krasner, L. *A Psychological Approach to Abnormal Behavior.* New Jersey : Prentice-Hall, 1975.

Victor, R.G., and Krug, C.M. "Paradoxical intention" in the treatment of compulsive gambling. *American Journal of Psychotherapy,* 1967, 21, 808–814.

Vogelaar, D.M. Skill versus chance: technical management. In McMillen, J. (ed.), *Gambling in the 80's.* Brisbane : National Association for Gambling Studies, 1986.

Volberg, R. Estimating the prevalence of pathological gambling in the United States. Paper presented at the *Eighth International Conference on Risk and Gambling,* London, August 1990. (To be published in Eadington, W.R., *Proceedings,* 1991.)

Volberg, R.A., and Steadman, H.J. Refining prevalence estimates of pathological gambling. *American Journal of Psychiatry,* 1988, 145, 502–505.

Volberg, R.A., and Steadman, H.J. Prevalence estimates of pathological gambling in New Jersey and Maryland. *American Journal of Psychiatry,* 1989, 146, 1618–1619.

Von Neumann, J., and Morganstern, O. *Theory of Games and Economic Behavior.* Princeton, N.J. : Princeton University Press, 1947.

Wagenaar, W.A. *Paradoxes of Gambling Behaviour*. London : Lawrence Erlbaum Associates, 1988.

Wagenaar, W.A., and Keren, G. Chance and luck are the same. *Journal of Behavioral Decision Making*, 1988, 1, 65–75.

Wagenaar, W.A., Keren, G., and Pleit-Kuiper, A. The multiple objectives of gamblers. *Acta Psychologica*, 1984, 56, 167–178.

Walker, G. The brief therapy of a compulsive gambler. *Journal of Family Therapy*, 1985, 7, 1–8.

Walker, M.B. The application of game theory to human behaviour. Unpublished D.Phil. thesis, University of Oxford, 1974.

Walker, M.B. Explanations for gambling. In Caldwell, G.T., Dickerson, M.G., Haig, B., and Sylvan, L. (eds.), *Gambling in Australia*. Sydney : Croom Helm, 1985.

Walker, M.B. Bridge for money: gambling with finesse. In Walker, M.B. (ed.), *Faces of Gambling*. Sydney : National Association for Gambling Studies, 1987.

Walker, M.B. Betting shops and slot machines: comparisons among gamblers. In Eadington, W.R. (ed.), *Gambling Research: Gamblers and Gambling Behavior*. Nevada : University of Nevada-Reno, 1988.

Walker, M.B. The presence of irrational thinking among poker machine players. In Dickerson, M.G., *200-UP*. Canberra : National Association for Gambling Studies, 1990.

Walker, M.B. A sociocognitive theory of gambling involvement. Paper presented at the *Eighth International Conference on Risk and Gambling*, London, August 1990. (To be published in Eadington, W.R., *Proceedings*, 1991.)

Weinstein, D., and Deitch, L. *The Impact of Legalized Gambling: The Socioeconomic Consequences of Lotteries and Off-Course Betting*. New York : Praeger, 1974.

Williams, J. How to be a better mug punter. In Dickerson, M.G., *200-UP*. Canberra : National Association for Gambling Studies, 1990.

Windross, A.J. Introduction of legal betting on rugby league. In Caldwell, G.T., Dickerson, M.G., Haig, B., and Sylvan, L. (eds.), *Gambling in Australia*. Sydney : Croom Helm, 1985.

Wise, R.A. The neurobiology of craving: Implications for the understanding and treatment of addiction. *Journal of Abnormal Psychology*, 1988, 97, 118–132.

Wolfgang, A., Zenker, S.I., and Viscusi, T. Control motivation and the illusion of control in betting on dice. *The Journal of Psychology*, 1984, 116, 67–72.

Wong, G. The obsessional aspects of compulsive gambling. Paper presented to the Society for the Study of Gambling, London, 1980. Reference in Dickerson, M.G., *Compulsive Gamblers*. London : Longman, 1984.

Wray, I., and Dickerson, M.G. Cessation of high frequency gambling and "withdrawal" symptoms. *British Journal of Addiction*, 1981, 76, 401–405.

Yaffee, R.A., Lorenz, V., and Politzer, R. A model explaining the severity of the gambling problem among pathological gambling patients in the State of Maryland: 1983–1989. Paper presented at the *Eighth International Conference on Risk and Gambling*, London, August 1990. (To be published in Eadington, W.R., *Proceedings*, 1991.)

Yardley, H.O. *The Education of a Poker Player*. Glasgow : Fontana/Collins, 1980. (First published 1957.)

Yokel, R.A., and Wise, R.A. Increased lever pressing for amphetamine after pimozide in rats: Implications for a dopamine theory of reward. *Science*, 1975, 187, 547–549.

Zola, J.K. Observations on gambling in a lower-class setting. *Social Problems*, 1963, 10, 353–361.

Zuckerman, M. *Sensation Seeking: Beyond the Optimal Level of Arousal*. New Jersey : Lawrence Erlbaum Associates, 1979.

Zuckerman, M. *The Biological Basis of Sensation-Seeking, Impulsivity and Anxiety*. Hillsdale, N.J. : Lawrence Erlbaum, 1983.

Zurcher, L. The "friendly" poker game: a study of an ephemeral role. *Social Forces*, 1970, 49, 173–186.

Author Index

Subject Index